CLYMER

BRIGGS & STRATTON
L-HEAD ENGINES

The world's finest publisher of mechanical how-to manuals

INTERTEC PUBLISHING CORPORATION

P.O. Box 12901, Overland Park, Kansas 66282-2901

Copyright ©1994 Intertec Publishing Corporation

FIRST EDITION
First Printing March, 1994

Printed in U.S.A.

ISBN: 0-89287-616-6

Library of Congress: 93-61210

Technical photography by Mike Morlan.

Technical illustrations by Steve Amos.

COVER: Photo courtesy of Briggs & Stratton.

CONTENTS

QUICK REFERENCE DATA

ENGINE OIL

Type	Viscosity	Ambient operating temperature
Regular grade	SAE 30	40° F (5° C) to 120° F (50° C)
Multigrade	5W-30, 10W-30	0° F (−18° C) to 40° F (5° C)
Synthetic	5W-20, 5W-30	−20° F (−30° C) to 0° F (−18° C)

ENGINE OIL CAPACITY

Model series (vertical crankshaft)	Capacity
60000, 80000, 90000, 100700, 110000, 120000	1.25 pints (0.6 L)
100900, 130000	1.75 pints (0.8 L)
170000, 190000	2.25 pints (1.1 L)
220000, 250000, 280000	3 pints (1.4 L)

Model series (horizontal crankshaft)	Capacity
60000, 80000, 90000, 100200, 130000	1.25 pints (0.6 L)
170000, 190000	2.75 pints (1.3 L)
220000, 250000	2.5 pints (1.2 L)

TUNE-UP SPECIFICATIONS

Spark plug
  Type — Champion J19LM or RJ19LM
  Gap — 0.030 in. (0.76 mm)
Breaker point gap — 0.020 in. (0.50 mm)
Ignition timing — Fixed
Valve clearance
  Intake — 0.005-0.007 in. (0.13-0.18 mm)
  Exhaust
    Model series numbers less than 130000 — 0.007-0.009 in. (0.18-0.23 mm)
    Model series numbers of 130000 and greater — 0.009-0.011 in. (0.23-0.28 mm)
Initial carburetor adjustment (turns open from seat)
  High speed needle — 1-1/2
  Low speed needle — 1-1/4
Idle speed — 1750

SPECIAL TIGHTENING TORQUES

Spark plug	140-200 in.-lb. (15.8-22.6 N•m)
Flywheel nut or starter clutch	
Series 60000, 80000, 81000, 82000, 90000, 92000, 93000, 94000, 95000, 100700, 110000, 120000	55 ft.-lb. (76 N•m)
Series 100200, 100900, 130000	60 ft.-lb. (81 N•m)
Series 170000, 171000, 190000, 192000, 193000, 220000, 250000, 280000	65 ft.-lb. (88 N•m)
Cylinder head	
Series 60000, 80000, 81000, 82000, 90000, 92000, 93000, 94000, 95000, 100200, 100700, 100900, 110000, 120000, 130000	140 in.-lb. (15.8 N•m)
Series 170000, 171000, 190000, 191000, 192000, 193000, 220000, 250000, 280000	165 in.-lb. (18.6 N•m)
Crankcase cover or oil pan	
Series 60000, 80000, 90000, 100700, 110000, 120000	85 in.-lb. (9.6 N•m)
Series 100200, 100900, 130000	120 in.-lb. (13.5 N•m)
Series 170000, 190000, 220000, 250000, 280000	140 in.-lb. (15.8 N•m)
Connecting rod	
Series 60000, 80000, 90000, 100000, 110000, 120000, 130000	100 in.-lb. (11.3 N•m)
Series 140000, 170000, 171000	165 in.-lb. (18.6 N•m)
Series 190000, 220000, 250000, 280000	190 in.-lb. (21.5 N•m)

CHAPTER ONE

GENERAL INFORMATION

SAFETY

Safety must be a constant concern for anyone working on or around machinery. Accidents can cause disabling injury to humans as well as damaging equipment. Although anticipating all manner of accidents possible is impossible, adhering to the following rules will reduce the possibility of accidents:

1. Never use gasoline as a cleaning solvent.

2. Never smoke or use a torch near flammable liquids such as cleaning solvent. Remember that open flames are present in some heaters, including water heaters and stoves.

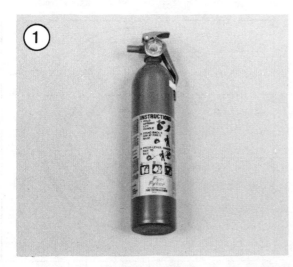

3. Never smoke or use a torch in an area where batteries are being charged. Highly explosive hydrogen gas is emitted during the charging process.

4. Place oil-soaked or solvent-soaked rags in a suitable closed metal container.

5. Disconnect the ground cable from the battery terminal when working on the electrical system. Never connect the posts on a battery either with wire or other metal objects, such as tools. The sparks may ignite hydrogen emitted from the battery, causing an explosion.

6. If welding or brazing, follow all recommended safety precautions prescribed by the American Welding Society. If in doubt as to proper procedure, take the work to an experienced welding shop.

7. Use the right tool for the job. Worn, improper or modified tools may cause injury and/or damage.

8. Be sure the parts meet the standards specified by the engine or equipment manufacturer. Installing incorrect or substandard parts can cause failure which may injure the technician or operator.

9. Keep the work area clean, uncluttered and well-lighted.

10. Wear appropriate safety equipment and clothing. Be sure safety equipment is designed to provide maximum protection and is properly used.

11. Be sure the shop is equipped with fire, safety and first aid equipment. An approved fire extinguisher (**Figure 1**) rated for gasoline (Class B) and electrical (Class C) fires should be nearby. A telephone should

be nearby with phone numbers of fire and medical service agencies highly visible on or near the phone.

12. Exercise extreme caution when using compressed air equipment, particularly blow guns. Always wear safety eyewear (**Figure 2**) when using compressed air. Do not use compressed air around other people and pets. Compressed air can hurl objects with sufficient force to cause injury. Never direct compressed air into skin or body openings, such as a cut, as this can cause severe injury or death.

13. When drying bearings or other rotating parts with compressed air, never allow the air jet to rotate the bearing or part. The air jet is capable of rotating them at speeds far in excess of those for which they were designed. The bearing or rotating part is very likely to disintegrate and cause serious injury and damage. To prevent bearing damage when using compressed air, hold the inner bearing race (**Figure 3**) by hand.

14. Small children, bystanders and pets should be kept out of the work area and away from equipment that is in an unsafe condition, i.e., equipment with safety guards removed while undergoing service.

15. Observe all safety notations on equipment. If safety systems must be defeated for servicing, be sure safety systems are functional before operating equipment.

16. If the equipment or engine must be lifted or supported, be sure proper equipment is used and in a safe manner. Be sure the equipment or engine is secure before applying great force to tools, such as when loosening or tightening cylinder head screws. Do not leave the equipment or engine in a position that someone else may inadvertently knock or bump over.

17. Be sure all electrical tools are in safe working order and properly grounded. The work area must be dry.

18. Do not use liquids from unmarked containers.

19. Follow directions and note safety precautions specified by manufacturers of fluids, cleaning solvents and adhesives.

20. Think through all procedures before-hand to anticipate possible problems.

21. Do not run an engine in an enclosed space. The area must be well-ventilated.

22. Wear rubber gloves and safety eyewear when handling a battery or battery acid.

NOTES, CAUTIONS AND WARNINGS

The terms NOTE, CAUTION and WARNING have specific meanings in this manual. A NOTE provides additional information to make a step or procedure easier or clearer. Disregarding a NOTE could cause inconvenience, but would not cause damage or personal injury.

A CAUTION emphasizes areas where equipment damage could occur. Disregarding a CAUTION could cause permanent mechanical damage; however, personal injury is unlikely.

A WARNING emphasizes areas where personal injury or even death could result from negligence. Mechanical damage may also occur. WARNINGS *are to be taken seriously.* In some cases, serious injury and death have resulted from disregarding similar warnings.

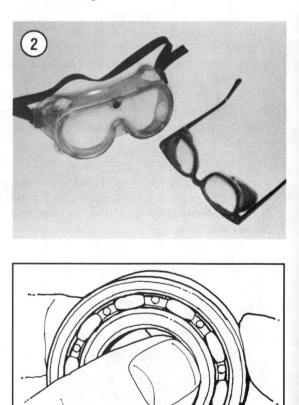

SERVICE HINTS

Most of the service procedures outlined in this manual are straightforward and can be performed by anyone reasonably competent with tools. It is suggested, however, that you consider your own capabilities carefully before attempting any operation involving major disassembly.

1. Safety first must be the overriding concern of any mechanic, regardless of experience. Read and follow the safety rules in the preceding *Safety* section.

2. With regard to procedural terms used in this manual, the term "replace" means to discard a defective part and install a new or exchange unit. "Overhaul" means to remove, disassemble, inspect, measure, repair or replace defective parts, reassemble and install major systems or parts.

3. Before undertaking any work on an engine or piece of equipment, be sure the unit is secured in a safe manner. Poorly supported or secured equipment can cause damage to the unit, as well as possible personal harm. Two hands are often needed to perform a task, which is difficult if one hand is required to hold the unit in place.

4. Repairs go much faster and easier if the engine or equipment is clean before work starts. There are several special cleaners for washing the engine and related parts. Spray or brush on the cleaning solution, following the manufacturer's directions. Rinse parts with a garden hose. Be sure the solution can be safely disposed of according to local regulations. Clean all oily or greasy parts with cleaning solvent when removed.

5. Much of the labor cost charged by mechanics is to remove and disassemble other parts to reach the defective unit. It is usually possible to perform the preliminary operations yourself and then take the defective unit to the dealer for repair.

6. Read the complete service procedure in this manual while looking at the actual parts before performing any work. Be sure the proper procedure is being used (the procedure may be different for various models). Study the illustrations and text until you have a good idea of what is involved in completing the job satisfactorily.

7. If special tools or replacement parts are required, make arrangements to get them before starting work. If special tools must be obtained, either by purchase or renting, determine whether it is better to have the job performed by a professional shop, keeping in mind that if the tool is purchased it will be available for future jobs. Also keep in mind that some jobs may require experience that is available only at a professional shop. This experience can often be acquired through adult-education courses, as well as experimentation, if the consequences of a mistake are understood.

8. Other than simple tests, electrical testing may require sophisticated test equipment and a knowledge of electronics.

CAUTION
Improper electrical testing can sometimes damage electrical components.

9. During disassembly, keep a few general cautions in mind. Excessive hand force is rarely needed to get things apart. If parts are a tight fit, such as a bearing in a case, there is usually a tool designed to separate them. Never use a screwdriver to pry parts with machined surfaces. You will mar the surfaces, which will promote leaks.

10. Make diagrams (or take a Polaroid picture) wherever similar-appearing parts are found. For instance, retaining screws may be of different lengths. Trying to remember where everything was originally located may prove costly. If the job must be stopped for a long period of time, which can occur when ordering parts, remembering details may be impossible.

11. Tag all similar internal parts for location and mark all mating parts for position. Record the number and thickness of any shims as they are removed (A, **Figure 4**); measure with a Vernier caliper or micrometer. Small parts such as screws can be iden-

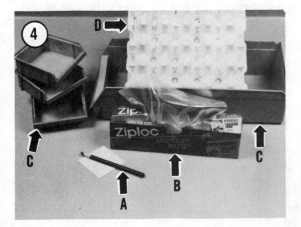

tified by placing them in plastic sandwich bags (B, **Figure 4**). Seal and label them with masking tape.

12. Place parts from a specific area of the engine (e.g. valves, camshaft, balancer, etc.) in boxes (C, **Figure 4**) to keep them separated.

13. When disassembling shaft assemblies, use an egg carton (D, **Figure 4**) and set the parts in the depressions in the order they are removed.

14. Wiring should be tagged with masking tape and marked as each wire is removed. Again, do not rely on memory alone, especially if the wiring has been altered.

15. Finished surfaces should be protected from physical damage and corrosion. Keep gasoline off painted surfaces.

16. Use penetrating oil on frozen or tight screws or bolts, then strike the screw or bolt head a few times with a hammer and punch (use a screwdriver on screws). Avoid the use of heat where possible, as it can warp, melt or affect the temper of parts. Heat also ruins paint and plastics.

17. No parts removed or installed (other than bushings and bearings) in the procedures found in this manual should require unusual force during disassembly or assembly. If a part is difficult to remove or install, find out why before proceeding.

18. Cover all openings after removing parts or components to prevent entrance of dirt or other foreign material.

19. When assembling parts, be sure all shims and washers are installed exactly as they were removed.

20. Whenever a rotating part butts against a stationary part, look for a shim or washer.

21. Installing new gaskets rather than reusing old gaskets is a good practice. Although using old gaskets may be the only possibility in some instances, the probability of a leak occurring is high, resulting in another teardown. Gaskets can be cut from sheets or rolls of gasket material of the same thickness as the old gaskets. Use of gasket forming compounds may be a better alternative to reusing old gaskets.

22. Heavy grease can be used to hold parts in place if they tend to fall out during assembly.

23. Never use wire to clean carburetor jets and air passages. The wire may disfigure the orifices, thereby affecting fuel or air flow.

24. Compressed air is helpful when drying parts and to dislodge debris from passages. Be sure compressed air is not directed against diaphragms or other delicate parts that may be damaged by the

sudden force of the air stream. Do not spin bearings or rotating parts with compressed air; the part can be damaged by rotating at high speed.

25. A baby bottle makes a good measuring device for liquids. Get one that is graduated in fluid ounces and cubic centimeters. DO NOT allow a baby to drink out of it after used in the workshop as residue from the oil or solvent will always remain.

26. Treat a rebuilt engine as a new engine and follow the proper break in procedure.

27. Rushing to complete a job usually creates mistakes that require repeating the job. Take your time and do it right the first time.

SPECIAL TOOLS

Briggs & Stratton offers tools that are designed to accomplish specific jobs on Briggs & Stratton engines. Where the use of a Briggs & Stratton tool is necessary to satisfactorily accomplish a particular job, the Briggs & Stratton tool is specified in the text. The tools are available either separately or as part of Briggs & Stratton Tool Kit 19300 (see Chapter Twelve). Briggs & Stratton tools can be obtained through a dealer or distributor. See Chapter Three for a list of Briggs & Stratton distributors who can provide the name of a local dealer. In some cases, the tool is also available from a tool manufacturer or from an aftermarket parts supplier. A small-engine dealer can usually obtain the tools or provide the name of a supplier.

Be careful when substituting a "home-made" tool for a recommended tool. Although time and money may be saved if an existing or fabricated tool can be made to work, consider the possibilities if the tool does not work properly. If the substitute tool damages the engine, the cost to repair the damage, as well

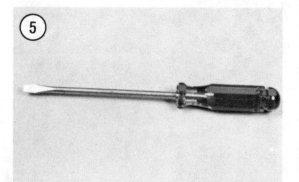

as losing time, may exceed the cost of the recommended tool.

BASIC HAND TOOLS

A good set of tools is essential to undertaking engine repair in a safe, efficient and satisfactory manner. The quality and extent of a mechanic's tool collection should be determined by the work to be performed and the frequency of use. Cheap, low-quality tools often break and do not perform well, often damaging the equipment as well as exposing the mechanic to injury if the tool should fail during a high-risk job. Buying a tool for use one time may be a waste of money if the tool could be rented instead, or the job requiring the special tool could be performed by a repair or machine shop for a nominal fee.

There is a collection of basic tools that is present in the tool set of any engine mechanic. A journeyman mechanic may purchase a complete "A to Z" set of tools at the outset, since the tools are essential for quality, productive work, but most experienced do-it-yourselfers build their tool collections based on what is needed. As experience is gained, more complex jobs are tackled and the tools needed are added to the collection.

The following points should be considered when purchasing tools. Quality tools may be expensive at the outset, but they last longer, fit better and may have features not found in cheaper tools. Tools can be purchased by mail order, at parts stores, at tool supply outlets, and from general merchandisers. All of the former offer high quality as well as cheap tools. A quality tool manufacturer will replace a tool if it breaks or wears out when used for jobs it was designed. Before purchasing tools, ask the supplier if free replacement is guaranteed by the tool manufacturer and what the procedure is; free replacement may be a waste of time if not easy and prompt.

Before purchasing tools, be sure of the type fasteners used on the engine, whether U.S. standard or metric. Be aware that both U.S. and metric tools may be needed as both types of fasteners may be present; the engine block may have U.S. fasteners while the engine components, such as the carburetor, may have metric fasteners.

Some of the more common hand tools that are frequently needed during engine service and repair are outlined in the following paragraphs.

Screwdrivers

The screwdriver is a very basic tool, but if used improperly it will do more damage than good. The slot on a screw has a definite dimension and shape. Through improper use or selection, a screwdriver can damage the screw head, making removal of the screw difficult. A screwdriver must be selected to conform to the shape of the screw head used. Two basic types of screwdrivers are required: standard (flat-blade or slot-blade) screwdrivers (**Figure 5**) and Phillips screwdrivers (**Figure 6**).

Note the following when selecting and using screwdrivers.

1. The screwdriver must always fit the screw head. If the screwdriver blade is too small for the screw slot, damage may occur to the screw slot and screwdriver. If the blade is too large, it cannot engage the slot properly and will result in damage to the screw head.

2. Standard screwdrivers are identified by the length of their blade. A 6 in. screwdriver has a blade 6 in. long. The width of the screwdriver blade will vary, so make sure that the blade engages the screw slot the complete width of the screw.

3. Phillips screwdrivers are sized according to their point size and numbered one through four. The degree of taper determines the point size with a number one being the most pointed. The points become more blunt as their number increases.

NOTE
You should also be aware of another screwdriver similar to the Phillips, and that is the Reed and Prince tip. Like the Phillips, the Reed and Prince screwdriver tip forms an "X" but with one

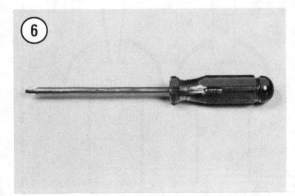

major exception, the Reed and Prince screwdriver has a much more pointed tip. The Reed and Prince screwdriver should never be used on Phillips screws and vice versa. Intermixing these screwdrivers will cause damage to the screw and screwdriver. If you have both types in your tool box and they are similar in appearance, you may want to identify them by painting the screwdriver shank underneath the handle.

4. When selecting screwdrivers, note that you can apply more power with less effort with a longer screwdriver than with a short one. Of course, there will be situations where only a short handled screwdriver can be used. Keep this in mind though, when removing tight screws.

5. Because the working end of a screwdriver receives quite a bit of abuse, you should purchase screwdrivers with hardened tips. The extra money will be well spent.

Screwdrivers are available in sets which often include an assortment of standard and Phillips blades. If you buy them individually, buy at least the following:

a. Standard screwdriver—5/16 × 6 in. blade.

b. Standard screwdriver—3/8 × 12 in. blade.

c. Phillips screwdriver—size 2 tip, 6 in. blade.

d. Phillips screwdriver—size 3 tip, 6 and 8 in. blade.

Use screwdrivers only for driving screws. Never use a screwdriver for prying or chiseling metal. Do not try to remove a Phillips, Torx or Allen head screw with a standard screwdriver (unless the screw has a combination head that will accept either type); you can damage the head so that the proper tool will be unable to remove it.

Keep screwdrivers in the proper condition and they will last longer and perform better. Always keep the tip of a standard screwdriver in good condition. **Figure 7** shows how to grind the tip to the proper shape if it becomes damaged. Note the symmetrical sides of the tip.

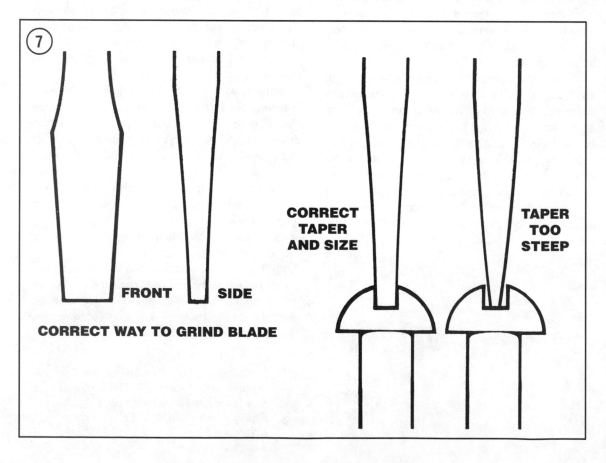

FRONT SIDE

CORRECT WAY TO GRIND BLADE

CORRECT TAPER AND SIZE

TAPER TOO STEEP

Pliers

Pliers come in a wide range of types and sizes. Pliers are useful for cutting, bending and crimping. They should never be used to cut hardened objects or to turn bolts or nuts. **Figure 8** illustrates several types of pliers useful for engine service and repair.

Each type of pliers has a specialized function. Slip-joint pliers are general purpose pliers and are used mainly for holding things and for bending.

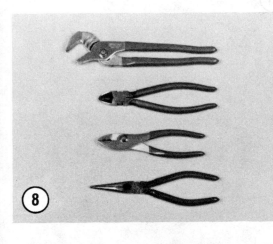

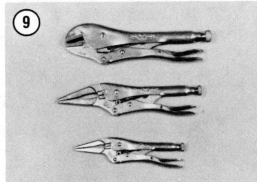

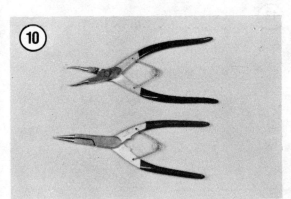

Needlenose pliers are used to hold or bend small objects. Water pump pliers can be adjusted to hold various sizes of objects; the jaws remain parallel to grip around objects such as pipe or tubing. There are many more types of pliers.

> *CAUTION*
> *Pliers should not be used for loosening or tightening nuts or bolts. The pliers' sharp teeth will grind off the nut or bolt corners and damage it.*

> *CAUTION*
> *If slip-joint or water pump pliers are going to be used to hold an object with a finished surface, wrap the object with heavy tape or rubber for protection.*

Locking Pliers

Locking pliers (**Figure 9**) are used to hold objects very tightly while another task is performed on the object. While locking pliers work well, caution should be followed with their use. Because locking pliers exert more force than regular pliers, their sharp jaws can permanently scar the object. In addition, when locking pliers are locked into position, they can crush or deform thin-walled material.

Locking pliers are available in many types for more specific tasks.

Snap Ring Pliers

Snap ring pliers (**Figure 10**) are special in that they are used to remove or install snap rings. When purchasing snap ring pliers, there are two kinds from which to choose. External pliers (spreading) are used to remove snap rings that fit on the outside of a shaft. Internal pliers (squeezing) are used to remove snap rings that fit inside a housing.

> *WARNING*
> *Because snap rings can sometimes slip and "fly off" during removal and installation, always wear safety glasses when servicing them.*

Box-end, Open-end and Combination Wrenches

Box-end and open-end wrenches (**Figure 11**) are available in sets or separately in a variety of sizes. The size number stamped near the end refers to the distance between two parallel flats on the hex head bolt or nut.

Box-end wrenches are usually superior to open-end wrenches. Open-end wrenches grip the nut on only two flats. Unless a wrench fits well, it may slip and round off the points on the nut. The box-end wrench grips on all six flats. Both 6-point and 12-point openings on box-end wrenches are available. The 6-point gives superior holding power; the 12-point allows a shorter swing.

Combination wrenches which are open on one side and boxed on the other are also available. Both ends are the same size.

No matter which style of wrench is used, proper use is important to prevent personal injury. When using a wrench, get into the habit of pulling the wrench toward you. This technique will reduce the risk of injuring your hand if the wrench should slip. If you have to push the wrench away from you to loosen or tighten a fastener, open and push with the palm of your hand; your fingers and knuckles will be out of the way if the wrench slips. Before using a wrench, always think ahead as to what could happen if the wrench should slip or if the fastener strips or breaks.

Adjustable Wrenches

An adjustable wrench can be adjusted to fit nearly any nut or bolt head which has clear access around its entire perimeter. Adjustable wrenches are best used as a backup wrench to keep a large nut or bolt from turning while the other end is being loosened or tightened with a proper wrench. See **Figure 12**.

Adjustable wrenches have only two gripping surfaces which makes them more subject to slipping off the fastener and damaging the part and possibly your hand. See *Box-end, Open-end and Combination Wrenches* in this chapter.

These wrenches are directional; the solid jaw must be the one transmitting the force. If you use the adjustable jaw to transmit the force, it will loosen and possibly slip off.

Adjustable wrenches come in a variety of sizes, but 6 in. and 8 in. wrenches are generally most useful.

Socket Wrenches

This type is undoubtedly the fastest, safest and most convenient to use. Sockets which attach to a ratchet handle (**Figure 13**) are available with 6-point or 12-point openings and 1/4, 3/8, 1/2 and 3/4 in. drives. The drive size indicates the size of the square hole which mates with the ratchet handle.

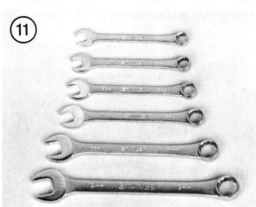

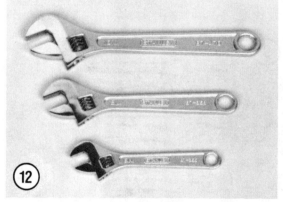

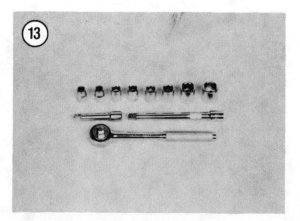

Torque Wrench

A torque wrench (**Figure 14**) is used with a socket to measure how tightly a nut or bolt is installed. They come in a wide price range and with either 3/8 or 1/2 in. square drives. The drive size indicates the size of the square drive which mates with the socket.

For general small engine repair, a torque wrench that measures 0-200 in.-lb. (0-23 N•m) and one that measures 0-150 ft.-lb. (0-200 N•m) will be most useful.

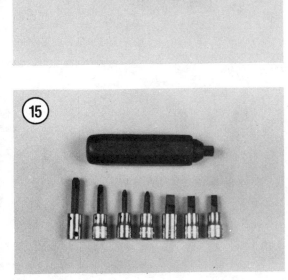

Impact Driver

This tool makes removal of tight fasteners easy and eliminates damage to bolts and screw slots. Impact drivers and interchangeable bits (**Figure 15**) are available at most large hardware and tool stores. Don't purchase a cheap impact driver as it won't operate as well as a moderately priced impact driver. Sockets can also be used with a hand impact driver. However, make sure the socket is designed for use with an impact driver or air tool. Do not use regular hand-type sockets, as they may shatter during use.

Hammers

The correct hammer (**Figure 16**) is necessary for repairs. Use only a hammer with a face (or head) of rubber or plastic or the soft-faced type that is filled with lead shot. These are sometimes necessary in engine teardowns. *Never* use a metal-faced hammer on engine components as severe damage will result in most cases. Ball-peen or machinist's hammers will be required when striking another tool, such as a punch or impact driver. When striking a hammer against a punch, cold chisel or similar tool, the face of the hammer should be at least 1/2 in. larger than the head of the tool. When it is necessary to strike hard against a steel part without damaging it, a brass hammer should be used. A brass hammer can be used because brass will give when striking a harder object.

When using hammers, note the following.

1. *Always* wear safety glasses when using a hammer.

2. Inspect hammers for damaged or broken parts. Repair or replace the hammer as required. *Do not* use a hammer with a taped handle.

3. Always wipe oil or grease off of the hammer before using it.

4. The head of the hammer should always strike the object squarely. Do not use the side of the hammer or the handle to strike an object.

5. Always use the correct hammer for the job.

Allen Wrenches

Allen wrenches (**Figure 17**) are available in sets or separately in a variety of sizes. These sets come in SAE and metric size. Allen screws are sometimes called socket screws. Note that a variety of tools are

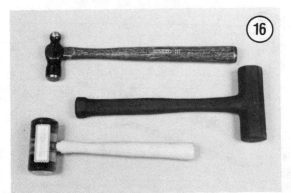

available as shown in **Figure 17** to fit Allen screws, which may be located in confined areas.

Chisels and Punches

Chisels and punches (**Figure 18**) are made of tool steel and configured in a variety of shapes and sizes. Punches can be used to create a locating dimple for drilling, aligning holes in mating parts, driving out pins and applying force in tight areas. Chisels are useful when metal must be chipped, gouged or cut, usually in a last-resort situation.

> *CAUTION*
> *Never use a screwdriver as a punch or chisel. The handle and metal in the blade are not capable of withstanding sharp hammer blows. The screwdriver will be ruined and a chisel or punch would probably have done the job better.*

Files

A selection of files (**Figure 19**) is needed to cut metal, such as smoothing large flat areas or removing burrs and irregularities. Files are available in various lengths, shapes and cutting patterns. Double-cut files are generally preferred for general engine work. A file handle should be attached to the file. A file card should be used to clean metal chips from the file teeth.

Tap and Die Set

A complete tap and die set (**Figure 20**) is a relatively expensive tool. But when you need a tap or die to restore a damaged thread, a tap and die set recoup the price over a period of time both in parts costs and lost time. Tap and die sets are available for both U.S. standard and metric threads.

Screw Extractors

When a screw or bolt is broken off in a hole, a screw extractor (**Figure 21**) can sometimes be used to remove the screw or bolt. After a hole is drilled in the screw or bolt, the extractor is inserted in the hole and the left-hand flutes on the extractor grip the screw or bolt so it can be unscrewed. Use of screw

extractors is discussed in Chapter Ten under *Removing Broken Screws or Bolts*.

Drivers and Pullers

These tools are used to remove and install oil seals, bushings, bearings, gears and flywheels. These will be called out as needed in the service sections of this manual.

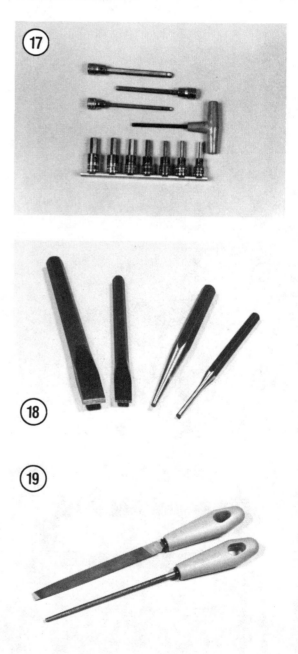

Engine Overhaul Tools

Tools such as valve spring compressors, cylinder ridge reamers, cylinder hones, piston ring compressors and valve service tools are discussed in Chapter Eleven.

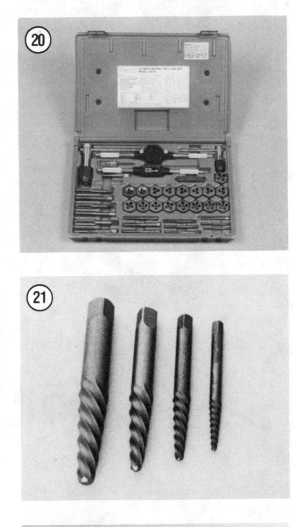

Spark Tester

A quick way to check the ignition system is to connect a spark tester (**Figure 22**) to the end of the spark plug wire and operate the engine's starter. A visible spark should jump the gap on the tester. A variety of spark testers is available from engine and aftermarket manufacturers. The gap distance is adjustable on some testers, while more sophisticated testers have a pressure chamber that simulates compression pressure in the cylinder.

Multimeter or Volt-Ohmmeter (VOM)

This instrument (**Figure 23**) is invaluable for electrical system troubleshooting and service. A few of its functions may be duplicated by homemade test equipment, but for the serious mechanic it is a must. Its uses are described in the applicable section of the book.

Compression Gauge

An engine with low compression cannot be properly tuned and will not develop full power. A compression gauge measures engine compression. The one shown in **Figure 24** has a flexible stem with an extension that permits more convenient reading of the gauge. The fitting on the hose end screws into the spark plug hole. Some types of compression gauges have a rubber tip (**Figure 25**) that is held manually in the spark plug hole.

Battery Hydrometer

A hydrometer (**Figure 26**) is the best way to check a battery's state of charge. A hydrometer measures the weight or density (specific gravity) of the battery acid.

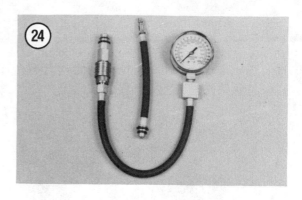

Portable Tachometer

A portable tachometer (**Figure 27**) is necessary for tuning the engine. Carburetor and governor adjustments must be performed at specific engine speeds. Two types are available, a mechanical type that uses a reed to sense engine rpm or an electrical type that senses engine rpm inductively at the spark plug wire.

PRECISION MEASURING TOOLS

Measurement is an important part of servicing any engine. When performing many of the service procedures in this manual, it will be necessary to make a number of measurements. These include basic checks such as engine compression and spark plug gap. Engine overhauling will require measurements to determine the condition of the piston, cylinder bore, crankshaft and other engine components. When making these measurements, the degree of accuracy will dictate which tool is required. Precision measuring tools are expensive. To avoid purchase of an expensive tool for one-time use, it may be wise to have the measurement performed by a professional shop. Some measuring tools, such as micrometers, require experience to be used accurately. This "feel" should be attained before making critical measurements. Following is a descriptive list of measuring tools that might be used during an engine overhaul.

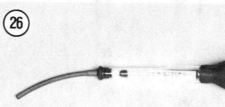

Feeler Gauges

Feeler gauges (**Figure 28**) are made of either a piece of a flat or round hardened steel of a specified thickness. Wire (round) gauges are used to measure spark plug gap. Flat gauges are used for all other measurements.

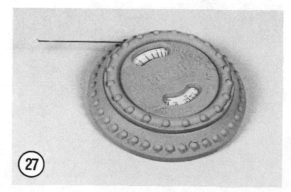

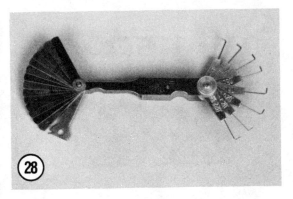

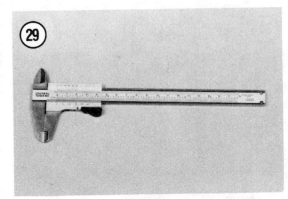

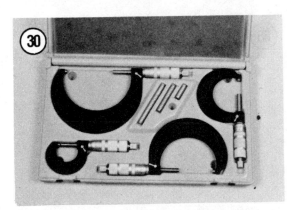

Vernier Caliper

A Vernier caliper (**Figure 29**) is invaluable when it is necessary to measure inside, outside and depth measurements with close precision. It can be used to measure the thickness of shims and thrust washers. Vernier calipers are available in a wide assortment of styles and price ranges.

Outside Micrometers

The outside micrometer (**Figure 30**) is used for very exact measurements of close-tolerance components. It can be used to measure the outside diameter of a piston as well as for shims and thrust washers. Outside micrometers will be required to transfer measurements from bore, snap and small hole gauges. Micrometers can be purchased individually or in a set.

Dial Indicator

Dial indicators (**Figure 31**) are precision tools used to check crankshaft runout and end play limits. Dial indicators may be purchased individually or as a set with adapters that facilitate mounting the indicator in a position for accurate measurement.

Cylinder Bore Gauge

The cylinder bore gauge is a very specialized precision tool. The gauge set shown in **Figure 32** is comprised of a dial indicator, handle and a number of length adapters to adapt the gauge to different bore sizes. The bore gauge can be used to make cylinder bore measurements such as bore size, taper and out-of-round. An outside micrometer must be

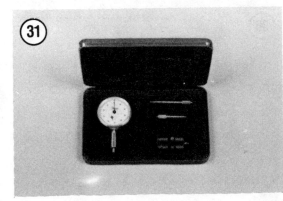

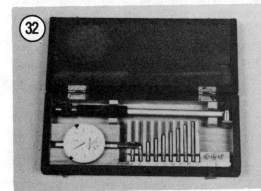

used together with the bore gauge to determine bore dimensions.

Telescoping Gauges

Telescoping gauges (**Figure 33**) can be used to measure hole diameters from 5/16 in. to 6 in. The telescoping gauge does not have a scale gauge for direct reading. Thus an outside micrometer must be used in conjunction with the telescoping gauges to determine bore dimensions.

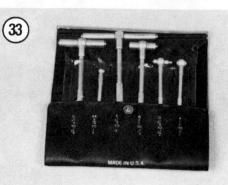

Small Hole Gauges

A set of small hole gauges (**Figure 34**) allows measurement of a hole, groove or slot ranging in size up to 1/2 in. An outside micrometer must be used together with the small hole gauge to determine bore dimensions.

Screw Pitch Gauge

A screw pitch gauge (**Figure 35**) determines the thread pitch of bolts, screws, and other threaded fasteners. The gauge is made up of a number of thin plates. Each plate has a thread shape cut on one edge to match one thread pitch. When using a screw pitch gauge to determine a thread pitch size, try to fit different blade sizes onto the bolt thread until both threads match.

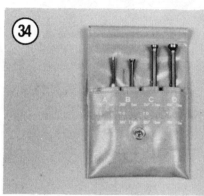

Surface Plate

A surface plate can be used to check the flatness of parts or to provide a perfectly flat surface for minor resurfacing of cylinder head or other critical gasket surfaces. While industrial quality surface plates are very expensive, a suitable substitute can be improvised using a thick metal plate. The metal plate shown in **Figure 36** has a piece of sandpaper glued to its surface that is used for cleaning and smoothing cylinder head and crankcase mating surfaces.

> *NOTE*
> *Check with a local machine shop on the availability and cost of having a metal plate machined for use as a surface plate.*

FASTENERS

Fasteners (screws, bolts, nuts, studs, pins, clips, etc.) are used to secure the various pieces of the engine together. Proper selection and installation of fasteners is important to ensure that the engine operates satisfactorily, otherwise, engine failure is possible.

Threaded Fasteners

Most of the components of an engine are held together by threaded fasteners, i.e. screws, bolts, nuts and studs. Most fasteners are tightened by turning clockwise (right-hand threads), although some fasteners may have left-hand threads if rotating parts can cause loosening.

Two dimensions are needed to match threaded fasteners: the number of threads in a given distance and the nominal outside diameter of the threads. Two standards are currently used in the United States to specify the dimensions of threaded fasteners, the U.S. common system and the metric system. Particular attention must be paid when working on a later

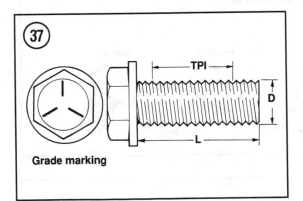

Grade marking

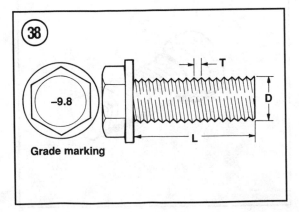

Grade marking

model engine as both U.S. and metric fasteners may be used, causing damage to threads if fasteners are mismatched during assembly.

NOTE
Threaded fasteners should be hand tightened during initial assembly to be sure mismatched fasteners are not being used and crossthreading is not occurring. If fasteners are hard to turn, determine cause before applying tool for final tightening.

Screws and bolts built to U.S. common system standard are classified by length (L, **Figure 37**), nominal diameter (D) and threads per inch (TPI). A typical bolt might be identified by the numbers 7/16—14 × 1-1/2, which would indicate that the bolt has a nominal diameter of 7/16 in., 14 threads per inch and a length of 1-1/2 in.

U.S. screws and bolts are graded according to Society of Automotive Engineers (SAE) specifications to indicate their strength. Slash marks are located on the top of the screw or bolt as shown in **Figure 37** to indicate the strength grade with a greater number of slashes indicating greater strength. Ungraded screws and bolts (no slash marks on head) are the weakest.

Metric screws and bolts are classified by length (L, **Figure 38**), nominal diameter (D) and distance between thread crests (T). A typical bolt might be identified by the numbers 12 × 1.25—130, which would indicate that the bolt has a nominal diameter of 12 mm, the distance between threads crests is 1.25 mm and bolt length is 130 mm.

The strength of metric screws and bolts is indicated by numbers located on the top of the screw or bolt as shown in **Figure 38**. The higher the number the stronger the screw or bolt. Unnumbered screws or bolts are the weakest.

CAUTION
***Do not** install screws or bolts with a lower strength grade classification than installed originally by engine or equipment manufacturer. Doing so may cause engine or equipment failure and possible injury.*

Tightening a screw or bolt increases the clamping force it exerts, the stronger the screw or bolt, the greater the clamping force. In most cases, the engine or equipment manufacturer specifies the tightening force (torque) to be used when tightening a specific screw or bolt. If not, recommended tightening torque specifications for general usage may be found in **Table 1**.

Screws and bolts are manufactured with a variety of head shapes to fit specific design requirements. Most machinery is equipped with the common hex and slotted head types, but other types, like those shown in **Figure 39** will also be encountered. As noted in the preceding *Basic Hand Tools* section, the proper tool must be used when turning a screw or bolt.

The most common nut used is the hex nut (**Figure 40**), often used with a lockwasher. Self-locking nuts have a nylon insert that prevents loosening; no lockwasher is required. Wing nuts, designed for fast removal by hand, are used for convenience in noncritical locations. Nuts are sized using the same system as screws and bolts. On hex-type nuts, the distance between two opposing flats indicates the proper wrench size to be used.

Self-locking screws, bolts and nuts may use a locking mechanism that utilizes an interference fit between mating threads. Interference is achieved in various ways: by distorting threads, coating threads with dry adhesive or nylon, distorting the top of an all-metal nut, using a nylon insert in the center or at the top of a nut, etc. Self-locking fasteners offer greater holding strength and better vibration resistance than standard fasteners. Some of these self-locking screws, bolts and nuts can be reused if in good condition; others, like the trilobial screw shown in **Figure 41**, are thread-rolling screws that form their own threads when installed and cannot be removed without displacement of the thread pattern. For greatest safety, self-locking fasteners should be discarded and new ones installed whenever components are disassembled.

Washers

There are two basic types of washers: flat washers and lockwashers. Flat washers are simple discs with

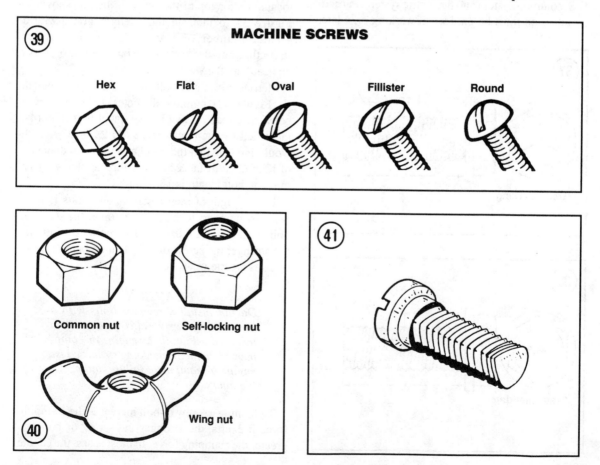

MACHINE SCREWS

Hex   Flat   Oval   Fillister   Round

Common nut   Self-locking nut

Wing nut

a hole to fit a screw or bolt. Lockwashers are designed to prevent a fastener from working loose due to vibration, expansion and contraction. Several types of washers are shown in **Figure 42**. Note that flat washers are often used between a lockwasher and a fastener to provide a smooth bearing surface. This allows the fastener to be turned easily with a tool.

Cotter Pins

Cotter pins (**Figure 43**) are used to secure special kinds of fasteners. The threaded stud must have a

hole in it; the nut or nut lock piece has castellations around which the cotter pin ends wrap. Cotter pins should not be reused after removal.

Retaining Rings

Retaining rings are designed to prevent or limit axial movement of shafts and bearings. Some examples of retaining rings are shown in **Figure 44**. A common type of retaining ring is known as a snap ring. Snap rings may have a rectangular or circular cross-section with plain ends or holes in the ends (Truarc) to accommodate special snap ring pliers. Another common retaining ring is the E-ring, which is usually found on linkage and other locations where appreciable force is not placed against the ring. Retaining rings fit in a groove that is machined to be used with a specific type retaining ring. Use of a retaining ring other than that specified by the manufacturer may cause engine damage and possible failure.

SEALANTS, CEMENTS AND CLEANERS

Sealants And Adhesives

Many mating surfaces of an engine require a gasket or seal between them to prevent fluids and gases from passing through the joint. At times, the

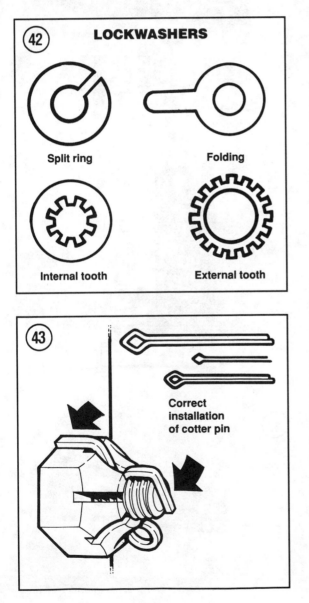

42 **LOCKWASHERS**

Split ring

Folding

Internal tooth

External tooth

43

Correct installation of cotter pin

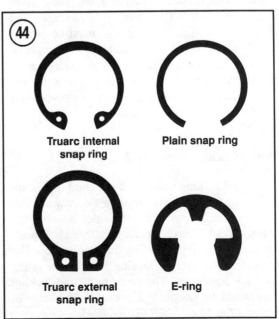

44

Truarc internal snap ring

Plain snap ring

Truarc external snap ring

E-ring

gasket or seal may be installed as is, however, most times some type of substance is applied to enhance the sealing capability of the gasket or seal. Note, however, that a sealing compound may be added to the gasket or seal during manufacture and adding sealant may cause premature failure of the gasket or seal.

RTV Sealants

One of the most common sealants is RTV (room temperature vulcanizing) sealant (**Figure 45**). This sealant hardens (cures) at room temperature over a period of several hours, which allows sufficient time to reposition parts if necessary without damaging the gaskets. RTV sealant is designed for different uses, including high temperatures. If in doubt as to correct type to use, ask vendor or read manufacturer's literature.

Cements and Adhesives

A wide variety of cements and adhesives is available (**Figure 46**), their use dependent on the type of materials to be sealed, and to some extent, the personal preference of the mechanic. Automotive parts stores offer the widest selection of cements and adhesives. Some points to consider when selecting cements or adhesives: the type of material being sealed (metal, rubber, plastic, etc.), the type of fluid contacting the seal (gasoline, oil, water, etc.) and whether the seal is permanent or must be broken periodically, in which case a pliable sealant might be desirable. Unless experienced in the selection of cements and adhesives, you should follow the engine or equipment manufacturer recommendation if a particular sealant is specified.

Thread Locking Compound

A thread locking compound is a fluid that is applied to fastener threads. After the fastener is tightened, the fluid dries to a solid filler between the mating threads, thereby locking the threads in position and preventing loosening due to vibration. The major manufacturer of locking compounds is the Loctite Corporation. The common thread locking compounds are Loctite 242 (a blue fluid) shown in **Figure 47** and Loctite 271 (a red fluid).

Loctite 242 (blue) has medium strength which allows unscrewing with normal hand tools. Loctite 271 (red) has high strength which may require special tools, such as a press or puller, as well as heat for disassembly.

Before applying Loctite, the contacting threads should be as clean as possible (aerosol electrical contact cleaner works well). Use only as much Loctite as necessary, usually one or two drops depending

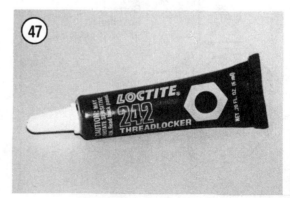

on the size of fastener. Excess fluid can work its way into adjoining parts.

Cleaners and Solvents

Cleaners and solvents are helpful in removing oil, grease and other residue found on engines and other equipment. Before purchasing cleaners and solvents, consider how they will be used and disposed of, particularly if they are not water soluble. Local ordinances may require special procedures for the disposal of certain cleaners and solvents.

> *WARNING*
> *Some cleaners and solvents are harmful and may be flammable. Be sure to adhere to any safety precautions noted on the container or in the manufacturer's literature. Petroleum-resistant gloves are recommended to protect hands from the harmful effect of cleaners and solvents.*

> *NOTE*
> *An alternative for a big job is to take the parts to an automotive machine shop that will clean them for a few dollars, but be sure to ask them what they can clean. Some shops can't clean aluminum and the cleaning solution will damage plastic parts. When returned, always clean the parts again with an aerosol cleaner to remove any residue.*

A variety of cleaners and solvents is shown in **Figure 48**. Cleaners designed for ignition contact cleaning are excellent for removing light oil from a part without leaving a residue. Cleaners designed to remove heavy oil and grease residue, called degreasers, contain a solvent that usually must "work" awhile. Some degreasers can be washed off with water. Removal of stubborn gaskets may be eased by using a solvent designed to remove gaskets.

One of the more powerful cleaning solutions is carburetor cleaner. It is designed to dissolve the varnish that may build up in carburetor jets and orifices. Good carburetor cleaner is usually expensive and requires special disposal. Carefully read directions before purchase; nonmetallic parts should not be immersed in carburetor cleaner.

LUBRICANTS

Lubricants are generally classified as oils if fluid, or greases if semi-solid. Grease is an oil which has been thickened by mixing with an additive.

Oil

Oil for four-stroke engines is graded by the American Petroleum Institute (API) and the Society of Automotive Engineers (SAE) in several categories. Oil containers display these ratings on the top of the oil container or on the label (**Figure 49**).

API oil grade is indicated by two letters, i.e., SE, SF, SG or SH. The first letter, "S," specifies that the oil is designed for use in a gasoline engine. The second letter indicates the API test grade that the oil meets. Based on engine performance and expected use, the engine manufacturer will specify the API grade that is approved for use in an engine.

Viscosity is an indication of the oil's thickness. The SAE uses numbers to indicate viscosity; thin oils have low numbers while thick oils have high numbers. A "W" after the number indicates that the viscosity testing was done at low temperature to

simulate cold-weather operation. Engine oils fall into the 5W-30 and 20W-50 range.

Multigrade oils (for example 10W-40) are less viscous (thinner) at low temperatures and more viscous (thicker) at high temperatures than straight-grade oils (for example SAE 30). This allows the oil to perform efficiently across a wide range of engine operating conditions. The lower the number, the better the engine will start in cold climates. Higher numbers are usually recommended for engines running in hot weather conditions.

Grease

Greases are graded by the National Lubricating Grease Institute (NLGI). Greases are graded by number according to the consistency of the grease; these range from number 000 to number 6 with number 6 being the most solid. A typical multipurpose grease is NLGI number 2. For specific applica-

tions, equipment manufacturers may require grease with an additive such as molybdenum disulfide (MOS2).

In some instances, an antiseize lubricant may be specified (**Figure 50**). The antiseize lubricant prevents the formation of corrosion that may lock parts together.

Table 1 GENERAL TORQUE SPECIFICATIONS

					SAE 2	SAE 5	SAE 7	SAE 8		
Type*					**Body size or outside diameter (in.)**					
	1/4	5/16	3/8	7/16	1/2	9/16	5/8	3/4	7/8	1
					Torque (ft.-lb.)					
SAE 2	6	12	20	32	47	69	96	155	206	310
SAE 5	10	19	33	54	78	114	154	257	382	587
SAE 7	13	25	44	71	110	154	215	360	570	840
SAE 8	14	29	47	78	119	169	230	380	600	700

* Fastener strength of SAE bolts can be determined by the bolt or screw head "grade markings." Unmarked bolt-heads and cap-screws are usually considered to be mild steel. Basically, the greater the number of "grade markings," the higher the fastener quality.

CHAPTER TWO

ENGINE FUNDAMENTALS

OPERATING PRINCIPLES

The Briggs & Stratton engines covered in this manual are classified as internal combustion reciprocating engines.

The source of power is heat generated when a mixture of air and fuel is directed into the engine and ignited. Heat causes expansion of air trapped in the closed cylinder of the engine (see **Figure 1** and **Figure 2**). A piston in the cylinder is forced through the cylinder in linear motion, which is translated into rotary motion through the connecting rod attached to the crankshaft crankpin. The process is repeated resulting in reciprocating piston movement.

There are five events that must occur for the engine to produce power. This series of events is called the "work cycle" and must be repeated for the engine to run. The events are named intake, compression, ignition, power and exhaust. The description and sequence are explained as follows:

1. *Intake*—As the piston moves downward, the exhaust valve is closed and the intake valve opens, allowing the new air:fuel mixture from the carburetor to be drawn into the cylinder (A, **Figure 3**). When the piston reaches the bottom of its travel, the intake valve closes, sealing the cylinder.

2. *Compression*—While the crankshaft continues to rotate, the piston moves toward the top of the cylinder, compressing the air:fuel mixture (B, **Figure 3**).

3. *Ignition*—As the piston almost reaches the top of its travel, the spark plug fires, igniting the compressed air:fuel mixture (C, **Figure 3**).

4. *Power*—The piston continues to top dead center, then is pushed downward by the rapidly expanding gases created as the air:fuel mixture burns in the cylinder (D, **Figure 3**).

5. *Exhaust*—When the piston reaches the bottom of its stroke, the exhaust valve opens. As the piston moves upward in the cylinder, combustion byproducts are forced out of the cylinder through the exhaust passage. After the piston has reached the top of its stroke, the exhaust valve closes and a new cycle begins with the intake event (E, **Figure 3**).

The succession of events in the work cycle may be accomplished in two or four strokes of the piston (the stroke is full piston travel in either direction). Note that the five events of the work cycle shown in **Figure 3** took place while the piston traveled through four strokes. Some engines are classified as two-stroke engines, performing the work cycle in two strokes of the piston. The Briggs & Stratton engines covered in this manual are four-stroke cycle engines.

MAJOR ENGINE COMPONENTS

The engine is comprised of components and systems that must operate properly for efficient engine operation. The fuel and electrical systems are discussed in later chapters of this manual. Refer to **Figure 4** to identify the major components of a typical four-stroke engine described below.

1. *Air filter*—prevents the entrance of dirt and other debris that will damage the engine if unfiltered.

2. *Carburetor*—mixes fuel with air in the proper ratio to produce a combustible mixture. See Chapter Six.

3. *Intake manifold*—directs fuel:air mixture from carburetor to engine.

4. *Flywheel*—inertia produced by the rotating flywheel maintains crankshaft rotation when not on power stroke; may house magnets for ignition; fins move air for engine cooling; may be part of starter mechanism.

5. *Ignition system*—generates electricity so a spark occurs at the spark plug gap just as the piston reaches a specified position in the cylinder. See Chapter Seven.

6. *Oil seal*—prevents oil in the crankcase from escaping.

7. *Crankcase*—houses internal engine components. Includes the cylinder which is cast as a one-piece unit with crankcase.

8. *Governor linkage*—transfers movement of internal governor assembly (26) to carburetor control linkage.

9. *Spark plug*—ignites fuel:air mixture. See *Electrical System*.

10. *Cylinder head*—encloses one end of the cylinder; may be removed for access to cylinder, piston and valves.

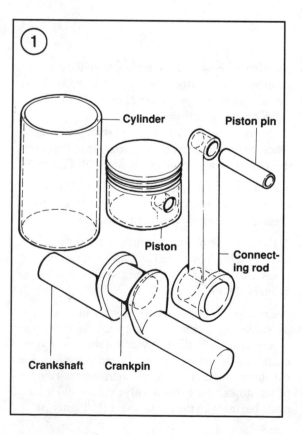

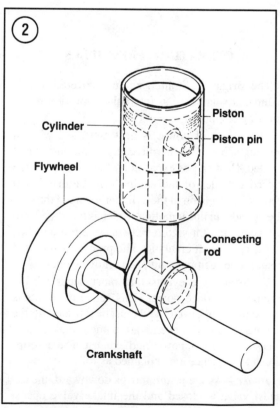

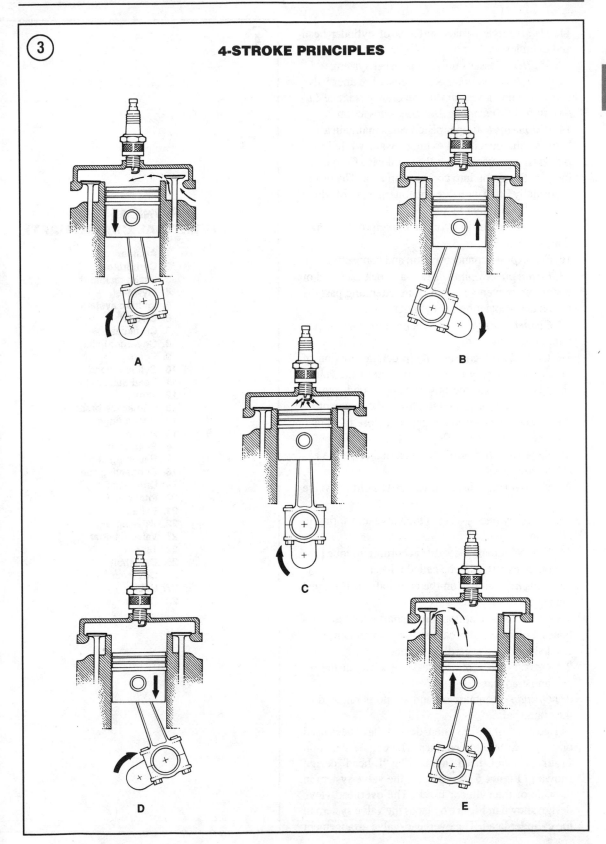

3

4-STROKE PRINCIPLES

A

B

C

D

E

2

11. *Head gasket*—seals surfaces of cylinder head and cylinder.

12. *Muffler*—lessens noise in exhaust system.

13. *Crankcase breather*—contains a breather valve that maintains a vacuum in the crankcase. See *Lubrication, Maintenance And Tune-up* section.

14. *Piston rings*—upper piston rings maintain a seal between the piston and cylinder wall, while lower piston ring prevents oil in the crankcase from flowing past the piston into combustion area. The piston is normally fitted with three piston rings, all of which are usually different in design.

15. *Piston*—slides in cylinder in reciprocating motion.

16. *Piston pin*—connects piston and connecting rod.

17. *Piston pin retaining clips*—a clip at each end of piston pin prevents the pin from extending past the piston and contacting the cylinder wall.

18. *Connecting rod*—transfers motion from the piston to the crankshaft.

19. *Crankshaft*—converts reciprocating motion of the piston to rotary motion. One end of the crankshaft is designated the power take-off end (pto) so power can be transmitted to powered equipment.

20. *Intake valve*—used to open and close the intake passage.

21. *Exhaust valve*—used to open and close the exhaust passage.

22. *Valve spring*—used on valves to hold the valve closed.

23. *Valve retainer*—secures the valve and spring in position.

24. *Tappet*—opens the valve according to lobe profile on camshaft. May be called a lifter.

25. *Camshaft*—lobes on the camshaft push against the tappets to open the valves.

26. *Governor*—Monitors crankshaft speed and actuates linkage to the carburetor to maintain a set crankshaft speed regardless of load.

27. *Gasket*—prevents oil leakage between the oil pan and crankcase.

28. *Oil pan*—contains oil and supports one end of the crankshaft.

Two types of valve system designs have been used on Briggs & Stratton engines. The engine shown in **Figure 4** is an L-head engine. The "L-head" design shown in **Figure 5** incorporates the valve system in the side of the cylinder block. The overhead-valve design shown in **Figure 6** places the valve system in the cylinder head. The overhead-valve arrangement

④

**ENGINE ASSEMBLY
(VERTICAL CRANKSHAFT)**

1. Air filter
2. Carburetor
3. Intake manifold
4. Flywheel
5. Ignition system
6. Oil seal
7. Crankcase
8. Governor linkage
9. Spark plug
10. Cylinder head
11. Head gasket
12. Muffler
13. Crankcase breather
14. Piston rings
15. Piston
16. Piston pin
17. Retaining clip
18. Connecting rod
19. Crankshaft
20. Intake valve
21. Exhaust valve
22. Valve spring
23. Valve retainer
24. Tappet
25. Camshaft
26. Governor
27. Gasket
28. Oil pan

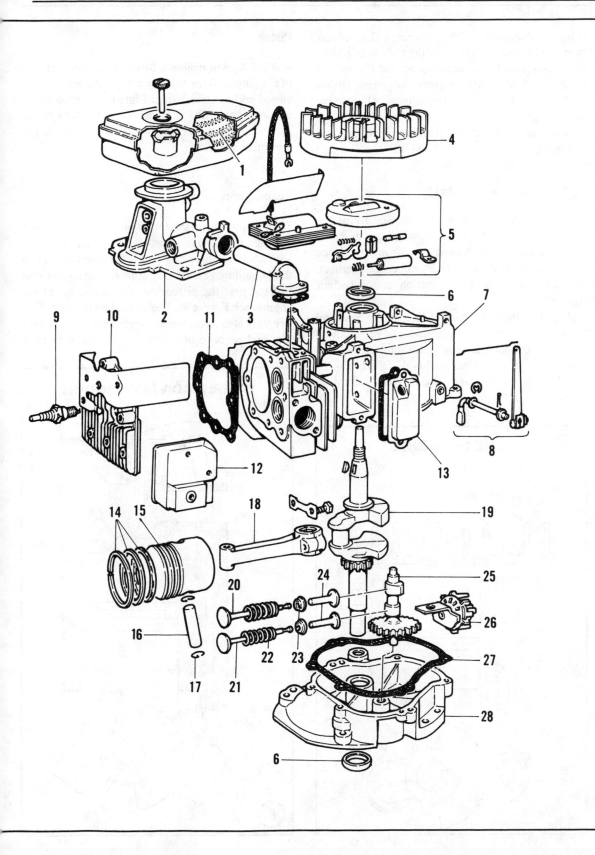

offers better engine cooling and more efficient combustion chamber design, but at the penalty of adding push rods and rocker arms to actuate the valves. Early Briggs & Stratton engines were all built using the L-head design, while later engines are built using both designs.

Additional information on major components and systems is outlined in the following.

Cylinder Head and Gasket

The cylinder head is removable and forms the closed end of the cylinder. The spark plug is mounted in the cylinder head. A cavity on the inside surface of the cylinder head, called the combustion chamber, is shaped to enhance combustion of the fuel:air mixture.

A gasket, located between the cylinder head and cylinder, seals the mating surfaces of the cylinder head and cylinder thereby preventing gases from escaping. The gasket material is designed to withstand the heat and pressure generated by combustion in the cylinder.

Piston

All pistons in Briggs & Stratton engines are made of aluminum. When the piston is positioned with the closed end up as shown in **Figure 7**, the top of the piston is called the "crown" while the area of the piston below the piston pin is called the "skirt" portion of the piston.

Piston Rings

Three piston rings are used on the piston (**Figure 8**). The top piston ring (nearest the piston crown) is a compression type ring that is designed to contain the expanding gases during combustion and prevent leakage past the piston into the crankcase of the engine (see **Figure 9**). The second piston ring (**Figure 9**) is also a compression type ring, but it serves the dual purpose of sealing gases that may have

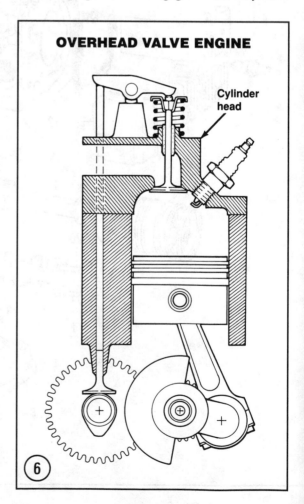

(5) L-HEAD ENGINE

Cylinder head

OVERHEAD VALVE ENGINE

Cylinder head

(6)

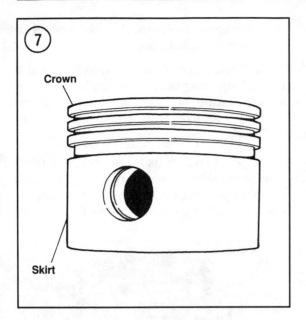

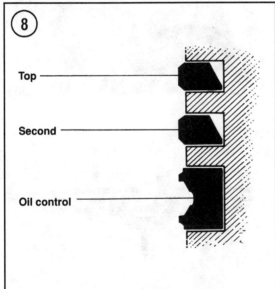

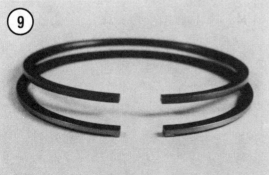

passed the top compression ring and also scraping oil off the cylinder wall that has passed the oil control ring (the second compression ring is sometimes called a scraper ring). The bottom piston ring (nearest the piston skirt) is called the oil control ring (**Figure 10**) and is designed to prevent oil in the crankcase from passing between the piston and cylinder wall into the combustion area. The oil control ring may be a single ring (**Figure 10**) or an assembled unit. The assembled oil control ring may consist of two pieces, the control ring plus an expander, or three pieces, two rails and an expander.

Due to their design, top and second compression pistons rings must be installed on a piston in the correct groove with the specified side of the ring towards the piston crown. An identifying mark (see **Figure 11**) is sometimes used to indicate which side must be towards the piston crown.

Piston Pin

A steel piston pin attaches the piston to the connecting rod. The piston pin is generally hollow and open at both ends, but some engines may be

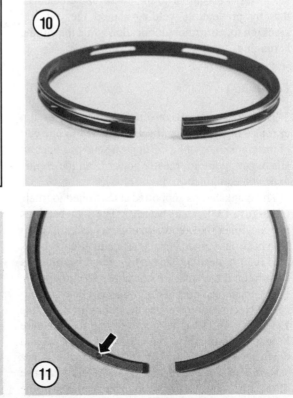

equipped with a piston pin that is closed at one end. Retaining clips are used to secure the pin in the piston, but some pistons are equipped with an internal stop on one side and a retaining clip on the opposite side. The retaining clip (**Figure 12**) fits in a groove in the piston.

Connecting Rod

The connecting rod serves as a link between the piston and crankshaft. For purposes of identification, the ends of the connecting rod are identified by their size, small end or big end. The steel piston pin connects the small end of the connecting rod to the piston, while the big end of the connecting rod attaches to the crankpin of the crankshaft. The big end is split to form a cap that is secured to the connecting rod either by screws or by nuts on studs.

The connecting rod on Briggs & Stratton engines covered in this manual is made of aluminum and rides directly on the crankshaft, no bearing insert is present between the connecting rod and crankshaft. Aluminum is used for its lightness, because its relative softness will absorb tiny particles of foreign material rather than scratch the crankpin surface, and the metal is dissimilar to the iron of the crankshaft thereby preventing welding should the rod and crankpin touch without lubrication while the engine is running.

Crankshaft

The iron crankshaft converts reciprocating motion to rotary motion. A flywheel is attached to one end of the crankshaft while the opposite end provides an attachment point to transfer power from the engine to driven equipment.

The crankshaft is supported at machined journals (A, **Figure 13**) by main bearings. The main bearings may be either the aluminum of the crankcase, plain type bearings (called bushings) or anti-friction bearings (ball or needle bearings). The ball bearing is a tight fit on the crankshaft of engines so equipped.

The machined area of the crankshaft that the connecting rod rides on is called the crankpin (B, **Figure 13**). The crankpin is hardened during manufacture to increase durability. The crankpin can be ground down to a smaller diameter if the damage is not severe. This is called regrinding and requires the use of a connecting rod with a smaller diameter at the

big end to obtain the desired clearance between the crankpin and connecting rod.

The flywheel end of the crankshaft is tapered to fit a corresponding taper in the flywheel. A key is used to match the keyways in the crankshaft and flywheel so the flywheel is properly indexed to the crankshaft.

The power take-off (pto) end of the crankshaft may be shaped in a variety of configurations to match the driven equipment coupled to the engine. Common variations include external or internal

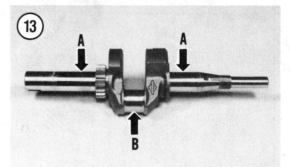

threads, with or without a keyway, and a plain shaft with a keyway.

Located on the crankshaft is a gear that drives the camshaft gear. The gear face on most Briggs & Stratton engines is marked with a chisel mark or dot (indentation) that aligns with a dot (indentation) on the camshaft gear (see **Figure 14**). The marks must align on every other revolution of the crankshaft so the valves operate at the proper time according to piston position.

Main Bearings

The crankshaft is supported by main bearings that may be either the aluminum of the crankcase, crankcase cover or oil pan (if made of aluminum), plain type bearings (called bushings) or anti-friction bearings (ball or needle bearings). See **Figure 15**.

Some engines that are manufactured with an aluminum crankcase support the crankshaft directly in the aluminum, which is a good bearing material. In most cases, the bearing bore can be machined if damaged and a plain type bearing (bushing) can be installed.

Plain type bearings (bushings) and anti-friction bearings (ball or needle bearings) can be removed and replaced if necessary.

Oil Seals

Oil seals are designed to keep foreign material from entering the engine and prevent oil leakage along the crankshaft. The seal has a rubber or neoprene lip (**Figure 16**) that rests against the shaft to form a seal. Depending on the application, the seal may have one or more lips, as well as a garter spring behind the lip to increase pressure on the seal lip. Correct installation of an oil seal is important if the seal is to function properly.

Camshaft and Tappets

The camshaft converts rotary motion into reciprocating motion to operate the valves. A gear on the end of the camshaft is driven by the gear on the crankshaft (see **Figure 17**). Machined on the camshaft are lobes for each of the valves. Riding against the cam lobe is a valve tappet, often called a valve lifter, that transfers motion from the cam lobe to the valve. When the camshaft turns, the raised portion of the cam lobe pushes against the tappet which in turn forces the valve to open. Each lobe is designed and machined so the respective valve opens and closes so that optimum engine performance is achieved. Excessive wear of either the cam lobe or tappet will cause a degradation in engine performance due to decreased valve action.

The valves must operate "in time" with the position of the piston for proper four-stroke engine operation. To achieve correct timing between the crankshaft and camshaft, timing marks are located on the crankshaft and camshaft gears. The gear face on most Briggs & Stratton engines is marked with a chisel mark that corresponds to a dot (indentation) on the camshaft gear (see **Figure 14**). The marks must align on every other revolution of the crankshaft so the valves operate at the proper time according to piston position.

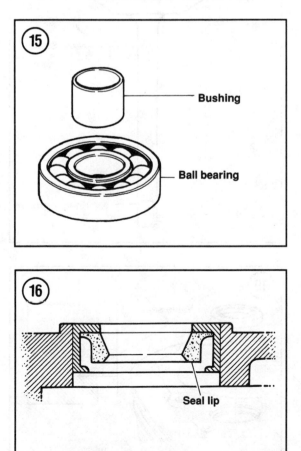

(15)

Bushing

Ball bearing

(16)

Seal lip

Valve System

All Briggs & Stratton engines are equipped with "poppet" type valves. On the engines covered by this manual, the valves are located in the cylinder block portion of the engine. This type of valve arrangement is called a side valve or "L-head" (also known as "flathead" due to the configuration of the cylinder head).

Two valves are used in the single-cylinder engine, an intake valve and an exhaust valve. Refer to **Figure 18** for terminology related to a valve. The intake and exhaust valves are usually constructed of different metals. The exhaust valve is manufactured from metal that is capable of withstanding the high temperature of the exhaust gas. A Cobalite exhaust valve that is more durable may be used on some engines.

When closed, the valve rests against a seat (**Figure 17**). Contact with the seat closes the air passage, as well as cooling the valve by providing a path for the heat to transfer from the valve head to the cylinder block. The valve seat may be machined directly into the metal of the engine, or a separate valve seat insert may be installed (**Figure 19**). Briggs & Stratton aluminum engines have seat inserts for both valves. Valve seat inserts are replaceable using special tools.

A more durable Cobalite exhaust valve seat may be used on some engines.

The valve is held in the closed position by a valve spring. The spring is held by a valve spring retainer (**Figure 17**), which on some engines has a slot that fits a groove in the end of the valve stem (**Figure 20**). On some engines, the valve spring retainer is secured by a pin or split collars (**Figure 20**).

Each valve rides in a valve guide (**Figure 17**). On some engines, the valve may ride directly in the aluminum crankcase, while on other engines, the valve may ride in a replaceable guide that is made of brass or sintered iron. Since the guide centers the valve on its valve seat, worn guides cause gradual engine power loss due to poor contact between the valve and seat, eventually resulting in valve system overhaul.

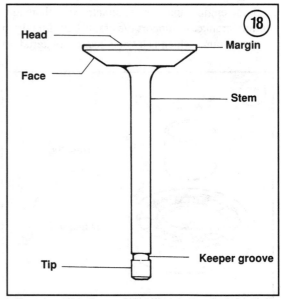

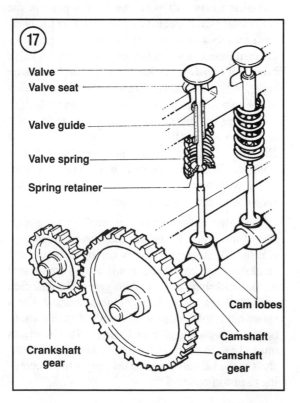

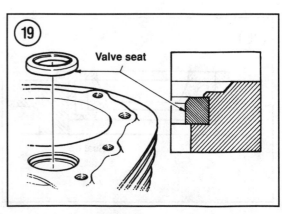

The exhaust valve on some engines may be equipped with a valve rotator (**Figure 21**) to extend service life of the valve and valve seat. Each time the valve opens, the rotator turns the valve a small amount, which helps clean the valve face and seat surfaces, as well as changing the contact surfaces of the valve face and seat when the valve closes.

Compression Release

Single-cylinder engines can be difficult to start using a manual starter. One problem is developing sufficient engine speed so the engine will continue to run after firing and reach the next ignition event. While starting, the starter must work against compression pressure, which tends to slow down the engine. To overcome this problem, a compression release device is used to bleed off compression pressure so the engine will rotate faster during starting.

Briggs & Stratton engines may be equipped with a mechanism on the camshaft that holds the exhaust valve open slightly during starting to reduce compression pressure. Some engines may be equipped with a spring-loaded yoke on the camshaft (**Figure 22**) that lifts the exhaust valve tappet at starting engine speed. When engine speed increases, weights pull the yoke away from the exhaust valve tappet for normal operation. The compression release mechanism on some engines is mounted on the back of the camshaft gear (**Figure 23**). When the engine is stopped, the spring-loaded actuator extends the rocker so it will contact the exhaust valve tappet during starting. When the engine is running, centrifugal force moves the actuator outward thereby withdrawing the rocker and allowing the exhaust valve tappet to fully contact the cam lobe.

Governor System

The purpose of the governor system is to maintain a desired engine speed regardless of the load imposed (within the limits of the engine power range).

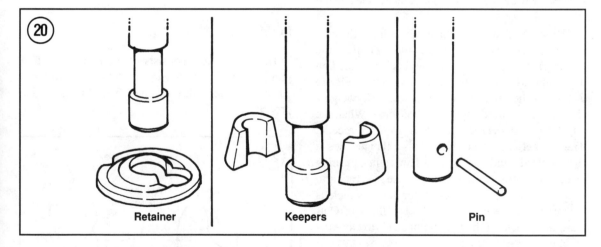

Retainer   Keepers   Pin

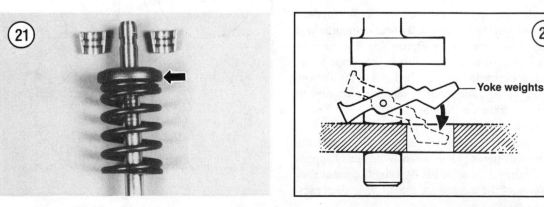

Yoke weights

The governor will open or close the throttle to adjust the engine power output to match the load, thereby maintaining the desired engine speed. On some engines, the engine speed may be varied (lawn mowers), while on other engines the engine speed is fixed (generators and pumps).

Two types of governor systems are used: mechanical or flyweight type and pneumatic or air vane type.

Both types of governor systems utilize a governor spring that is connected to the throttle linkage. The governor spring tension opposes the action of the governor and tends to open the throttle, increasing engine speed and power. For variable speed governors, the governor spring is connected to an adjustable control of some type so that the tension of the spring can be changed by the operator. Increasing the spring tension will raise the engine speed. Decreasing the spring tension will lower engine speed. For fixed speed governors, the spring is connected to a fixed point to provide a constant engine speed. The desired governed speed is maintained when the force created by the governor counterbalances the tension of the governor spring.

The mechanical governor system utilizes the centrifugal force of rotating flyweights to oppose the governor spring. A set of flyweights is mounted on a gear that is driven by the camshaft gear (see **Figure 24**). When the engine speed increases, the flyweights are thrown outward by centrifugal force. When the engine speed decreases, the flyweights recede. Trapped between the flyweights is a flanged sleeve that moves in and out with the flyweights, pushing against a governor arm. Externally, the governor arm transfers motion to the governor lever, which is connected to the carburetor throttle linkage. Outward movement of the flyweights tends to close the carburetor throttle plate.

Engines equipped with a pneumatic governor use air flow from the fan on the flyweel to monitor and adjust engine speed (see **Figure 25**). The air flow pushes against an air vane that is connected to the carburetor throttle linkage. The force of the air flow against the air vane tends to move the air vane to close the carburetor throttle plate.

The operation of either type governor system is the same. As the load on the engine is increased, the engine will start to slow down. When this happens the centrifugal force of the flyweights decreases or the force of the air against the air vane decreases, reducing the opposing force against the governor spring. This allows the governor spring to open the throttle, increasing engine power to compensate for the increased load and thus maintain the desired engine speed.

The opposite effect occurs when the load on the engine decreases. The engine speed starts to increase which increases the centrifugal force of the flyweights or the air pressure against the air vane, increasing the opposing force against the governor spring. The movement of the governor linkage will stretch the governor spring and close the throttle to reduce engine power to match the load and maintain the desired engine speed.

Based on a variety of factors, including the intended application of the engine, an engine is designed to operate at a specific fixed governed speed or in an operating range. The most critical governed speed is maximum governed speed as it sets the upper limit of engine operation. Exceeding the maximum governed speed can cause overspeeding which may result in engine failure.

Fuel System

The fuel system consists of the carburetor, fuel pump, intake manifold and air inlet system. Refer to Chapter Six for a discussion of fuel system service procedures.

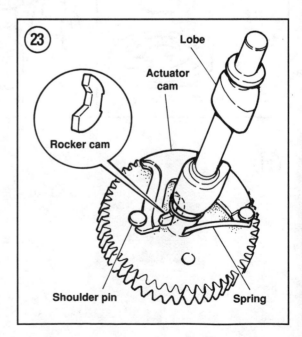

(23)

Lobe

Actuator cam

Rocker cam

Shoulder pin

Spring

Ignition System

Service procedures covering the components that deliver spark to the engine are outlined in Chapter Seven.

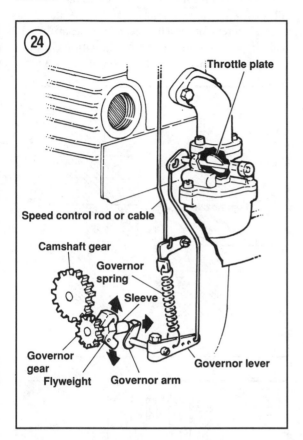

Speed control rod or cable
Throttle plate
Camshaft gear
Governor spring
Sleeve
Governor gear
Flyweight
Governor arm
Governor lever

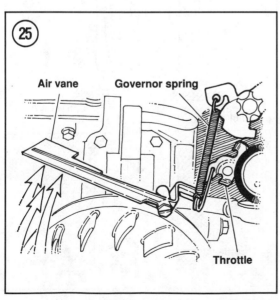

Air vane
Governor spring
Throttle

FUEL SYSTEM

The Briggs & Stratton engines covered in this manual use gasoline for the fuel and are equipped with a carburetor. Some Briggs & Stratton engines are designed to run on gaseous fuels, such as propane, but they are beyond the scope of this manual.

Carburetor Operating Principles

The function of the carburetor on a spark-ignition engine is to atomize the fuel and mix the atomized fuel in proper proportions with air flowing to the engine intake port or intake manifold. Carburetors used on engines that are to be operated at constant speeds and under even loads are of simple design since they only have to mix fuel and air in a relatively constant ratio. On engines operating at varying speeds and loads, the carburetor must be more complex because different fuel:air mixtures are required to meet the varying demands of the engine.

Fuel:air mixture ratio requirements

To meet the demands of an engine being operated at varying speeds and loads, the carburetor must mix fuel (gasoline) and air at different mixture ratios. Fuel:air mixture ratios required for different operating conditions are shown in **Table 1**.

Basic design

Carburetor design is based on the venturi principle which simply means that a gas or liquid flowing through a necked-down section (venturi) in a passage undergoes an increase in velocity (speed) and a decrease in pressure as compared to the velocity and pressure in the full size sections of the passage. The principle is illustrated in **Figure 26**, which shows air passing through a carburetor venturi. The figures given for air speeds and vacuum are approximate for a typical wide-open throttle operating condition. Due to low pressure (high vacuum) in the venturi, fuel is forced out through the fuel nozzle by the atmospheric pressure (0 vacuum) on the fuel; as fuel is emitted from the nozzle, it is atomized by the high velocity air flow and mixes with the air.

In **Figure 27**, the carburetor choke plate and throttle plate are shown in relation to the venturi. Downward pointing arrows indicate air flow through the carburetor.

At cranking speeds, air flows through the carburetor venturi at a slow speed; thus, the pressure in the venturi does not usually decrease to the extent that atmospheric pressure on the fuel will force fuel from the nozzle. If the choke plate is closed as shown by the dotted line in **Figure 27**, air cannot enter into the carburetor and pressure in the carburetor decreases greatly as the engine is turned at cranking speed. Fuel can then flow from the fuel nozzle. In manufacturing the carburetor choke plate, a small hole or notch (**Figure 28**) is cut in the plate so that some air can flow through the plate when it is in closed position to provide air for the starting fuel:air mixture. In some instances after starting a cold engine, it is advantageous to leave the choke plate in a partly closed position as the restriction of air flow will decrease the air pressure in the carburetor venturi, thus causing more fuel to flow from the nozzle, resulting in a richer fuel:air mixture. The choke plate should be in fully open position for normal engine operation.

If, after the engine has been started, the throttle plate is in the wide-open position as shown by the solid line in **Figure 27**, the engine can obtain enough fuel and air to run at dangerously high speeds. Thus, the throttle plate must be partly closed as shown by the dotted lines to control engine speed. At no load, the engine requires very little air and fuel to run at its rated speed and the throttle must be moved toward the closed position as shown by the dash lines. As more load is placed on the engine, more fuel and air are required for the engine to operate at its rated speed and the throttle must be moved closer to the wide open position as shown by the solid line. When the engine is required to develop maximum power or speed, the throttle must be in the wide open position.

A simple carburetor which relies only on the venturi principle will supply a progressively richer mixture as engine speed is increased, but the engine will not run at all at idle speeds. The carburetor must therefore be built with additional elements so the engine will run efficiently at varying speeds.

An idle or slow speed circuit uses a separate fuel mixing and metering system like that shown in **Figure 29**. An idle passage leads from the fuel chamber to the air horn at the approximate location of the throttle plate (1). When the throttle plate is closed,

air flow is shut off. This reduces the pressure in the intake manifold, which results in insufficient air passing through the venturi to draw fuel from the main fuel nozzle. However, fuel is drawn up the idle passage through idle jet (5), then through primary idle orifice (2) into the intake manifold. At the same time, air enters through the secondary idle orifice (3) and air metering orifice (4) to mix with fuel in the idle passage. The sizes of the two orifices (2 and 3)

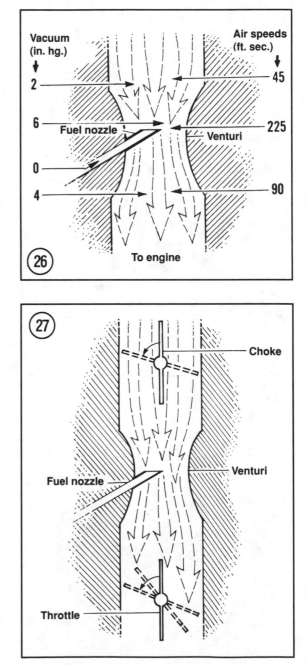

and the idle jet (5) are carefully designed to obtain desired engine idle speed performance. An idle mixture screw (6) is used on some carburetors so the mixture can be adjusted to fine tune engine idle speed performance.

When throttle plate (1) is opened slightly to a fast idle position (as indicated by the broken lines) both the primary and secondary idle orifices (2 and 3) are subjected to high manifold vacuum. The incoming flow of air through the secondary orifice (3) is cut

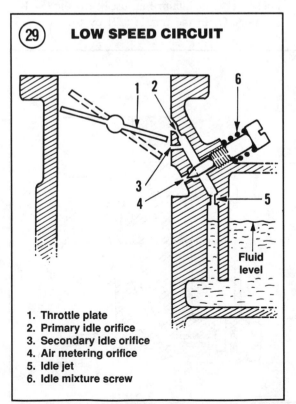

LOW SPEED CIRCUIT

Fluid level

1. **Throttle plate**
2. **Primary idle orifice**
3. **Secondary idle orifice**
4. **Air metering orifice**
5. **Idle jet**
6. **Idle mixture screw**

off, which increases the speed of fuel flow through the idle jet (5). This supplies the additional fuel needed to properly mix with the greater volume of air passing around the throttle plate. As the throttle plate is further opened, the idle fuel system ceases to operate and the fuel mixture is again controlled by the venturi of the main fuel system.

The fuel:air mixture of the main fuel system (generally called the high speed mixture system) is determined by either a fixed jet (orifice) or an adjustment screw (see **Figure 30**). The jet is often available in different sizes to accommodate different engine applications and operating conditions, while the adjustment screw may be turned to alter the mixture setting.

Although some simple carburetors use just the systems previously described, most carburetors require more complex features to supply a fuel:air mixture that will produce efficient engine operation over a wide range of engine speeds and in a variety of operating conditions. These design features are described in the following paragraphs which outline the different carburetor types.

Carburetor Types

The carburetors used on Briggs & Stratton engines fall into one of two carburetor types, suction-lift or float. Lower horsepower engines generally use the suction-lift carburetor, while high horsepower engines are equipped with a float type carburetor, and intermediate horsepower engines may use either type carburetor.

Suction lift and float carburetors use the fundamental carburetor principles regarding air flow and fuel atomization as previously outlined. The basic difference between the two types is the manner in which fuel is delivered to the carburetor fuel metering system. Suction lift carburetors draw the fuel from the fuel tank to the carburetor, while float carburetors require gravity or a fuel pump to fill the carburetor's fuel bowl.

Suction lift carburetor

A drawing of a typical suction lift carburetor is shown in **Figure 31**. The carburetor's fuel pipe is immersed in fuel in the fuel tank. Due to a vent in the fuel tank cap, atmospheric pressure is present in the fuel tank. When the engine is running, low pressure (suction) is created at the nozzle orifice (**Figure 31**) and atmospheric pressure forces fuel up through the fuel pipe and out of the nozzle into the carburetor venturi where it is mixed with the air flowing through the venturi. A check ball is located in the lower end of the fuel pipe on some carburetors to prevent pulsations of air pressure in the venturi from forcing fuel back down through the fuel pipe. The lower end of the fuel pipe has a fine mesh screen to prevent foreign material or dirt in the fuel from entering the fuel nozzle. Turning the mixture screw will change the fuel:air mixture.

A typical suction lift type Briggs & Stratton carburetor is shown in a cross-sectional view in **Figure 32**. The basic principles of carburetor operation as previously outlined apply to this carburetor, but two features should be noted. Rather than using a choke plate disc to enrich the fuel:air mixture during cold weather operation, the carburetor is equipped with a sliding choke tube. Just as a choke plate closes the carburetor air inlet so increased fuel will be drawn into the carburetor bore, the choke tube also closes the carburetor air inlet.

When the engine is running at idle or slow speed, the fuel:air mixture is determined by the position of the throttle plate in relation to two holes (**Figure 32**) in the side of the carburetor bore. Both holes are calibrated to a specific size so the desired fuel:air mixture is obtained. Due to changes in air pressure past the holes caused by the position of the throttle plate, either one or both of the holes will emit fuel.

Float type carburetor

The principle of float type carburetor operation is illustrated in **Figure 33**. Fuel is delivered to inlet (1) by gravity when the fuel tank is located above the carburetor, or by a fuel lift pump when the tank is located below the carburetor inlet. Fuel flows through the open fuel inlet valve (2) until fuel level (3) in the fuel bowl lifts the float (4) sufficiently to close the valve (2). When the engine is running, fuel will be emitted from the nozzle (5), lowering the fuel level. When the fuel level drops, the float will also drop, thereby opening the valve (2) and allowing more fuel into the carburetor fuel bowl.

A typical float type Briggs & Stratton carburetor is shown in a cross-sectional view in **Figure 34**. Atmospheric pressure is maintained in the fuel bowl through the vent passage (20) which opens into the carburetor air horn ahead of the choke plate (21). Fuel level is maintained at just below the level of opening (O) in the nozzle (22) by the float (19)

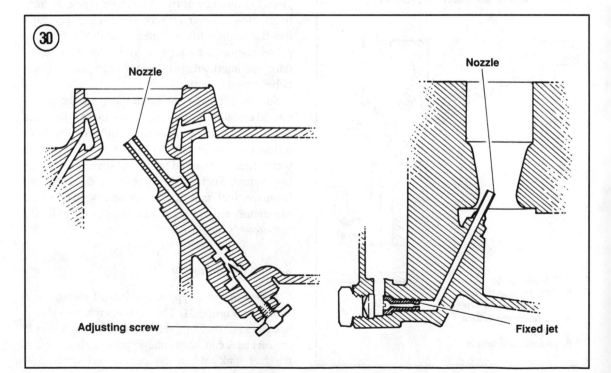

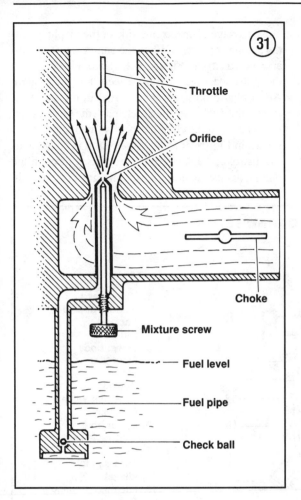

actuating the inlet valve needle (8). Float height can be adjusted by bending the float tang (5).

When the engine is running at slow idle speed (throttle plate nearly closed), air pressure above the throttle plate is low and atmospheric pressure in the fuel bowl forces fuel up through the nozzle and out through the orifice in seat (14) where it mixes with the air passing the throttle plate. The idle fuel mixture is adjustable by turning the idle fuel needle (15) in or out as required. Idle speed is adjustable by turning the throttle stop screw (not shown) in or out to control the amount of air passing the throttle plate.

When the throttle plate is opened to increase engine speed, air flow velocity through the venturi (18) increases, air pressure at the venturi decreases and fuel will flow from openings (O) in the nozzle instead of through the orifice in the idle seat (14). When the engine is running at high speed, pressure in the nozzle (22) is less than at the vent (12) opening in the carburetor throat above the venturi. Thus, air will enter the vent and travel down the vent into the nozzle and mix with the fuel in the nozzle. Vents that introduce air into the carburetor metering system are referred to as air bleed holes.

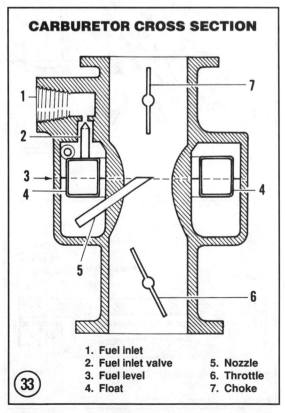

CARBURETOR CROSS SECTION

1. Fuel inlet
2. Fuel inlet valve
3. Fuel level
4. Float
5. Nozzle
6. Throttle
7. Choke

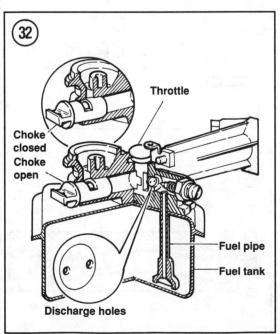

Fuel Pump

A fuel pump is used to transfer fuel from a fuel tank to the carburetor. The fuel pump may be a separate unit, or in some cases, it may be an integral part of the carburetor.

The most common type of fuel pump is equipped with a diaphragm and valves. Although design of the pump may vary as to type of check valves, etc., all operate on the principle shown in **Figures 35-37**. A

pulse passage connects one side of the diaphragm to the engine crankcase. When the engine's piston is on an upward stroke (**Figure 36**), vacuum is created in the pulse passage which deflects the diaphragm. Atmospheric pressure against fuel in the fuel tank forces the fuel into the inlet, past the inlet check valve and into the chamber below the diaphragm as shown in **Figure 36**. When the piston is on a downward stroke, crankcase pressure passes through the pulse passage against the diaphragm as shown in

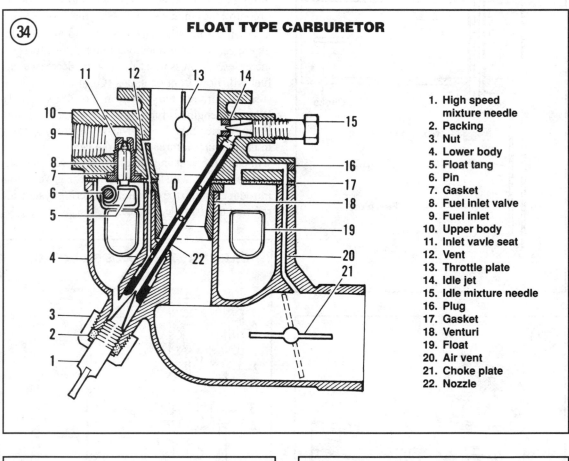

FLOAT TYPE CARBURETOR

1. High speed mixture needle
2. Packing
3. Nut
4. Lower body
5. Float tang
6. Pin
7. Gasket
8. Fuel inlet valve
9. Fuel inlet
10. Upper body
11. Inlet vavle seat
12. Vent
13. Throttle plate
14. Idle jet
15. Idle mixture needle
16. Plug
17. Gasket
18. Venturi
19. Float
20. Air vent
21. Choke plate
22. Nozzle

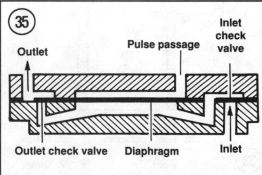

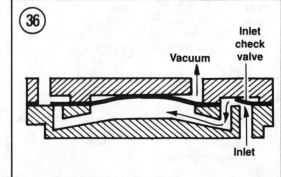

2

Figure 37. The diaphragm forces the fuel out of the chamber below the diaphragm, past the outlet check valve and out the pump outlet.

IGNITION SYSTEM

The Briggs & Stratton engines covered in this manual are equipped with magneto ignition systems. The basic design is similar for all systems, with the greatest difference being the use of a breakerless solid-state design on later engines. All systems utilize flywheel magnets, a generating coil, a switching device (breaker points or solid-state module), a transformer (coil) and a spark plug to ignite the

fuel:air mixture at the appropriate time in the cylinder. A typical breaker point-type magneto ignition system is shown in **Figure 38**. Fundamental operating principles are discussed in the following paragraphs.

Ignition System Operating Principles

The heart of the ignition system is the ignition coil and armature assembly. The ignition coil consists of two sets of windings, the primary and the secondary, which are wound around an armature. Each set of windings is connected to other components to form the primary and secondary circuits. The interaction of the flywheel magnets, primary and secondary circuits comprises the ignition event during engine operation.

The ignition event begins when magnets in the flywheel induce an electric current in the primary windings of the ignition coil through the armature legs as shown in **Figure 39**. Note that the breaker points are closed. As the flywheel continues to rotate (**Figure 40**), the magnetic field changes direction, although the primary current continues flowing because magnetic lines through the center remain the same due to the design of the armature. The primary current also results in an electromagnetic field around the primary and secondary coil windings. The breaker points open, stopping primary circuit current flow. The condenser serves as a buffer to prevent arcing across the breaker points. When the primary current stops, the electromagnetic field collapses which induces high voltage in the secondary coil windings. The high voltage in the secondary windings passes through the secondary wiring (high

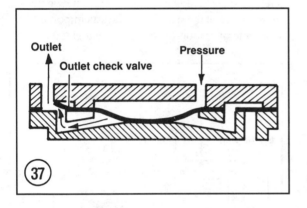

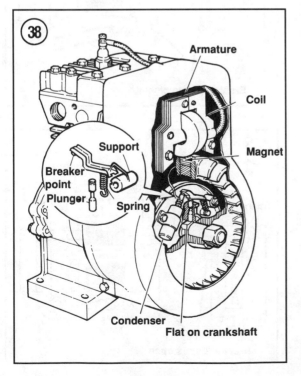

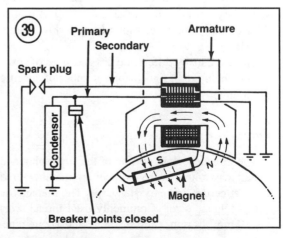

tension spark plug lead) and fires the spark plug (**Figure 41**). The sequence of events is timed so the spark plug fires when the piston is located at a specified point in the cylinder usually noted as degrees of crankshaft rotation before top dead center (BTDC), i.e., 10° BTDC.

To prevent engine starting or to stop the engine, the primary circuit is grounded, usually through the ignition switch. Grounding the primary circuit prevents buildup of the electromagnetic field, thereby stopping operation of the secondary circuit and spark plug firing.

The breaker points are operated by a cam and plunger arrangement. A cam on the crankshaft or camshaft operates the breaker points via a plunger.

On later engines, the breaker points and condenser are replaced by an ignition module. The electrical components in the module perform the same function electronically as the mechanical breaker points, switching the primary circuit on and off as required.

Spark Plug

In any spark-ignition engine, the spark plug (see **Figure 42**) provides the means for igniting the compressed fuel:air mixture in the cylinder. Before an electric charge can pass across an air gap, the intervening air must be charged with electricity, or ionized. If the spark plug is properly gapped and the system is not shorted, not more than 7000 volts may be required to initiate a spark. Higher voltage is required as the spark plug warms up, or if compression pressure or the distance of the air gap is increased. Compression pressures are highest at full throttle and relatively slow engine speeds, therefore, high voltage requirements or a lack of available secondary voltage most often shows up as a miss during maximum acceleration from a slow engine speed.

There are many different types and sizes of spark plugs which are designed for a number of specific requirements.

Thread size

The threaded, shell portion of the spark plug and the attaching hole in the cylinder are manufactured to meet certain industry standards. The diameter is called "thread size." Commonly used thread sizes are 10 mm, 14 mm, 18 mm, 7/8 in. and 1/2 in. pipe.

Reach

The length of thread and the thread depth in the cylinder head or wall are also standardized dimensions. The dimension is measured from the gasket seat on the spark plug to the end of the threads. Common sizes for spark plug reach are 3/8 in., 7/16 in., 1/2 in. and 3/4 in.

Heat range

During engine operation, part of the heat generated during combustion is transferred to the spark plug, and from the plug to the cylinder through the shell threads and gasket, if used. The operating temperature of the spark plug plays an important part in engine operation. If too much heat is retained by

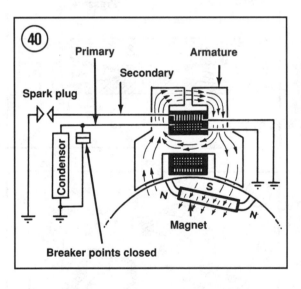

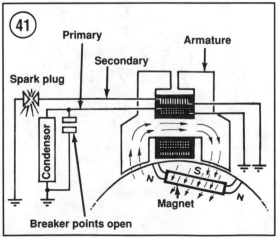

the plug, the fuel:air mixture may be ignited by contact with the heated surface before the ignition spark occurs. If insufficient heat is retained, partially burned combustion products (soot, carbon and oil) may build up on the plug tip resulting in "fouling" or shorting out of the plug. If this happens, the secondary ignition current is dissipated uselessly as it is generated instead of bridging the plug gap as a useful spark, and the engine will misfire.

The operating temperature of the spark plug tip can be controlled, within limits, by altering the length of the path the heat must follow to reach the threads and gasket of the plug. Thus a plug with a short, stubby insulator around the center electrode will run cooler than one with a long, slim insulator. Refer to **Figure 43**. Most spark plugs in the more popular sizes are available in a number of heat ranges. Engine manufacturers specify the correct spark plug heat range for normal and severe engine usage.

ELECTRICAL SYSTEM

The electrical system consists of the alternator, regulator/rectifier, battery and electric starter motor. Additional components, such as lights and accessories, may be found on the engine-driven equipment and are connected to the engine's electrical system. The design of the engine's electrical system depends on the engine's application, some engines may be equipped with only an alternator, while a battery must be used on engines equipped with an electric starter, as well as the electrical devices required to charge the battery.

Alternator

The most common type of alternator used on small engines is the flywheel alternator. Magnets located in the flywheel induce a current in the alternator coils (stator) that are located under the flywheel. The electrical principle is the same as previously outlined in the *Ignition System* section. Refer to views in **Figure 44** and the following description:

View A—As the flywheel rotates, a magnetic field is induced in the stator.

View B—During flywheel rotation, the magnetic field reverses and an electric current is created in the wires surrounding the stator.

View C—At some point during flywheel rotation, the magnetic field reverses and electric current returns to zero.

View D—Continued flywheel rotation results again in the creation of electric current in the alternator, but the direction of the current is reversed.

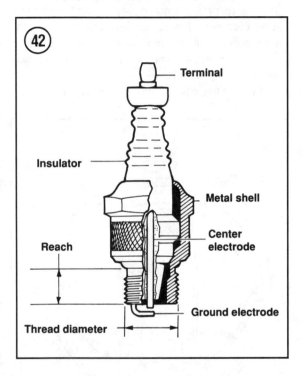

(42)

Terminal

Insulator

Metal shell

Center electrode

Reach

Ground electrode

Thread diameter

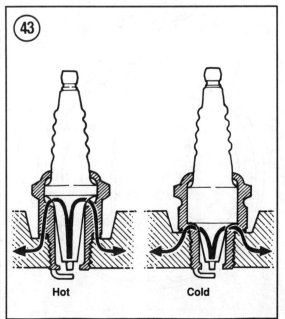

(43)

Hot   Cold

The electric current from an alternator forms a sinusoidal wave as shown in **Figure 45** that is alternately oriented negative and positive, hence the term alternating current. The alternator is designed to produce the desired output to fit the requirements of the output device or circuit.

In some cases, the alternator circuit is connected directly to lights, which must be properly selected to match the alternator output. A bulb with insufficient capacity will burn out when alternator output exceeds bulb capacity. Conversely, a bulb with excessive capacity will burn dimly when connected to an alternator with lesser output.

Rectifier

Alternating currect must be converted to direct current for output to a battery or a device requiring direct current (batteries and DC equipment have negative and positive terminals). Alternating current may be converted to direct current by using a rectifier. The rectifier consists of one or more diodes that allow current to flow in one direction, but not in the reverse direction. A circuit using a simple diode is shown in **Figure 46**. The circuit consists of an alternator coil (A), rectifier diode (B), battery (C) and a load (D). After passing through the rectifier, a pul-

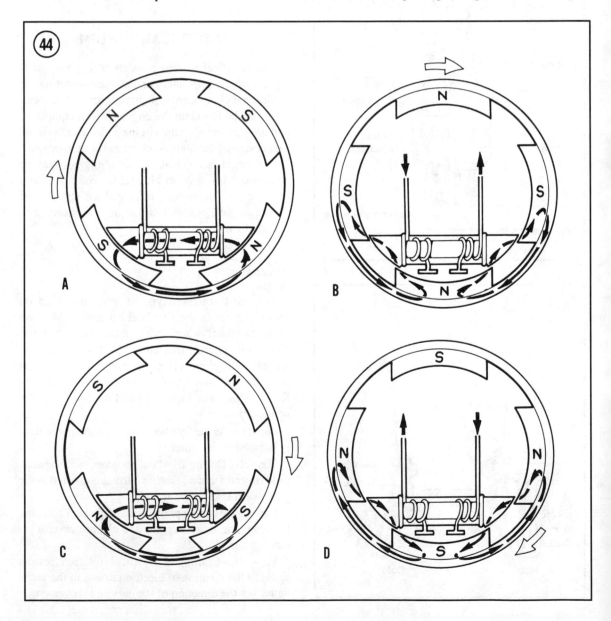

sating direct current is produced as shown by the graph wave. Note that half of the current is lost (shown by broken lines) because the rectifier diode allows current to flow in only one direction, which is half of the alternating current. This type of rectifier is often called a half-wave rectifier.

To use all of the current, a rectifier is designed with four diodes as shown in **Figure 47**. All current flows through the rectifier diodes (B) which results

in the graph wave shown. This type of rectifier is often called a full-wave or bridge rectifier. All of the alternating current is converted to direct current.

Regulator

The regulator maintains the correct charging system voltage so the battery is not undercharged or overcharged regardless of variations in engine speed and load.

Virtually all later small engine models are equipped with a modular, solid-state regulator. The regulator senses the voltage in the charging system and automatically either opens or completes the circuit as required to maintain the desired voltage. The rectifier and regulator are usually contained in a single unit. Service is generally limited to testing and replacement.

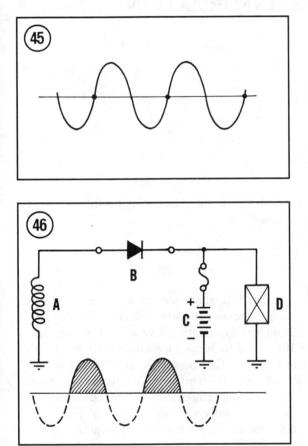

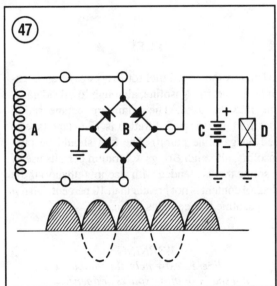

Table 1 FUEL:AIR MIXTURE RATIOS		
	Fuel	Air
Starting, cold weather	1 lb.	7 lb.
Accelerating	1 lb.	9 lb.
Idling (no load)	1 lb.	11 lb.
Part open throttle	1 lb.	15 lb.
Full load, wide open throttle	1 lb.	13 lb.

CHAPTER THREE

GENERAL ENGINE INFORMATION

FUEL

The recommended fuel for Briggs & Stratton engines is lead-free gasoline, although low-lead gasoline may be used. The minimum octane rating specified by Briggs & Stratton is 77 octane (specified on gasoline pump). The fuel should be pure gasoline, although Briggs & Stratton permits use of gasoline that is blended with alcohol (ethanol) if the alcohol content is not greater than 10 percent. *Do not use gasoline that contains methanol.*

WARNING

*Gasoline is extremely flammable. **Do not** smoke or allow sparks or open flame around fuel or in presence of fuel vapor. Be sure area is well-ventilated. Observe fire prevention rules.*

Stored gasoline, either in the engine's fuel tank or in a gasoline can, degrades as time passes. The gasoline becomes less volatile and if present in an engine, harmful deposits form on engine parts causing erratic engine operation and possible damage. A stabilizing agent that retards gasoline degradation should be added to gasoline that is to be stored more than one month. Two brands of stabilizing agent are Briggs & Stratton Gasoline Additive 5041 and Sta-Bil. When in doubt concerning the quality of gasoline, drain the old gasoline and refill with fresh gasoline.

OIL

Briggs & Stratton recommends using oil with an API service classification of SE, SF or SG. Use SAE 30 oil for temperatures above 40° F (4° C); use SAE 10W-30 oil for temperatures between 0° F (–18° C) and 40° F (4° C); below 0° F (–18° C) use petroleum based SAE 5W-20 or a suitable synthetic oil. Due to high operating temperature of an air-cooled engine, the use of multiviscosity oil above 40° F (4° C) is not recommended as high oil consumption and possible engine damage may result.

If unfamiliar with oil grade and viscosity terms, refer to *Lubricants* section in Chapter One.

The engine is filled with oil by pouring oil through the opening for the oil fill plug or the oil dipstick cap. If the engine is equipped with an oil fill plug (**Figure 1**), unscrew the plug and add oil until the oil level is even with the top threads in the plug hole (**Figure 2**).

> *CAUTION*
> *Debris, dirt and other foreign material can easily enter the engine crankcase*

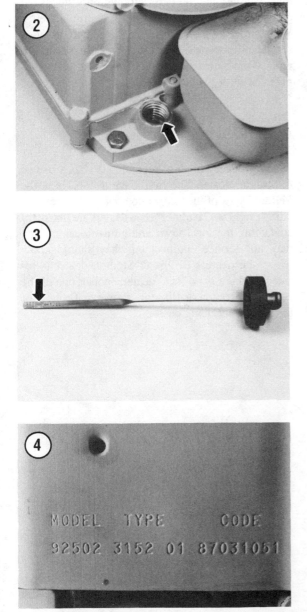

through the oil fill plug hole causing increased engine wear. Thoroughly clean around oil fill plug before removing the plug.

Some engines are equipped with an extended oil fill tube and a dipstick attached to the oil fill cap. The oil level should be between the ADD and FULL marks on dipstick (**Figure 3**).

> *NOTE*
> *The dipstick must be screwed firmly into place, then remove it to check oil level.*

On any engine, do not overfill engine with oil. Excess oil is forced into the cylinder where it burns, resulting in exhaust smoke and carbon deposits on the piston, cylinder head, valves and valve seats. Excess oil also prevents the oil slinger from working properly, which can cause engine damage due to inadequate lubrication in the top of the engine.

ENGINE IDENTIFICATION

Before servicing engine and ordering parts, the Briggs & Stratton engine model and type numbers must be determined. Although engines may be similar in appearance, specific differences that affect service specifications and parts configuration are only defined by the model and type numbers. Although rarely required, provide the code number also when ordering parts.

Engine identification numbers, including the model number, type number and code number, are located on the blower housing around the flywheel. The numbers are stamped in an identification plate or directly in the metal. See **Figure 4**.

The engine model number identifies the basic engine family. Refer to **Table 1** for a breakdown of Briggs & Stratton engine model numbers. As an example, an engine model number of 130202 would indicate that the engine has an approximate displacement of 13 cubic inches, is design series "0," the crankshaft is horizontal, the carburetor is a Pulsa-Jet, the main bearings are plain type, and a rewind starter is used.

The type number specifies the parts configuration of the engine, as well as cosmetic details such as paint color and decals. The type number also determines governor speed settings depending on the engine's application, i.e., lawn mower, tractor, pump, etc.

The code number provides information concerning the manufacturing of the engine, for instance, a code number of 90012201 indicates the engine was built in 1990, the first month of the year, on the 22nd day of the month, in manufacturing plant "01."

BASIC ENGINE SPECIFICATIONS

Table 2 lists basic engine specifications for Briggs & Stratton engines covered in this manual.

PURCHASING PARTS

Virtually all parts necessary to maintain and repair a Briggs & Stratton engine are available from Briggs & Stratton dealers, including Briggs & Stratton oil and filters. Parts are also available from outside vendors that may be purchased in hardware stores, lawn equipment dealers and mass merchandise stores. The quality of aftermarket parts may not meet the design standards specified by Briggs & Stratton resulting in reduced engine life or performance. When in doubt as to the quality of an aftermarket part, ask the supplier if he will pay for costs incurred should the part not perform properly.

Before ordering parts, refer to *Engine Identification* in this chapter and note all engine identifying information on engine. All of it may be necessary for the parts supplier to identify the part needed in the parts book.

If possible, the old part should be taken along when ordering parts. The old and new parts can then be matched to be certain the proper part is obtained. In some cases, a knowledgeable parts supplier can provide the correct part after seeing the old part, even if the engine identification numbers are unavailable.

There are components that are available only as an assembly, such as piston rings, which are available only as a set of piston rings and not individually. Some components, such as carburetors, may have individual components that can be ordered from the manufacturer, but the parts supplier only stocks the complete assembly to reduce inventoried items. When ordering parts, be aware that although only a single component is faulty, it may be necessary to replace the entire assembly. Contact the parts supplier for parts availability.

Where to Get Parts

Almost every town of medium size has a Briggs & Stratton dealer. The first place to look is in the Yellow Pages of the telephone book under the category "Engines-Gasoline." If no dealers are listed, try contacting the local lawn and garden dealer. They may not service engines, but they should know where the nearest Briggs & Stratton dealer is located. If there is no local dealer, contact one of the Briggs & Stratton distributors shown in **Table 3** for the nearest servicing dealer.

Table 1 ENGINE MODEL NUMBER BREAKDOWN

CUBIC INCH DISPLACEMENT	FIRST DIGIT AFTER DISPLACEMENT — BASIC DESIGN SERIES	SECOND DIGIT AFTER DISPLACEMENT — CRANKSHAFT/ CARBURETOR/ GOVERNOR	THIRD DIGIT AFTER DISPLACEMENT — BEARINGS/ REDUCTION GEARS/ AUXILIARY DRIVES	FOURTH DIGIT AFTER DISPLACEMENT — TYPE OF STARTER
6	0	0: Horizontal Diaphragm	0: Plain bearing	0: Without starter
8	1	—	—	1: Rope starter
9	2	—	—	2: Rewind starter
10	3	1: Horizontal Vacu-Jet	1: Flange mounting Plain bearing	3: Elecric - 110 volt, gear Drive
11	4	—	—	4: Electric starter- generator - 12 volt, belt drive
12	5	—	—	
13	6	2: Horizontal Pulsa-Jet Pneumatic	2: Ball bearing —	5: Electric starter only - 12 volt, gear drive
16	7			
17	8			
19	9	3: Horizontal Flo-Jet Mechanical	3: Flange mounting Ball bearing —	6: Alternator only*
22				
23				
24		4: Horizontal Flo-Jet	4: Pressure lube —	7: Electric starter, 12 volt gear drive, with Alternator
25				
26		—	—	
28		5: Vertical Vacu-Jet	5: — 6 to 1 gear drive	8: Vertical-pull starter
29				
30		—		
32		6: —	6: — 6 to 1 reverse rotation	
35		—		
40		—		
42		7: Vertical Flo-Jet	7: Pressure lube —	*Digit 6 formerly used for "Wind-Up" Starter on 60000, 80000 and 92000 series
		—	—	
		8: —	8: — — Perpendicular to crankshaft	
		— —		
		9: Vertical Pulsa-Jet	9: — — Parallel to crankshaft	
		—		

EXAMPLE

To identify Model 121702:

12	1	7	0	2
12 cubic inch	Design series 4	Vertical shaft Flo-Jet	Plain bearing	Rewind starter

Table 2 ENGINE SPECIFICATIONS

Model series	Bore	Stroke	Displacement	Power rating
60000 (early), 61000 (early)	2.31 in. (58.7 mm)	1.50 in. (38.1 mm)	6.3 cu.in. (103 cc)	2.25 hp (1.7 kW)
60000 (late), 61000 (late)	2.38 in. (60.3 mm)	1.50 in. (38.1 mm)	6.7 cu.in. (109 cc)	2.25 hp (1.7 kW)

(continued)

Table 2 ENGINE SPECIFICATIONS (continued)

Model series	Bore	Stroke	Displacement	Power rating
80000, 81000, 82000, 83000	2.38 in. (60.3 mm)	1.75 in. (44.5 mm)	7.8 cu.in. (127 cc)	3 hp (2.2 kW)
90000, 91000, 92000, 93000, 94000, 95000	2.56 in. (65.0 mm)	1.75 in. (44.5 mm)	9.0 cu.in. (148 cc)	3.5 hp (2.6 kW)
96000	2.56 in. (65.0 mm)	1.75 in. (44.5 mm)	9.0 cu.in. (148 cc)	3.75 hp (2.8 kW)
100200, 100900	2.50 in. (63.5 mm)	2.12 in. (54.0 mm)	10.4 cu.in. (169 cc)	3.5 hp 2.6 kW)
100700	2.56 in. (65.0 mm)	1.94 in. (49.3 mm)	10 cu.in. (164 cc)	3.5 hp (2.6 kW)
110000, 111000, 112000, 113000, 114000	2.78 in. (70.6 mm)	1.88 in. (47.6 mm)	11.4 cu.in. (186 cc)	4 hp (3 kW)
121000	2.69 in. (68.0 mm)	2.04 in. (51.8 mm)	11.57 cu.in. (190 cc)	3.5 hp (2.6 kW)
122000	2.69 in. (68.0 mm)	2.04 in. (51.8 mm)	11.57 cu.in. (190 cc)	4 hp (3 kW)
124000, 126000	2.69 in. (68.0 mm)	2.04 in. (51.8 mm)	11.57 cu.in. (190 cc)	5 hp (3.8 kW)
130000, 131000, 132000	2.56 in. (65.0 mm)	2.44 in. (60.9 mm)	12.6 cu.in. (203 cc)	5 hp (3.8 kW)
140000	2.75 in. (69.9 mm)	2.38 in. (60.3 mm)	14.1 cu.in. (231 cc)	5-6 hp (3.8-4.5 kW)
170000, 171000	3.00 in. (76.2 mm)	2.38 in. (60.3 mm)	16.8 cu. in. (275 cc)	7 hp (5.2 kW)
190000, 191000*, 192000, 193000*, 194000, 195000, 196000	3.00 in. (76.2 mm)	2.75 in. (69.8 mm)	19.44 cu. in. (318 cc)	8 hp (6 kW)
220000, 221000, 222000	3.44 in. (87.3 mm)	2.38 in. (60.3 mm)	22.04 cu. in. (361 cc)	10 hp (7.5 kW)
251000, 252000, 253000, 254000, 255000, 256000, 257000, 258000, 259000	3.44 in. (87.3 mm)	2.62 in. (66.6 mm)	24.36 cu. in. (399 cc)	11 hp (8.2 kW)
280000, 281000, 282000, 283000	3.44 in. (87.3 mm)	3.06 in. (77.7 mm)	28.4 cu. in. (465 cc)	12 hp (9 kW)
285000, 286000, 289000	3.44 in. (87.3 mm)	3.06 in. (77.7 mm)	28.4 cu. in. (465 cc)	12.5 hp (9.4 kW)

*Early models 191000 and 193000 had a cast iron crankcase with different specifications and are not covered in this manual.

Table 3 BRIGGS AND STRATTON CENTRAL PARTS DISTRIBUTORS
(Arranged Alphabetically by States)

BEBCO, Inc.
Phone (205) 251-4600
2221 Second Avenue, South
Birmingham, Alabama 35233

Power Equipment Co.
Phone (602) 272-3936
#7 North 43rd Avenue
Phoenix, Arizona 85107

Pacific Western Power
Phone (415) 692-3254
1565 Adrain Road
Burlingame, California 94010

Power Equipment Co.
Phone (805) 684-6637
1045 Cindy Lane
Carpinteria, California 93013

Pacific Power Equipment Co.
Phone (303) 744-7891
1441 W. Bayaud Avenue #4
Denver, Colorado 80223

Spencer Engine, Inc.
Phone (813) 253-6035
1114 W. Cass St.
Tampa, Florida 33606

Sedco, Inc.
Phone (404) 925-4706
4305 Steve Reynolds Blvd.
Norcross, Georgia 30093

Small Engine Clinic, Inc.
Phone (808) 488-0711
98019 Kam Highway
Aiea, Hawaii 96701

Midwest Engine Warehouse
Phone (708) 833-1200
515 Roman Road
Elmhurst, Illinois 60126

Commonwealth Engine, Inc.
Phone (502) 267-7883
11421 Electron Drive
Louisville, Kentucky 40229

Delta Power Equipment
Phone (504) 465-9222
755 E. Airline Highway
Kenner, Louisiana 70062

Atlantic Power
Phone (508) 543-6911
77 Green Street
Foxboro, Massachusetts 02035

Wisconsin Magneto, Inc.
Phone (612) 780-5585
8010 Ranchers Road
Minneapolis, Minnesota 55432

Diamond Engine Sales
Phone (314) 652-2202
3134 Washington
St. Louis, Missouri 63103

Original Equipment, Inc.
Phone (406) 245-3081
905 Second Avenue, North
Billings, Montana 59101

Midwest Engine Warehouse
of Omaha
Phone (402) 339-4700
7706-30 "I" Plaza
Omaha, Nebraska 68127

Atlantic Power
Phone (908) 356-8400
650 Howard Avenue
Somerset, New Jersey 08873

Power Equipment Co.
Phone (505) 345-8851
7209 Washington Street, N.E.
Albuquerque, New Mexico 87109

AEA, Inc.
Phone (704) 377-6991
700 West 28th Street
Charlotte, North Carolina 28206

Central Power Systems
Phone (614) 876-3533
2555 International Street
Columbus, Ohio 43228

Engine Warehouse, Inc.
Phone (405) 946-7800
4200 Highline Blvd.
Oklahoma City, Oklahoma 73108

Brown & Wiser, Inc.
Phone (503) 692-0330
9991 South West Avery Street
Tualatin, Oregon 97062

Three Rivers Engine Distributors
Phone (412) 321-4111
1411 Beaver Avenue
Pittsburgh, Pennsylvania 15233

Automotive Electric Corporation
Phone (901) 345-0300
3250 Millbranch Road
Memphis, Tennessee 38116

Grayson Co., Inc.
Phone (214) 630-3272
1234 Motor Street
Dallas, Texas 75207

Engine Warehouse, Inc.
Phone (713) 937-4000
7415 Empire Central Drive
Houston, Texas 77040

Frank Edwards Co.
Phone (801) 972-0128
1284 South 500 West
Salt Lake City, Utah 84101

RBI Corporation
Phone (804) 550-2210
101 Cedar Ridge Drive
Ashland, Virginia 23005

Wisconsin Magneto, Inc.
Phone (414) 445-2800
4727 North Teutonia Avenue
Milwaukee, Wisconsin 53209

CANADIAN DISTRIBUTORS

Briggs & Stratton Canada, Inc.
Phone (403) 435-9265
9519 49th Avenue
Edmonton, Alberta T6E 5Z5

Briggs & Stratton Canada, Inc.
Phone (604) 520-1294
1360 Cliveden Avenue
Delta, British Columbia V3M 6K2

Briggs & Stratton Canada, Inc.
Phone (204) 633-5400
89 Paramount Road
Winnipeg, Manitoba R2X 2W6

Briggs & Stratton Canada, Inc.
Phone (416) 625-6557
1815 Sismet Road
Mississauga, Ontario L4W 1P9

Briggs & Stratton Canada, Inc.
Phone (514) 366-6891
112-116 Lindsay Avenue
Dorval, Quebec H9P 2T8

3

CHAPTER FOUR

TROUBLESHOOTING

OPERATING REQUIREMENTS

For any engine to operate, several conditions must be met. Before troubleshooting an engine, be sure the following items are checked and found satisfactory.

Fuel

The engine requires clean, fresh gasoline to operate at maximum efficiency. See *Fuel* in Chapter Three for fuel recommendation. Two fuel-related problems usually cause the most cases of erratic engine operation or an inability to start an engine: poor fuel and water in the fuel.

The engines covered in this manual use gasoline or alcohol/gasoline for fuel. Stored gasoline, either in the engine's fuel tank or in a gasoline can, degrades as time passes. The gasoline becomes less volatile and if present in an engine, harmful deposits form on engine parts causing erratic engine operation and possible damage. When in doubt concerning the quality of gasoline, drain the old gasoline and refill with fresh gasoline.

Fuel that is contaminated with water will cause erratic engine operation and may prevent the engine from starting. Water can enter the fuel system from a contaminated fuel can, open fuel tank cap or condensation in the fuel tank. The water may be difficult to detect in the fuel tank, although a significant amount will appear as a bubble in the gasoline. If water-contaminated gasoline is a continuing prob-

lem, identify the cause. Testing kits are available from some small-engine shops that will detect water in gasoline.

Controls

Before operating the engine, be sure all controls are in good, safe operating condition. Maladjusted, disconnected, bent or otherwise damaged controls can prevent engine starting, cause erratic engine operation, damage the engine and possibly injure the operator.

> *WARNING*
> **Do not** *operate engine or any equipment unless all safety-related devices are functional.*

If the engine is mounted on a piece of equipment and will not start or operate properly, the problem may be caused by electrical or mechanical problems on the equipment that affect the engine. For instance, faulty ignition switches and safety interlocks may prevent engine starting. It may be necessary to isolate the engine from the equipment to determine whether the problem is with the engine or with the equipment.

Starter

The starter system, whether manual or electrical, must be capable of turning the engine's crankshaft with sufficient speed to start the engine. A manual starter should operate freely without binding or slippage so the crankshaft is turned through several revolutions. The electric starter system must be in good operating condition. If so equipped, the battery should be charged periodically if the engine is not used frequently enough to maintain battery charge.

TROUBLESHOOTING

Every small engine requires an uninterrupted supply of fuel and air, proper ignition and adequate compression. If any of these are lacking, the engine will not run.

Diagnosing mechanical problems is relatively simple if you use orderly procedures and keep a few basic principles in mind.

The troubleshooting procedures in this chapter analyze typical symptoms and show logical methods of isolating causes. These are not the only methods. There may be several ways to solve a problem, but only a systematic approach can guarantee success.

Never assume anything. Do not overlook the obvious. If the engine suddenly quits, check the easiest, most accessible problem spots first. Is there gasoline in the tank? Has the spark plug wire fallen off?

If nothing obvious turns up in a quick check, look a little further. Learning to recognize and describe symptoms will make repairs easier for you or a mechanic at the shop. How fast was the engine running when it quit? How long had the engine been running before it quit? If the engine was smoking, what color was the smoke?

Gather as many symptoms as possible to aid in diagnosis. Note whether the engine lost power gradually or all at once. Remember that the more complicated a machine is, the easier it is to troubleshoot because symptoms point to specific problems.

After the symptoms are defined, areas which could cause problems are tested and analyzed. Guessing at the cause of a problem may provide the solution, but it can easily lead to frustration, wasted time and a series of expensive, unnecessary parts. When analyzing a problem, be aware that an underlying problem may be the root cause. For instance, replacing a soot-fouled spark plug may get the engine running again. However, a maladjusted carburetor is the real problem and the engine will continue stopping until the carburetor is fixed.

You do not need fancy equipment or complicated test gear to determine whether repairs can be attempted. A few simple checks could save a large repair bill and lost time should the engine be sent to a professional shop. On the other hand, be realistic and do not attempt repairs beyond your abilities. Professional shops tend to charge heavily for putting together a disassembled engine that may have been abused. Some shops won't even take on such a job—so use common sense, don't get in over your head.

Some common problems and remedies are outlined in the following paragraphs. Also refer to the troubleshooting information found in **Table 1**.

Engine Will Not Start

Failure to start is usually caused by fuel not reaching the cylinder or spark not occurring at the spark plug. Do not neglect to check obvious causes (fuel tank empty, stop switch actuated, safety switch malfunctioning, etc.). Be sure that the problem is not due to a faulty starter or an internal problem is causing sufficient drag that the crankshaft will not rotate normally. If the engine is mounted on equipment, be sure that the clutch is operating properly or devices connected directly to the engine are not slowing crankshaft rotation. If the ambient temperature is very cold, the use of incorrect viscosity oil can cause excessive drag against internal engine parts.

> *NOTE*
> *On engines equipped with Oil Gard, insufficient oil in the crankcase will allow the internal float to ground the ignition thereby preventing engine starting.*

Test for fuel and spark

Fuel and a timed spark are essential for the engine to run. Remove the spark plug and check the condition of the spark plug. The spark plug should have an odor of gasoline and may be slightly damp appearing. If the spark plug insulator is not tan or light gray, refer to **Figure 1** which depicts defective spark plugs and lists possible causes.

Reinstall the spark plug and check for ignition spark by disconnecting the spark plug lead from the spark plug and holding the spark plug lead approximately 1/8 in. (3 mm) from the spark plug as shown

① **SPARK PLUG CONDITION**

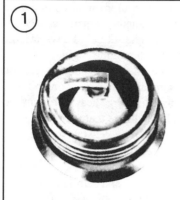

NORMAL

- Identified by light tan or gray deposits on the firing tip.
- Can be cleaned.

GAP BRIDGED

- Identified by deposit buildup closing gap between electrodes.
- Caused by oil or carbon fouling. If deposits are not excessive, the plug can be cleaned.

OIL FOULED

- Identified by wet black deposits on the insulator shell bore and electrodes.
- Caused by excessive oil entering combustion chamber through worn rings and pistons, excessive clearance between valve guides and stems or worn or loose bearings. Can be cleaned. If engine is not repaired, use a hotter plug.

CARBON FOULED

- Identified by black, dry fluffy carbon deposits on insulator tips, exposed shell surfaces and electrodes.
- Caused by too cold a plug, weak ignition, dirty air cleaner, too rich a fuel mixture or excessive idling. Can be cleaned.

LEAD FOULED

- Identified by dark gray, black, yellow or tan deposits or a fused glazed coating on the insulator tip.
- Caused by highly leaded gasoline. Can be cleaned.

WORN

- Identified by severely eroded or worn electrodes.
- Caused by normal wear. Should be replaced.

FUSED SPOT DEPOSIT

- Identified by melted or spotty deposits resembling bubbles or blisters.
- Caused by sudden acceleration. Can be cleaned.

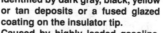

OVERHEATING

- Identified by a white or light gray insulator with small black or gray brown spots and with bluish-burnt appearance of electrodes.
- Caused by engine overheating, wrong type of fuel, loose spark plugs, too hot a plug or incorrect ignition timing. Replace the plug.

PREIGNITION

- Identified by melted electrodes and possibly blistered insulator. Metallic deposits on insulator indicate engine damage.
- Caused by wrong type of fuel, incorrect ignition timing or advance, too hot a plug, burned valves or engine overheating. Replace the plug.

in **Figure 2**. A spark plug tester like that shown in **Figure 3** can also be used. Set engine control to run position and operate starter. A bright electrical spark should jump across the gap between the spark plug lead and spark plug. A spark indicates the ignition is operating.

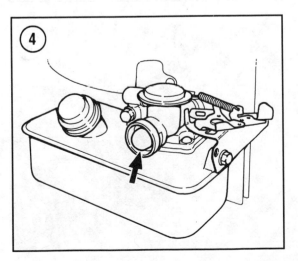

WARNING
The engine can start during test. Be sure all safety precautions concerning starting the equipment are observed.

If the ignition will not provide a spark, check the ignition electrical system further to locate cause for lack of spark. Especially check condition of the engine stop switch wiring for shorts, correct operation of safety switch and condition of breaker points and condenser on models so equipped.

If the test indicates a good spark, but the removed spark plug is dry with no evidence of fuel, be sure the engine is getting fuel. The carburetor choke valve should be closed when attempting to start engine. Some engines are equipped with a primer (**Figure 4**) that injects additional fuel for starting when the primer is pushed. Check the carburetor for proper operation.

NOTE
A prime cause of failure to start or erratic operation is water in the fuel. If water is present in the fuel, drain the fuel tank and refill with fresh fuel.

If testing indicates a good spark and the removed spark plug is damp, the spark plug may be faulty or the plug wire connector is corroded. Clean the connector and recheck. If the problem remains, install a new spark plug and attempt to start the engine (be sure the spark plug electrode gap is correct).

If testing indicates a good spark and the removed spark plug is damp, but the engine will not start or runs erratically with a new spark plug, remove the flywheel and check for a sheared flywheel key (**Figure 5**) and excessive wear in the flywheel and crankshaft keyways. A sheared flywheel key or excessive keyway wear will affect ignition timing.

If testing indicates a good spark and the removed spark plug was exceedingly wet with fuel, the engine may be flooded due to a carburetor malfunction. Check for proper adjustment of carburetor controls, and if correct, check carburetor adjustment. If all adjustments are correct, inspect and, if required, overhaul the carburetor.

NOTE
*To clear a flooded engine, set the engine control so the throttle is in wide open position and operate the starter. **Do not** attempt to expel fuel in the cylinder by removing the spark plug as fuel may be*

ignited by ignition spark or other sources.

Check compression

If the ignition spark is good and the fuel system is operating properly, compression in the cylinder may be insufficient for engine operation.

> *NOTE*
> *Briggs & Stratton does not specify compression pressure. Briggs & Stratton states that compression should be satisfactory if the flywheel rebounds sharply when the flywheel is rotated rapidly counterclockwise against the compression stroke.*

An alternate method of checking compression pressure can be performed as follows: To check compression, disconnect the spark plug wire from the spark plug and then remove the spark plug. Ground the spark plug wire against the cylinder head as shown in **Figure 6**.

> *WARNING*
> *When grounding the spark plug wire, be sure the wire end is securely held against the cylinder head, otherwise, a loose wire end may emit a spark that can shock you or ignite fuel expelled from the cylinder.*

Hold finger against the spark plug hole in the cylinder head and operate the starter. If finger is blown off the spark plug hole each time the engine completes its compression stroke, compression is adequate for the engine to start. If pressure is minimal, the following internal engine problems may exist.

Insufficient compression pressure may be due to:

1. Defective cylinder head gasket.
2. Warped cylinder head.
3. Worn or broken piston rings.
4. Sticking valves.
5. Worn valve guides.
6. Worn or damaged valves or seats.
7. Insufficient valve spring tension.
8. Mistimed camshaft gear.

Engine Hard to Start

The same conditions that prevent the engine from starting can also cause hard starting. See preceding section.

If the engine sounds like it is firing, but just won't continue to run, some of the more common causes are a fouled spark plug, contaminated fuel, improperly adjusted carburetor and improperly adjusted engine controls.

Engine Starts Then Stops

If the engine starts, runs a minute or two, then dies, check the fuel tank cap. The cap must have a vent so

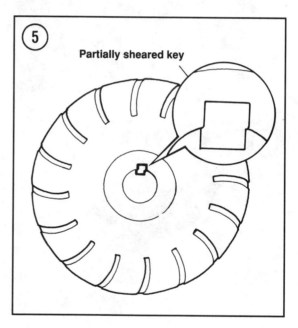

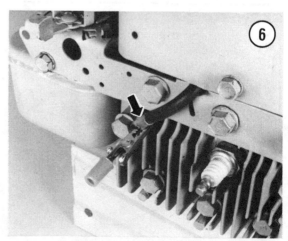

fuel will properly feed into the carburetor or the fuel system. The baffled vent hole (**Figure 7**) prevents fuel from sloshing out of the fuel cap while permitting air to enter the fuel tank. If the vent is absent (an incorrect fuel cap may have been installed) or plugged, fuel will cease to flow when sufficient vacuum builds in the tank.

Engine Runs Rough or Lacks Power

An intermittent miss may be caused by a malfunctioning ignition system or fuel system. Conduct a spark test as outlined in *Engine Will Not Start* section.

A spark plug may produce a good spark when tested outside the engine, but produce a weak or sporadic spark when subjected to compression pressure inside the engine. The weak spark may be due to a defective spark plug or ignition coil. Install a new spark plug and run the engine. If an intermittent miss continues, the ignition coil may be faulty. Refer to *Ignition System* in Chapter Seven.

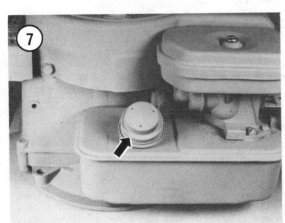

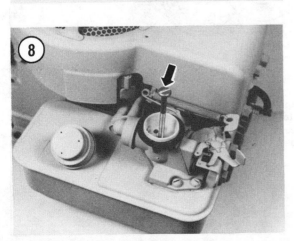

An intermittent miss caused by the fuel system may be due to an improperly adjusted carburetor or sticking choke causing an excessively rich fuel:air mixture (exhaust smoke will be black), a dirty carburetor, contaminated fuel or a clogged fuel filter. Check the fuel and the fuel system lines and filters before servicing carburetor.

Lack of power without an apparent miss may be caused by improper carburetor adjustment, incorrect governor adjustment, incorrect ignition timing, a dirty air cleaner, a plugged muffler, a dirty carburetor or a malfunctioning governor. Also check equipment connected to the engine which may cause a seeming lack of power, such as a dull lawn mower blade.

The engine may be run *temporarily* without an air cleaner to check performance. On some engines, the air cleaner screw must be installed as shown in **Figure 8** before running the engine.

CAUTION
Running an engine for even a short time in dusty conditions without an air filter causes rapid engine wear.

Engine power may be decreased due to overheating, which can be caused by a lean fuel:air mixture or inadequate cooling. A lean fuel:air mixture is usually caused by an improperly adjusted carburetor, but may also be a result of an air intake leak (bad gaskets) or limited fuel supply. Inadequate cooling is usually due to debris covering the cooling fins on the cylinder and cylinder head. Broken flywheel fan blades, as well as running without proper air shrouds will also cause overheating.

Reduced engine compression also results in a lack of power, usually producing hard engine starting as well.

NOTE
Briggs & Stratton does not specify compression pressure. Briggs & Stratton states that compression should be satisfactory if the flywheel rebounds sharply when the flywheel is rotated rapidly counterclockwise against the compression stroke.

Engine Surges

If the engine surges (rhythmically speeds up and slows down) while running, the trouble is probably caused by incorrect carburetor adjustment, incorrect

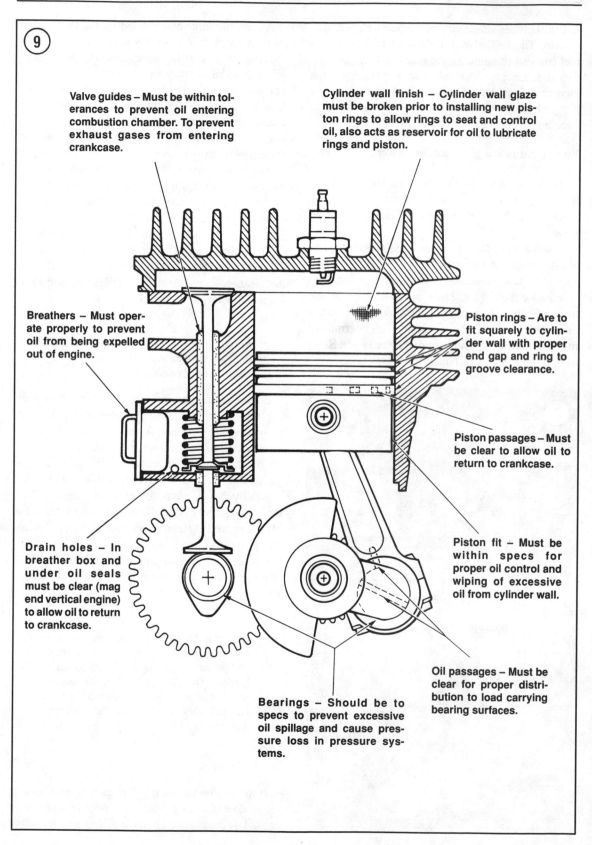

9

Valve guides – Must be within tolerances to prevent oil entering combustion chamber. To prevent exhaust gases from entering crankcase.

Cylinder wall finish – Cylinder wall glaze must be broken prior to installing new piston rings to allow rings to seat and control oil, also acts as reservoir for oil to lubricate rings and piston.

Breathers – Must operate properly to prevent oil from being expelled out of engine.

Piston rings – Are to fit squarely to cylinder wall with proper end gap and ring to groove clearance.

Piston passages – Must be clear to allow oil to return to crankcase.

Drain holes – In breather box and under oil seals must be clear (mag end vertical engine) to allow oil to return to crankcase.

Piston fit – Must be within specs for proper oil control and wiping of excessive oil from cylinder wall.

Oil passages – Must be clear for proper distribution to load carrying bearing surfaces.

Bearings – Should be to specs to prevent excessive oil spillage and cause pressure loss in pressure systems.

governor adjustment or malfunctioning carburetor or governor. Refer to the appropriate section in this manual for adjustment or service.

Excessive Engine Vibration

The usual cause of excessive engine vibration is a bent crankshaft.

> *WARNING*
> *Do not attempt to straighten a bent crankshaft. The crankshaft may have incurred stress fractures when bent and attempting to straighten the crankshaft will increase the possibility of the crankshaft breaking, which can cause personal injury if the engine is running.*

Engine vibration may also be caused by loose mounting bolts and out-of-balance equipment at-tached to the crankshaft, such as a loose mower blade.

Excessive Oil Consumption

An engine that uses too much oil may be damaged due to a low oil level. Oil serves as both lubricant and coolant in an engine and when the oil supply is reduced to a critical level, engine damage will result. Leaking oil seals are usually readily apparent, as well as leaking gaskets. Overfilling the engine with oil will cause high oil consumption, as will excessive engine speeds. Malfunctioning internal components can result in high oil consumption, usually evidenced by blue exhaust smoke. Refer to **Figure 9** for a drawing showing internal engine areas that can cause high oil consumption.

4

Table 1 COMMON TROUBLESHOOTING PROBLEMS

SYMPTOM	CAUSE	CORRECTION
Fails to start		
No fuel to carburetor	No fuel in tank	Fill tank
	Shut-off valve closed	Open valve
	Inlet screen plugged	Clean screen
	Fuel line plugged	Clean line
	Tank cap plugged	Open vent
No fuel to cylinder	No fuel to carburetor	See above
	Float stuck	Clean carburetor
	Inlet valve stuck	Clean carburetor
	Incorrect float level	Adjust float
	Choke inoperative	Overhaul carburetor
	Fuel passages clogged	Overhaul carburetor
	Water in fuel	Use fresh fuel
Engine flooded	Float stuck	Clean carburetor
	Incorrect float level	Adjust float
	Overchoked	Purge engine
	No spark at plug	See below
	Air cleaner plugged	Clean air filter

(continued)

Table 1 COMMON TROUBLESHOOTING PROBLEMS (continued)

SYMPTOM	CAUSE	CORRECTION
No spark at plug	Plug fouled	Clean plug
	Incorrect plug gap	Adjust gap
	No spark at plug wire	See below
No spark at plug wire	Breaker points coated	Clean points
	Breaker points not opening	Adjust points
	Breaker points not closing	Adjust points
	Breaker points burned	Install new points
	Kill switch shorted	Repair/replace switch
	Condenser shorted	Install new condenser
	Ignition coil shorted	Install new coil
	Incorrect magneto air gap	Adjust gap
	Ignition module faulty	Install new module
	Safety switch malfunction	Repair/replace switch
	Cranking speed slow	Repair as needed
Ignition timing incorrect	Flywheel key sheared	Install new key
No compression	Valves stuck	Free valves
	Valves burned	Install new valves
	Piston damaged	Overhaul engine
	Cylinder damaged	Overhaul engine
	Connecting rod damaged	Overhaul engine
Lacks power		
Engine smokes	Rich fuel mixture	Adjust carburetor
	Choke partially closed	Open choke
	Air filter plugged	Clean air filter
	Worn piston rings	Overhaul engine
Lean fuel mixture adjustment	Carburetor faulty	Adjust carburetor
	Manifold gasket leaking	Install new gasket
	Fuel tank vent plugged	Clean vent
	Fuel tank screen plugged	Clean screen
Partial miss under load	Spark plug fouled	Clean spark plug
	Plug gap incorrect	Regap spark plug
	Spark plug faulty	Replace spark plug
	Breaker points faulty	Replace breaker points
	Carburetor faulty	Adjust carburetor
	Weak valve spring	Replace valve spring
	Valve clearance	Adjust clearance
Engine overheats		
	Engine dirty	Clean engine
	Low oil level	Add oil
	Engine overloaded	Reduce load
	Cooling fins missing/broken	Install new parts
	Shrouds missing	Install shrouds
	Lean fuel mixture	See above
Engine knocks	Carbon in combustion chamber	Clean carbon from piston and head
	Connecting rod faulty	Replace connecting rod
	Flywheel loose	Check flywheel
	Worn cylinder	Replace cylinder

LUBRICATION AND MAINTENANCE

LUBRICATION

All engines are lubricated using splash lubrication. Oil in the oil pan is thrown onto internal engine parts by an oil dipper on the connecting rod or by a slinger driven by the camshaft gear.

Some engines are equipped with a low-oil level system (Oil Gard) that uses a float which is located inside the crankcase and connected by a wire lead to the ignition. If there is insufficient oil in the crankcase, the ignition is grounded so the engine stops or will not start.

All engines are equipped with a breather system that prevents a pressure build-up in the engine crankcase (just as the piston creates pressure in the cylinder on the up stroke, it also creates pressure in the crankcase on the down stroke). Excessive pressure in the crankcase can cause oil leakage past gaskets and seals. An open type breather is used on some engines, which allows gases to flow through the breather in both directions. Some engines are equipped with a breather valve that permits gases to flow out of the engine only, which creates a vacuum in the engine crankcase. Proper operation of the breather system is necessary to prevent excessive oil consumption and leakage.

Oil Requirements

Briggs & Stratton recommends using oil with an API service classification of SE, SF or SG. Use SAE 30 oil for temperatures above 40° F (4° C); use SAE 10W-30 oil for temperatures between 0° F (−18° C) and 40° F (4° C); below 0° F (−18° C) use petroleum based SAE 5W-20 or a suitable synthetic oil. Due to the high operating temperature of an air-cooled engine, do not use multiviscosity oil above 40° F (4° C) as high oil consumption and possible engine damage may result.

If unfamiliar with oil grade and viscosity terms, refer to *Lubricants* in Chapter One.

Refer to the following section for oil change intervals and procedure.

MAINTENANCE

Most machinery requires periodic maintenance so it will operate efficiently for as long as possible. Engine manufacturers specify the maintenance work that must be performed on the engine and when the work should be accomplished. If the engine is not maintained as specified, engine life and performance will be reduced. Neglecting maintenance work may save time and money initially, but the cost of early engine replacement or overhaul will cost more than any early cost savings.

The maintenance program prescribed by the manufacturer may only apply to normal operating conditions. The engine operator will have to determine if operating conditions are more severe and adjust the maintenance schedule accordingly. If in doubt as to recommended maintenance procedures and frequency for abnormally severe usage, contact a dealer or the manufacturer's service department.

Maintenance should include cleaning and inspection of the engine and any related equipment, such as controls and drive components. Any debris on or around the engine, particularly in or on the cooling fins, must be removed or the engine will overheat. Inspection will reveal problems that can be corrected before a more costly, major problem results. Any malfunctioning safety components must be corrected before further operation.

The maintenance paragraphs included in the following section describe maintenance jobs that pertain to most Briggs & Stratton engines. However, due to the wide range of applications, usage and operating environments that Briggs & Stratton engines encounter, a maintenance program tailored to a particular engine must be developed by the engine operator. As a general rule, maintenance jobs should be performed frequently at first while monitoring engine condition. Then a long-term schedule can be constructed.

The following jobs are generally listed in order of importance, however the order and frequency may require alteration due to the engine operating conditions. For instance, spark plug service may require frequent attention due to chronic fouling.

NOTE
Keep a log and write down the time of service as well as any abnormalities found, then refer to the log the next time maintenance is performed so minor problems can be spotted and cured before major, costly repairs are necessary.

Safety Devices

The engine and equipment the engine is mounted on may be equipped with safety devices to protect the operator. The equipment should be periodically checked to be sure all safety devices operate as designed. Any faulty devices should be replaced or repaired before the engine and/or equipment are operated.

Some later Briggs & Stratton engines are equipped with a flywheel brake that simultaneously stops the flywheel and grounds the ignition. The brake should stop the engine within three seconds when the operator releases the mower safety control

and the speed control is in high speed position. Refer to Chapter Seven for service information.

Oil Change

Briggs & Stratton specifies that the engine oil should be changed after the first five hours of operation, and then, if used normally, after every 50 hours of operation or seasonally, whichever is less. If the engine is operating in severe conditions, such as under heavy load or in high ambient temperatures,

the oil should be changed weekly or after every 25 hours of operation, whichever occurs first.

Engine oil should be changed with the engine warm. Unscrew the drain plug and remove the oil. The drain plug is located on the underside of the crankcase on vertical crankshaft engines (**Figure 1**) and on the side of horizontal crankshaft engines (**Figure 2**). Some engines may have more than one drain plug.

> *NOTE*
> *Properly discard used oil. Oil should not be placed in the trash for collection or poured on the ground. Used oil should be taken to a recycling center or to a retailer with an oil disposal container.*

Fill the engine with oil specified in the preceding *Oil Requirements* section. Approximate oil capacities are listed in **Table 1**.

Fill the engine with oil by pouring oil through the opening for the oil fill plug or the oil dipstick cap. If the engine is equipped with an oil fill plug (**Figure 3**), unscrew the plug and add oil until the oil level is

even with the top threads in the plug hole (**Figure 4**).

> *CAUTION*
> *Debris, dirt and other foreign material can easily enter the engine crankcase through the oil fill plug hole causing increased engine wear. Thoroughly clean around the oil fill plug before removing the plug.*

Some engines are equipped with an extended oil fill tube and a dipstick attached to the oil fill cap. When checking the oil level, screw the dipstick into place until the cap bottoms on the filler tube, then unscrew the dipstick and observe oil level on dipstick. The oil level should be between the ADD and FULL marks on the dipstick (**Figure 5**).

On any engine, do not overfill the engine with oil. Excess oil is forced into the cylinder where it burns, resulting in exhaust smoke and carbon deposits on the piston, cylinder head, valves and valve seats.

Air Cleaner

Grit is one of the major causes of premature engine wear and most grit enters the engine through the intake tract. The air cleaner is designed to prevent the entrance of grit and other debris into the engine, but the air cleaner can only function effectively if it is maintained properly. Dirty air cleaners will affect engine performance by restricting air flow while an improperly serviced or assembled air cleaner will allow grit to enter the engine. A filter is relatively inexpensive when compared to engine repairs and it should be discarded if it cannot be cleaned, if it has holes or tears or if it does not seal properly against the canister.

> *NOTE*
> *When obtaining a replacement air filter, be sure the filter meets Briggs & Stratton specifications for fit and filtering capability. Installing a low quality filter can shorten engine life.*

> *CAUTION*
> *Never run an engine without an air filter. Ingesting only a small amount of grit will damage an engine.*

The air cleaner consists of a canister and the filter element it contains. The canister is secured by one

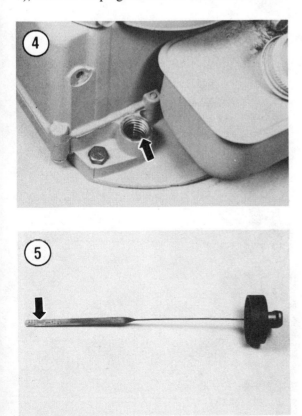

or two wing nuts, screws or knobs. The filter element may be made of foam or paper, or a combination of both foam and paper. The recommended maintenance interval depends on the type of filter element.

Foam type filter

Foam type filter elements (**Figure 6**) should be cleaned, inspected and re-oiled after every 25 hours of engine operation, or after three months, whichever occurs first. Clean the filter in kerosene or soapy water and squeeze until dry. Inspect the filter for tears and holes or any other opening. Discard the filter if it cannot be cleaned satisfactorily or if the filter is torn or otherwise damaged. Soak the filter with *clean* engine oil, then squeeze the filter to remove the excess oil and distribute oil throughout the filter. Clean the filter canister. Inspect and, if necessary, replace any defective gaskets.

When installing the filter element in the canister, be sure the filter seals properly. On round type filters, the filter must seal at the top and bottom of the inner screen (**Figure 7**). On rectangular filters, the filter protrudes so there is a seal between the upper and lower covers (**Figure 8**). If the filter does not seal properly, grit can bypass the filter and enter the engine.

If the air cleaner has a flanged cup, install the cup so one of the depressed areas (**Figure 8**) on the flange is towards the narrow side of the filter.

If the air cleaner has a cup with tangs, position the cup so the tangs (**Figure 9**) are aligned with the long side of the canister.

Be sure any spacers are properly positioned during assembly. If air cleaner has a screen, the screen should be placed on top of the filter.

Paper type filter

Paper type filter elements (**Figure 10**) should be cleaned and inspected after every 25 hours of engine operation, or after three months, whichever occurs first. Tap the filter gently to dislodge accumulated dirt. The filter may be washed using warm water and nonsudsing detergent directed from the inside of the filter to the outside. *Do not* use petroleum-based cleaners or solvents to clean the filter. *Do not* direct pressurized air towards the filter. Let the filter air dry thoroughly, then inspect the filter and discard it if damaged or uncleanable. Clean the filter canister.

Inspect and, if necessary, replace any defective gaskets.

Combination foam and paper type filter

The combination type air cleaner consists of a foam type filter, known as the precleaner, wrapped around or in front of a paper type filter. See **Figure 11**. The foam precleaner should be cleaned weekly or after every 25 hours of operation, whichever occurs first. The paper filter should be cleaned

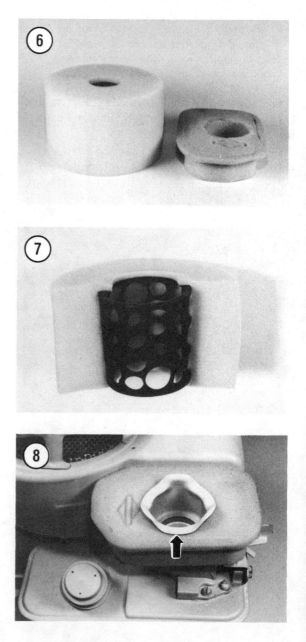

yearly or after every 100 hours of operation, whichever occurs first. Clean the foam precleaner or paper filter using the cleaning methods previously outlined for foam and paper filters.

Cooling System

The Briggs & Stratton engines covered in this manual use air to cool the engine. Any stoppage or disruption of the flow of air around the engine can cause overheating of the engine and subsequent damage. The fins on the flywheel force air around the cooling fins on the cylinder head and cylinder, while shrouds are used to direct cooling air as needed. Depending on the operating environment of the engine, the cooling system should be inspected yearly or after 100 hours of operation, whichever occurs first, or more frequently if conditions are severe.

Inspect the engine and remove any shrouds or other components as necessary to remove any dirt or debris on the engine. All foreign matter in the cooling fins must be removed (**Figure 12**). Remove the blower shroud (may require removal of rewind starter) surrounding the flywheel and look for debris (**Figure 13**). Be sure that the flywheel screen (**Figure 14**) is free of debris. Check the flywheel for broken or missing fins.

> *WARNING*
> *Do not operate engine if flywheel fins are broken or missing. The flywheel can crack when the engine is running and*

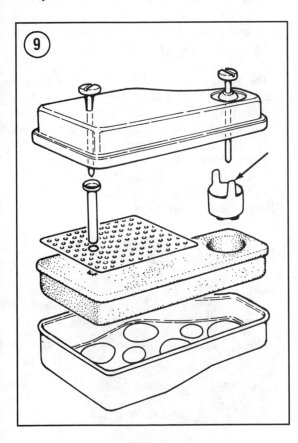

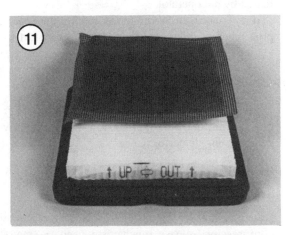

hurl harmful pieces. Replace a damaged flywheel.

Hoses and Wires

Whenever maintenance is performed, check all hoses and wires for looseness at connections and any damage. Old, hard hoses should be replaced with new hoses. Be sure any clamps and locating clips are in place. If hoses or wires are worn or damaged by moving parts, determine and correct the problem. Wire connections should be clean and tight.

Operating Cable and Controls

Some engines are controlled by a remote control. Periodically apply a dry lubricant such as liquid graphite to the cable to lubricate between the housing and steel wire inside. Oil can be used, but dirt and debris will adhere to the oil film.

Check all operating controls for proper operation. The choke should close fully during starting and the throttle should open fully when full throttle operation is required. The engine should stop when directed by the operator.

If any malfunctions are found, refer to the appropriate chapter and correct the problem before further engine operation.

Muffler

Periodically remove and inspect the muffler. A blocked muffler or exhaust pipe can significantly decrease engine performance.

Compression Test

Briggs & Stratton does not specify the compression pressure for its engines. This is due to the compression release mechanism used on many Briggs & Stratton engines, which affects compression pressure at starting speed.

To check compression pressure, disconnect the spark plug lead from the spark plug and ground the lead to the engine. Remove parts as needed so the flywheel is accessible. Rapidly rotate the flywheel counterclockwise against the compression stroke (**Figure 15**). The flywheel should come to an abrupt stop then sharply rebound if compression is adequate. If the flywheel does not change direction or does so sluggishly, compression pressure is abnormal. Low compression pressure may be due to worn,

broken or stuck piston rings, a warped cylinder head, a leaking cylinder head gasket, sticking or leaking valves or a combination of all. The cause of the low compression pressure should be corrected, otherwise, the engine will suffer from a significant power loss and satisfactory engine operation cannot be achieved.

Spark Plug

The spark plug is an important item in a good maintenance program because it is the point of ignition as well as an indicator of how well combustion is occurring in the engine. Refer to Chapter Two for a discussion of spark plug operation and terminology.

The spark plug should be removed, inspected, cleaned and regapped after every 100 hours of operation. If spark plug fouling is a problem, the inspection interval must be adjusted accordingly. Refer to **Figure 1** in Chapter Four for possible engine problems when inspecting spark plug.

The original spark plug may be either 1-1/2 in. or 2 in. long. Briggs & Stratton recommends Champion or Autolite spark plugs.

If a Champion spark plug is used and the spark plug is 1-1/2 in. (38 mm) long, the recommended spark plug is a CJ8 or J19LM. Install a Champion RCJ8 or RJ19LM if a resistor type spark plug is required. If the spark plug is 2 in. (51 mm) long, the recommended spark plug is a J8C or J19LM. Install a Champion RJ8C or RJ19LM if a resistor type spark plug is required.

If an Autolite spark plug is used and the spark plug is 1-1/2 in. (38 mm) long, the recommended spark plug is 235. Install an Autolite 245 if a resistor type spark plug is required. If the spark plug is 2 in. (51 mm) long, the recommended spark plug is 295. Install an Autolite 306 if a resistor type spark plug is required.

Before removing a spark plug, clean the area around the spark plug so dirt or debris will not enter the engine through the spark plug hole. Use a suitable spark plug socket and wrench to remove the spark plug.

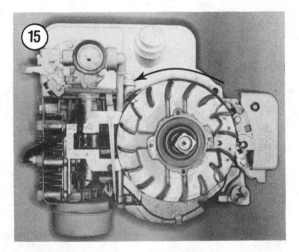

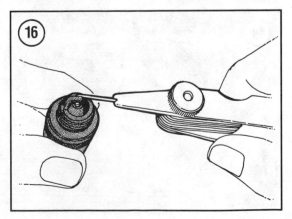

NOTE
*Allow the engine to cool completely before removing the spark plug. The spark plug should "break free" when it is turned initially with moderate force. If the spark plug will not turn or is hard to turn, it may be frozen or tearing the threads in the cylinder head. Do not turn further. Apply penetrating oil such as WD-40 or Liquid Wrench around the base of the spark plug and let stand for 10-20 minutes. If the threads of the cylinder head are damaged, a thread repair insert can be installed (see **Repair Techniques** in Chapter Ten).*

After removing the spark plug, note the condition of the plug. The material on the end of the plug will offer clues on the combustion event. Compare the spark plug with the examples shown in Chapter Four and note the possible causes.

The electrodes of a spark plug must be clean and sharp. A contaminated spark plug will "leak" voltage rather than producing an intense spark, causing misfiring. Worn electrodes require greater voltage to produce a spark, which may be greater than the ignition system is capable of generating, and misfiring results. A spark plug with light, soft deposits (such as a plug with soot from an over-rich mixture) can be cleaned with a soft wire brush, but a plug with heavy deposits should be discarded and a new plug installed.

NOTE
Briggs & Stratton does not recommend using abrasive blasting to clean spark plugs as this may introduce abrasive material into the engine which could cause extensive damage.

On both new and old spark plugs, the gap between the spark plug electrodes must be adjusted to the dimension specified by the engine manufacturer. Briggs & Stratton specifies a gap of 0.030 in. (0.76 mm) for all engines. Measure the electrode gap with a round feeler gauge (a flat feeler gauge will not accurately measure the gap, particularly on a worn plug) as shown in **Figure 16**. If the gap is correct, a slight drag will be felt when the gauge is pulled through the electrode gap. If the gap is incorrect, use a suitable gap setting tool (**Figure 17**) to adjust the electrode gap.

Before installing the spark plug, be sure the area where the spark plug seats on the cylinder head is clean. Any dirt or debris in this area can prevent solid seating of the plug, which can cause damage from hot escaping combustion gases.

Although often overlooked, it is a good practice to apply a small amount of antiseize compound to the spark plug threads to lessen the possibility of thread-tearing during removal.

When installing the spark plug, screw the plug in by hand. If the plug binds, unscrew it and determine the cause. Excessive force may cause cross-threading. Hand-tighten the spark plug, then use a torque wrench and tighten the plug to 140-200 in.-lb. (15.8-22.6 N•m).

To install the spark plug without using a torque wrench, proceed as follows: When installing a new spark plug (with new gasket), tighten spark plug finger tight, then tighten an additional 1/4 to 1/2 turn. When reinstalling a spark plug (with a used gasket), tighten spark plug finger tight, then tighten an additional 1/8 to 1/4 turn.

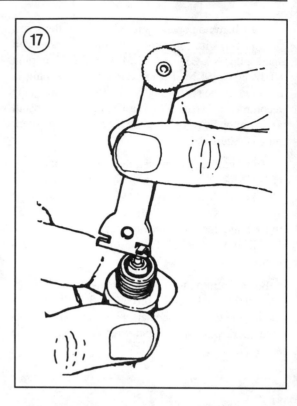

NOTE
Do not overtighten. Overtightening may damage the spark plug hole threads.

Reconnect the spark plug lead being sure it fits securely.

Ignition Breaker Points
(Models So Equipped)

Some Briggs & Stratton engines are equipped with ignition breaker points. Properly operating breaker points are critical to engine performance. The position of the breaker point mounting plate cannot be moved, so ignition timing, as well as control of the primary ignition circuit, is determined by the breaker point gap.

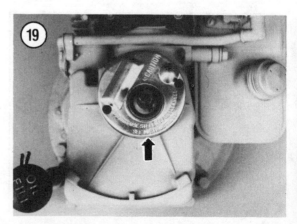

NOTE
*On some engines originally equipped with breaker points, a Magnetron breakerless ignition system or aftermarket ignition module (**Figure 18**) can be retrofitted. Contact a Briggs & Stratton or small engine dealer for information.*

Remove breaker points

The breaker points and condenser are contained under a metal cover (**Figure 19**) behind the flywheel. On some model 251000, 252000 and 253000 en-

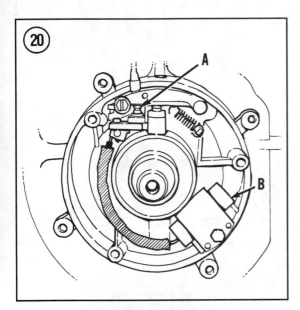

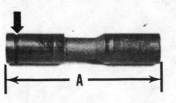

gines, the breaker points (A, **Figure 20**) and condenser (B) are separate pieces, similar to automotive engines. On all other later engines with breaker points, the condenser and the fixed breaker point comprise a single unit (A, **Figure 21**) while the movable breaker point (B) is separate. The breaker point arm on all engines is actuated by a plunger that rides against a cam on the crankshaft.

1. Refer to Chapter Eleven for flywheel removal procedure.

2. Unscrew and remove the metal cover (**Figure 19**).

3. Unscrew the mounting screws and remove the breaker points and condenser. Note on models with the integral condenser and breaker point (**Figure 21**) that the primary wire is held in a hole in the breaker point shaft by a spring. Depress the spring using the button supplied with breaker point parts set, or other suitable tool, to release the primary wire.

4. Remove the breaker point actuating plunger shown in **Figure 22** and measure plunger length (A). Install a new plunger if the length is 0.870 in. (22.10 mm) or less. Install the plunger so the grooved end is visible.

5

Install breaker points on engines with a separate condenser

1. Refer to **Figure 23** and attach ignition coil wire (1), stop switch wire (2) and condenser wire (3) to breaker points as viewed from backside.

2. Install breaker points on engine.

3. Adjust breaker point gap.

4. Apply RTV sealant around breaker point cover and wires to prevent entrance of moisture and oil.

Adjust breaker point gap on engines with a separate condenser

The breaker point gap should be set as accurately as possible. If breaker points are eroded, oxidized or dirty, service or replace them. The gap between worn points cannot be measured accurately.

1. Remove the breaker point cover as previously outlined.

2. Rotate the crankshaft so the breaker point gap is maximum.

3. Loosen the breaker point mounting screw (1, **Figure 24**).

4. Insert a screwdriver in slot (2, **Figure 24**) and move the breaker point bracket to adjust the breaker point gap.

5. Adjust the breaker point gap so that a 0.020 in. (0.5 mm) feeler gauge inserted between the breaker points will move while a slight drag is felt.

6. Retighten the mounting screw, then recheck the breaker point gap to be sure the gap did not change while tightening the screw.

Install breaker points on engines with integral condenser and breaker point

1. Attach open loop end of spring to movable breaker point (the closed loop end fits over a stud on the engine). Note that breaker point ground wire must be over the post (**Figure 25**).

2. Install movable point arm post while noting that groove (A, **Figure 25**) in post must index with a projection (B) in the boss on the engine. Tighten post retaining screw.

3. Insert flat end of movable breaker point arm into groove (A, **Figure 26**) on post and attach spring end to stud (B).

4. Depress spring (**Figure 27**) using button supplied with breaker point parts set, or other suitable tool, and insert ignition coil wire and stop switch wire through hole in breaker point shaft.

5. Install condenser on engine.

6. Adjust breaker point gap.

7. Apply RTV sealant around breaker point cover and wires to prevent entrance of moisture and oil.

NOTE
Some engines designed for winter operation may have a vent hole in the breaker point cover.

Adjust breaker point gap on engines with integral condenser and breaker point

The breaker point gap should be set as accurately as possible. If breaker points are eroded, oxidized or dirty, service or replace them. The gap between worn points cannot be measured accurately.

1. Remove the breaker point cover as previously outlined.

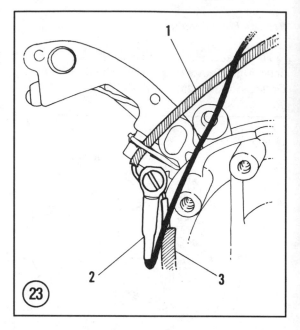

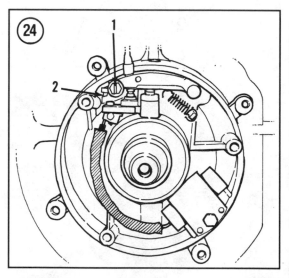

2. Rotate the crankshaft so the breaker point gap is maximum.

3. Loosen condenser clamp screw (**Figure 28**) so condenser will slide in clamp with some resistance.

4. Place a 0.020 in. (0.5 mm) feeler gauge between breaker points as shown in **Figure 28**. The movable breaker point must rest against the plunger.

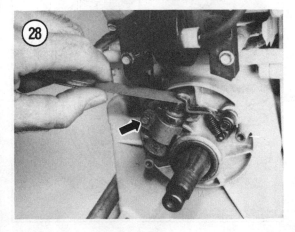

5. Move condenser so there is a slight drag when feeler gauge is withdrawn from between breaker points.

6. Tighten condenser clamp screw and recheck gap. Be sure to recheck gap after tightening condenser clamp screw as tightening the screw may move the condenser slightly.

Service breaker points

Virtually all problems concerning breaker points are related to the contacting surfaces of the breaker points. If the surfaces are not clean and sufficiently aligned so good contact is made, the primary circuit current will not flow and the engine will run erratically or not at all. Poor electrical contact between the surfaces is usually due to oxidation, erosion or oil contamination.

Breaker points that are excessively worn or pitted should be replaced. If there is excessive protrusion on one breaker point then the condenser is faulty and must be replaced. Replace both breaker points, not just one.

If breaker points are coated with oil, spray electrical contact cleaner to clean the points. Determine the source of the oil. Oil may be leaking from the crankshaft oil seal or around the breaker plunger, either of which should be serviced if the breaker points must be cleaned frequently. Refer to Chapter Eleven for procedure to replace the crankshaft oil seal. If oil is leaking past the breaker plunger, the plunger hole is worn and will require service. Refer to Chapter Eleven for procedure (before repairing the worn hole, see the following *NOTE*).

NOTE
*On some engines originally equipped with breaker points, a Magnetron breakerless ignition system or after-market ignition module (**Figure 18**) can be retrofitted. Contact a Briggs & Stratton or small engine dealer for information.*

Unless excessively worn or pitted, the breaker points can be dressed using a breaker point file. The surface should be nearly flat and slightly rounded. Some small pits are acceptable, but there must be no protrusions. Do not use emery cloth or sandpaper to dress points as material may be embedded in point surface. Burnish the points by rubbing with stiff paper, such as a business card, then spray with electrical contact cleaner.

Ignition Coil Armature Air Gap

To obtain best performance from the ignition system, the engine manufacturer specifies the width of the air gap (**Figure 29**) between the ignition coil armature legs and the magnets in the flywheel.

The type of ignition coil armature must be identified before adjusting the armature air gap. A two-leg armature is shown in **Figure 30** while a three-leg armature is shown in **Figure 31**. Specified armature air gap for engines with a three-leg armature is 0.012-0.016 in. (0.30-0.41 mm). If the engine is equipped with a two-leg armature, refer to **Table 2** for air gap specification.

Adjust Armature Air Gap

1. Disconnect and properly ground the spark plug lead.
2. Remove the blower shroud so the flywheel and ignition coil are exposed.
3. Loosen the armature retaining screws (**Figure 32**), move the armature away from the flywheel and hand tighten the screws.
4. Rotate the flywheel so the magnets on its outer edge are away from the armature legs.
5. Insert a thickness gauge between flywheel and armature legs (**Figure 33**) with a thickness that is in the middle of the desired specified air gap, i.e. use a gauge 0.012 in. (0.30 mm) thick if specified air gap is 0.010-0.014 in. (0.25-0.36 mm).
6. Rotate flywheel so magnets are directly opposite armature legs.
7. Loosen armature retaining screws and allow flywheel magnets to pull armature legs against thickness gauge, then tighten screws.
8. Rotate flywheel so thickness gauge is ejected.

CARBURETOR

Adjustment

Before attempting carburetor adjustment, be sure:
1. The air cleaner is properly serviced (a dirty filter will affect carburetor mixture).
2. The fuel tank is approximately half full of clean, fresh gasoline.

3. The ignition system is operating properly.
4. Carburetor and governor linkage operates properly.
5. The engine is at normal operating temperature.
6. The engine is installed on equipment with all engine-driven components installed, otherwise, readjust carburetor after engine is installed.

> *NOTE*
> *The carburetor must operate properly for successful adjustment. If abnormal mixture screw adjustments are required*

or the engine does not respond to mixture screw adjustments, the carburetor may be dirty, excessively worn or otherwise damaged. Overhaul the carburetor as outlined in Chapter Six.

Most carburetors are equipped with three adjustment screws: the idle mixture adjusting screw, the high speed mixture adjusting screw and the idle speed adjusting screw. Some carburetors are not equipped with a high speed mixture adjusting screw, in which case, the high speed mixture is controlled by a jet or orifice that may or may not be removable for adjustment purposes.

Initial settings for mixture screws are given as turns out from a lightly seated position, for instance, 1-1/2 turns out. The initial setting will usually allow the engine to start and run so final adjustments can be performed with the engine at normal operating temperature.

CAUTION
Do not tighten mixture screws against their seats. Doing so may damage the tapered needle point of the screw tip, which will affect fuel flow, as well as possibly damaging the seat, which will require carburetor replacement.

Before proceeding with adjustment, determine whether the carburetor is mounted directly on the gas tank. If the carburetor is mounted on the gas tank, follow adjustment procedure for Pulsa-Jet and Vacu-Jet carburetors. If the carburetor is separate from the fuel tank, refer to the adjustment procedure for float type carburetors.

Pulsa-Jet and Vacu-Jet carburetors

The Pulsa-Jet and Vacu-Jet carburetors are mounted directly on the fuel tank (**Figure 34**) and have adjustment screws for adjusting the fuel:air mixture and idle speed. On all Pulsa-Jet or Vacu-Jet carburetors, except those with a fixed jet, the mixture screw adjusts the high speed fuel:air mixture. On carburetors with a fixed jet (identified by threaded attachment holes for the air cleaner as shown in **Figure 35**), the mixture screw adjusts the idle speed fuel:air mixture.

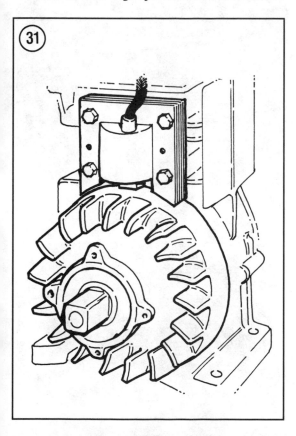

NOTE
Engine models 93900, 95900 and 96900 are equipped with a Pulsa-Prime carburetor that is mounted on the fuel tank like a Pulsa-Jet carburetor, but there are no adjustments possible on the Pulsa-Prime carburetor.

The mixture screw is located on the side of the Pulsa-Jet or Vacu-Jet carburetor. It may be visible through a hole in a bracket as shown in **Figure 36**. The idle speed screw is located on the throttle arm as shown in **Figure 37**.

Adjustable jet carburetor

1. Turn high speed mixture screw clockwise until it is lightly seated, then turn screw counterclockwise 1-1/2 turns.
2. Run engine until engine is at normal operating temperature (approximately 5-7 minutes).

NOTE
Be sure the choke is open, if not, be sure the speed control is properly adjusted, or if the choke is faulty, refer to Chapter Six for choke adjustment.

3. Run engine with speed control in fast position.
4. Turn high speed mixture screw clockwise until engine begins to stumble and note screw position.
5. Turn high speed mixture screw counterclockwise until engine begins to stumble and note screw position.

NOTE
When turning the high speed mixture screw from clockwise position (lean) to counterclockwise position (rich), the engine will run smoother and engine speed will increase until the engine slows and stumbles again.

6. Turn the high speed mixture screw clockwise to a position that is midway from the clockwise (lean) and counterclockwise (rich) positions.
7. Place a tachometer on the engine (**Figure 38**).
8. With engine running at idle, adjust idle speed screw so engine speed is 1750 rpm.
9. With engine running at idle, rapidly move speed control to full throttle position. If engine stumbles or hesitates, slightly turn high speed mixture screw counterclockwise and repeat test.

10. Recheck idle speed and, if necessary, readjust idle speed screw.

Fixed jet carburetor

1. Turn idle mixture screw clockwise until it is lightly seated, then turn screw counterclockwise 1-1/2 turns.

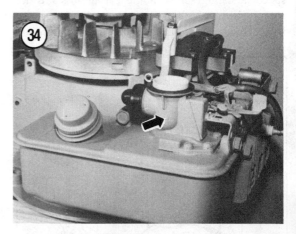

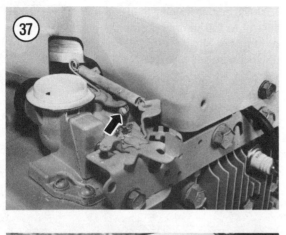

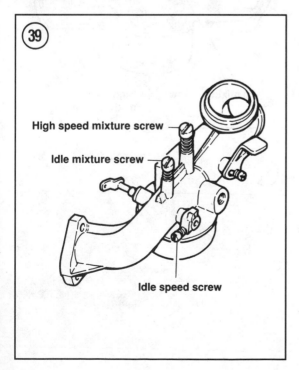

High speed mixture screw

Idle mixture screw

Idle speed screw

2. Run engine until engine is at normal operating temperature (approximately 5-7 minutes).

> *NOTE*
> *Be sure the choke is open, if not, be sure the speed control is properly adjusted, or if the choke is faulty, refer to Chapter Six for choke adjustment.*

3. Run engine with speed control in slow position.

4. Place a tachometer on the engine (**Figure 38**).

5. With engine running at idle, adjust idle speed screw so engine speed is 1750 rpm.

6. Turn idle mixture screw clockwise until engine begins to stumble and note screw position.

7. Turn idle mixture screw counterclockwise until engine begins to stumble and note screw position.

> *NOTE*
> *When turning the idle mixture screw from clockwise position (lean) to counterclockwise position (rich), the engine will run smoother and engine speed will increase until the engine slows and stumbles again.*

8. Turn the idle mixture screw clockwise to a position that is midway from the clockwise (lean) and counterclockwise (rich) positions.

9. With engine running at idle, rapidly move speed control to full throttle position. If engine stumbles or hesitates, slightly turn idle mixture screw counterclockwise and repeat test.

10. Recheck idle speed and, if necessary, readjust idle speed screw.

Float type carburetors

The float type carburetors used on Briggs & Stratton engines are identified by the fuel bowl (**Figure 39**) that contains the float. Two types have been used, either a Flo-Jet, manufactured by Briggs & Stratton, or a Walbro. Refer to Chapter Six and identify the carburetor being serviced, then refer to appropriate following paragraphs for adjustment information.

One-piece Flo-Jet carburetor

The location of the idle speed screw and idle mixture screw is the same on all one-piece Flo-Jet carburetors. See **Figures 39-40**. The high speed mixture screw may be located either on top of the carburetor or on the bottom of the fuel bowl. To adjust the carburetor, proceed as follows:

1. Turn idle mixture screw and high speed mixture screw clockwise until they are lightly seated, then turn both screws counterclockwise 1-1/2 turns.

2. Run engine until engine is at normal operating temperature (approximately 5-7 minutes).

> *NOTE*
> *Be sure the choke is open, if not, be sure the speed control is properly adjusted, or if the choke is faulty, refer to Chapter Six for choke adjustment.*

3. Run engine with speed control in fast position.

4. Turn high speed mixture screw clockwise until engine begins to stumble and note screw position.

5. Turn high speed mixture screw counterclockwise until engine begins to stumble and note screw position.

> *NOTE*
> *When turning the high speed mixture screw from clockwise position (lean) to counterclockwise position (rich), the engine will run smoother and engine speed will increase until the engine slows and stumbles again.*

6. Turn the high speed mixture screw clockwise to a position that is midway from the clockwise (lean) and counterclockwise (rich) positions.

7. Run engine with speed control in slow position.

8. Place a tachometer on the engine (**Figure 38**).

9. With engine running at idle, adjust idle speed screw so engine speed is 1750 rpm.

10. Turn idle mixture screw clockwise until engine begins to stumble and note screw position.

11. Turn idle mixture screw counterclockwise until engine begins to stumble and note screw position.

> *NOTE*
> *When turning the idle mixture screw from clockwise position (lean) to counterclockwise position (rich), the engine will run smoother and engine speed will increase until the engine slows and stumbles again.*

12. Turn the idle mixture screw clockwise to a position that is midway from the clockwise (lean) and counterclockwise (rich) positions.

13. With engine running at idle, rapidly move speed control to full throttle position. If engine stumbles or hesitates, slightly turn idle mixture screw counterclockwise and repeat test.

14. Recheck idle speed and, if necessary, readjust idle speed screw.

> *NOTE*
> *The operation of the idle and high speed mixture screws is related. After adjusting one mixture screw it may be necessary to adjust the other mixture screw.*

> *NOTE*
> *Some engines equipped with the one-piece Flo-Jet carburetor may require adjustment of the governed idle speed as outlined in the **Governor Linkage** section.*

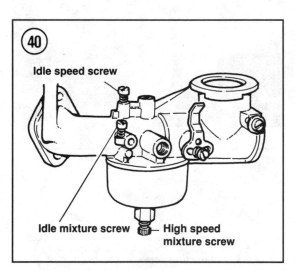

Idle speed screw

Idle mixture screw — **High speed mixture screw**

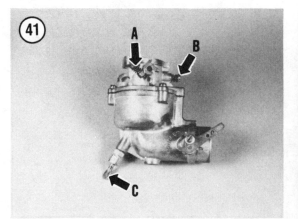

Two-piece Flo-Jet carburetor

All variations of the two-piece Flo-Jet have the adjustment screws in the same location. See **Figure 41** for location of the idle speed screw (A), idle mixture screw (B) and high speed mixture screw (C). To adjust the carburetor, proceed as follows:

1. Turn idle mixture screw (A) and high speed mixture screw (C) clockwise until they are lightly seated. Turn idle mixture screw counterclockwise 1-1/4 turns. Turn high speed mixture screw counterclockwise 1-1/2 turns.

2. Follow steps 2 through 14 as previously outlined for one-piece Flo-Jet while referring to **Figure 41**.

> *NOTE*
> *Some engines equipped with the two-piece Flo-Jet carburetor may require adjustment of the governed idle speed as outlined in the **Governor Linkage** section.*

Cross-Over Flo-Jet carburetor

The location of the adjusting screws is shown in **Figure 42**. To adjust carburetor, proceed as follows:

1. Turn idle mixture screw and high speed mixture screw clockwise until they are lightly seated, then turn both screws counterclockwise 1-1/2 turns.

2. Run engine until engine is at normal operating temperature (approximately 5-7 minutes).

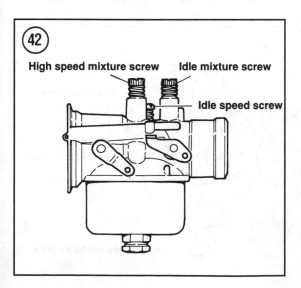

(42)

High speed mixture screw   **Idle mixture screw**

Idle speed screw

> *NOTE*
> *Be sure the choke is open, if not, be sure the speed control is properly adjusted, or if the choke is faulty, refer to Chapter Six for choke adjustment.*

3. Run engine with speed control in slow position.
4. Place a tachometer on the engine (**Figure 38**).
5. With engine running at idle, adjust idle speed screw so engine speed is 1750 rpm.
6. Turn idle mixture screw clockwise until engine begins to stumble and note screw position.
7. Turn idle mixture screw counterclockwise until engine begins to stumble and note screw position.

> *NOTE*
> *When turning the idle mixture screw from clockwise position (lean) to counterclockwise position (rich), the engine will run smoother and engine speed will increase until the engine slows and stumbles again.*

8. Turn the idle mixture screw clockwise to a position that is midway from the clockwise (lean) and counterclockwise (rich) positions.
9. Run engine with speed control in fast position.
10. Turn high speed mixture screw clockwise until engine begins to stumble and note screw position.
11. Turn high speed mixture screw counterclockwise until engine begins to stumble and note screw position.

> *NOTE*
> *When turning high speed mixture screw from clockwise position (lean) to counterclockwise position (rich), the engine will run smoother and engine speed will increase until the engine slows and stumbles again.*

12. Turn the high speed mixture screw clockwise to a position that is midway from the clockwise (lean) and counterclockwise (rich) positions.
13. With engine running at idle, rapidly move speed control to full throttle position. If engine stumbles or hesitates, slightly turn idle mixture screw counterclockwise and repeat test.
14. Recheck idle speed and, if necessary, readjust idle speed screw.

> *NOTE*
> *The operation of the idle and high speed mixture screws is related. After adjust-*

5

ing one mixture screw it may be necessary to adjust the other mixture screw.

NOTE
Some engines equipped with the Cross-Over Flo-Jet carburetor may require adjustment of the governed idle speed as outlined in **Governor Linkage** *section.*

Small Walbro carburetor

Refer to **Figure 43** for the location of the adjusting screws on the small Walbro carburetor used on Briggs & Stratton engines. Some carburetors are not equipped with the adjustable high speed mixture screw on the bottom of the fuel bowl; a fixed main jet is located inside the carburetor. To adjust carburetor, proceed as follows:

1. Turn idle mixture screw and high speed mixture screw, if so equipped, clockwise until they are lightly seated, then turn both screws counterclockwise 1-1/4 turns.

2. Run engine until engine is at normal operating temperature (approximately 5-7 minutes).

NOTE
Be sure the choke is open, if not, be sure the speed control is properly adjusted, or if the choke is faulty, refer to Chapter Six for choke adjustment.

3. Run engine with speed control in slow position.

4. Place a tachometer on the engine (**Figure 38**).

5. With engine running at idle, adjust idle speed screw so engine speed is 1750 rpm.

6. Turn idle mixture screw clockwise until engine begins to stumble and note screw position.

7. Turn idle mixture screw counterclockwise until engine begins to stumble and note screw position.

NOTE
When turning the idle mixture screw from clockwise position (lean) to counterclockwise position (rich), the engine will run smoother and engine speed will increase until the engine slows and stumbles again.

8. Turn the idle mixture screw clockwise to a position that is midway from the clockwise (lean) and counterclockwise (rich) positions.

NOTE
If carburetor is not equipped with a high speed mixture screw, disregard adjustment Steps 9 through 12 and proceed to Step 13.

9. Run engine with speed control in fast position.

10. Turn high speed mixture screw clockwise until engine begins to stumble and note screw position.

11. Turn high speed mixture screw counterclockwise until engine begins to stumble and note screw position.

NOTE
When turning the high speed mixture screw from clockwise position (lean) to counterclockwise position (rich), the engine will run smoother and engine speed will increase until the engine slows and stumbles again.

12. Turn the high speed mixture screw clockwise to a position that is midway from the clockwise (lean) and counterclockwise (rich) positions.

13. With engine running at idle, rapidly move speed control to full throttle position. If engine stumbles or hesitates, slightly turn idle mixture screw counterclockwise and repeat test.

14. Recheck idle speed and, if necessary, readjust idle speed screw.

NOTE
If the carburetor is equipped with both idle and high speed mixture screws, note that the operation of the screws is related. After adjusting one mixture screw

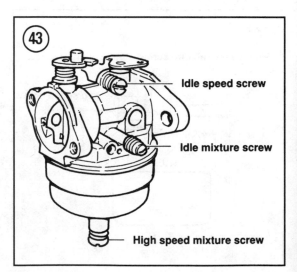

Idle speed screw

Idle mixture screw

High speed mixture screw

it may be necessary to adjust the other mixture screw.

Large Walbro carburetor

Refer to **Figure 44** for the location of the idle speed screw (A) and idle mixture screw (B) on the large Walbro carburetor used on Briggs & Stratton engines. To adjust the carburetor, proceed as follows:

1. Turn idle mixture screw clockwise until it is lightly seated, then turn screw counterclockwise 1-1/2 turns.

2. Run engine until engine is at normal operating temperature (approximately 5-7 minutes).

> *NOTE*
> *Be sure the choke is open, if not, be sure the speed control is properly adjusted, or if the choke is faulty, refer to Chapter Six for choke adjustment.*

3. Run engine with speed control in slow position.

4. Place a tachometer on the engine (**Figure 38**).

5. With engine running at idle, adjust idle speed screw so engine speed is 1750 rpm.

6. Turn idle mixture screw clockwise until engine begins to stumble and note screw position.

7. Turn idle mixture screw counterclockwise until engine begins to stumble and note screw position.

> *NOTE*
> *When turning the idle mixture screw from clockwise position (lean) to counterclockwise position (rich), the engine will run smoother and engine speed will increase until the engine slows and stumbles again.*

8. Turn the idle mixture screw clockwise to a position that is midway from the clockwise (lean) and counterclockwise (rich) positions.

9. With engine running at idle, rapidly move speed control to full throttle position. If engine stumbles or hesitates, slightly turn idle mixture screw counterclockwise and repeat test.

10. Recheck idle speed and, if necessary, readjust idle speed screw.

> *NOTE*
> *Some engines equipped with the large Walbro carburetor may require adjustment of the governed idle speed as outlined in the **Governor Linkage** section.*

Governor Linkage

The governor is designed to maintain a constant engine speed while the engine is subjected to varying loads, as well as limiting maximum engine speed. A malfunctioning governor can cause poor operation and possible engine damage.

> *CAUTION*
> *Modifying components of the governor mechanism or installing parts other than those specified by the manufacturer can cause engine failure.*

Inspection

Check the following when inspecting the governor mechanism.

1. Operate the governor linkage and check for binding. Any obstruction to free movement will cause erratic governor operation.

2. Check for missing or damaged pieces in the mechanism.

3. Check for excessively worn components that will affect governor operation.

4. Check the governor spring for stretching; the coils should be evenly spaced.

5. If the governor linkage is faulty or malfunctioning, refer to Chapter Six and correct the problem.

Governed idle speed adjustment

On some larger engines with a mechanical governor, the engine idle speed is regulated by the governor. On these models, the idle speed screw on the

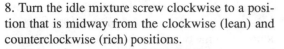

carburetor is set to a speed lower than the desired governed idle speed, then the governed idle speed is adjusted. Some typical applications are described in the following paragraphs.

Models 170000 and 190000

Some remote controlled model 170000 and 190000 engines with a vertical crankshaft and lever actuator, may be equipped with a governed idle speed. The governed idle speed may be determined by a movable stop plate (left view, **Figure 45**) or a stop screw (right view, **Figure 45**). To adjust governed idle speed, proceed as follows:

1. Adjust carburetor as previously outlined.

2. Loosen stop plate retaining screw (left view, **Figure 45**), if so equipped, and move stop plate away from remote control lever.

3. Back out governed idle speed screw (right view, **Figure 45**), if so equipped.

4. Set remote control to idle position.

5. With carburetor throttle held in idle position, adjust idle speed screw on carburetor so engine idles at 1550 rpm.

6. Adjust position of remote control so engine idles at 1750 rpm.

7. If equipped with stop plate (left view, **Figure 45**), position plate so it contacts remote control lever and tighten retaining screw.

8. If equipped with screw (right view, **Figure 45**), turn screw in until it just contacts remote control lever.

Models 170400, 171400, 190400, 195400, 221400, 222400, 252400 and 254400 with governed idle speed screw

If model 170400, 171400, 190400, 195400, 221400, 222400, 252400 or 254400 with a sliding block actuator is equipped with the governed idle speed screw shown in **Figure 46**, proceed as follows:

1. Adjust carburetor as previously outlined.

2. Set remote control to idle position.

3. With carburetor throttle held in idle position, adjust idle speed screw on carburetor so engine idles at 1550 rpm.

4. Adjust position of remote control so engine idles at 1750 rpm.

5. Rotate governed idle speed screw as needed so it just contacts remote control lever.

Models 170700, 190700, 191700, 192700, 193700, 220700, 252700, 253700, 255700, 256700, 258700, 280700 and 281700 with governed idle speed screw

If model 170700, 190700, 191700, 192700, 193700, 220700, 252700, 253700, 255700, 256700,

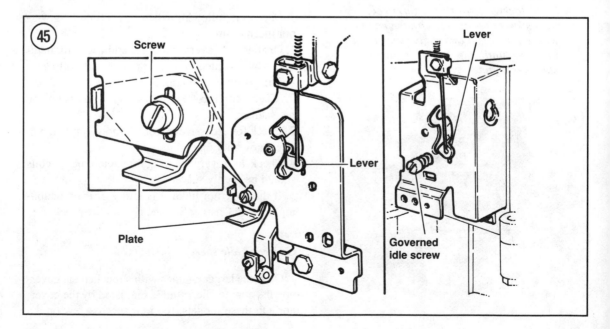

258700, 280700 or 281700 with a sliding block actuator is equipped with the governed idle speed screw shown in **Figure 47**, proceed as follows:

1. Adjust carburetor as previously outlined.
2. Set remote control to idle position.
3. With carburetor throttle held in idle position, adjust idle speed screw on carburetor so engine idles at 1550 rpm.

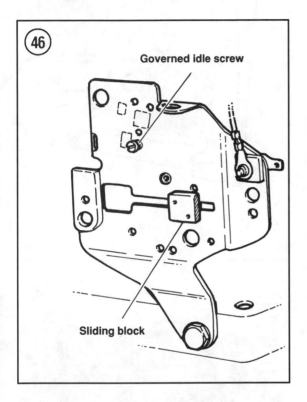

Governed idle screw

Sliding block

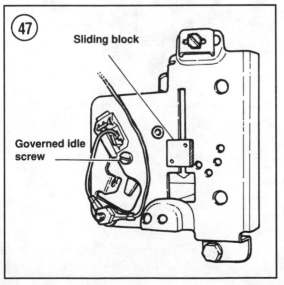

Sliding block

Governed idle screw

4. Adjust position of remote control so engine idles at 1750 rpm.
5. Rotate governed idle speed screw as needed so it just contacts remote control lever.

Models 194700, 196700, 254700, 257700, 283700 and 286700 with governed idle speed screw

If model 194700, 196700, 254700, 257700, 283700 or 286700 with a sliding block actuator is equipped with the governed idle speed screw shown in **Figure 47**, proceed as follows:

1. Adjust carburetor as previously outlined.
2. Set remote control to idle position.
3. With carburetor throttle held in idle position, adjust idle speed screw on carburetor so engine idles at 1200 rpm.
4. Adjust position of remote control so engine idles at 1750 rpm.
5. Rotate governed idle speed screw as needed so it just contacts remote control lever.

Models 194700, 196700, 254700, 257700, 258700, 259700, 282700, 283700, 285700, 286700 and 289700 with governed idle speed adjusting tang

If model 194700, 196700, 254700, 257700, 258700, 259700, 282700, 283700, 285700, 286700 or 289700 with a sliding block actuator is equipped with the governed idle speed adjusting tang shown in **Figure 48**, proceed as follows:

1. Adjust carburetor as previously outlined.

5

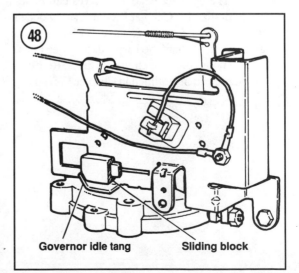

Governor idle tang   **Sliding block**

2. Set remote control to idle position.

3. With carburetor throttle held in idle position, adjust idle speed screw on carburetor so engine idles at 1200 rpm.

4. Adjust position of remote control so engine idles at 1750 rpm.

5. Bend governed idle speed adjusting tang as needed so it just contacts remote control lever.

Models 253400 and 255400 with governed idle speed adjusting tang

If model 253400 or 255400 is equipped with the governed idle speed adjusting tang shown in **Figure 49**, proceed as follows:

1. Adjust carburetor as previously outlined.

2. Set remote control to idle position.

3. With carburetor throttle held in idle position, adjust idle speed screw on carburetor so engine idles at 1550 rpm.

4. Bend governed idle speed adjusting tang so engine idles at 1750 rpm.

COMBUSTION CHAMBER

Cleaning

Engines are susceptible to the formation of deposits on the cylinder head, piston crown and valves (see **Figure 50**). These deposits, which are primarily carbon, reduce engine performance. On all engines the deposits should be removed after every 150 hours of operation or whenever the cylinder head is removed. The cylinder head and valves can be removed as outlined in Chapter Eleven. Use a wooden or plastic scraper to remove the deposits. Spray a suitable solvent on hardened deposits to soften them. Be careful not to damage engine surfaces. Reinstall the cylinder head as outlined in Chapter Eleven.

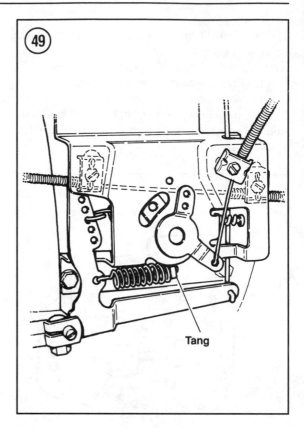

Tang

Table 1 APPROXIMATE OIL CAPACITIES

Models	
60000, 61000, 80000, 81000, 82000, 83000, 90000, 91000, 92000, 93000, 94000, 95000, 96000, 100200, 100700, 110000, 111000, 112000, 113000, 114000, 121000, 122000, 124000, 126000	1 1/4 pints (0.6 L)
100900	1 3/4 pints (0.8 L)
130000, 131000, 132000:	
Horizontal crankshaft	1 1/4 pints (0.6 L)
Vertical crankshaft	1 3/4 pints (0.8 L)
140000, 170000, 171000, 190000, 191000, 192000, 193000, 194000, 195000, 196000:	
Horizontal crankshaft	2 3/4 pints (1.3 L)
Vertical crankshaft	2 1/4 pints (1.1 L)
220000, 221000, 222000, 250000, 251000, 252000, 253000, 254000, 255000, 256000, 257000, 258000, 259000, 280000, 281000, 282000, 283000, 285000, 286000, 289000:	
Vertical crankshaft	3 pints (1.4 L)
Horizontal crankshaft	2 1/2 pints (1.2 L)

5

Table 2 TWO-LEG ARMATURE AIR GAP

Model	Armature air gap
60000 & 61000	0.006-0.010 in. (0.15-0.25 mm)
80000, 81000, 82000, 83000	0.006-0.010 in. (0.15-0.25 mm)
90000, 91000, 92000, 93000, 94000, 95000, 96000	0.006-0.010 in. (0.15-0.25 mm)
100200 & 100900	0.010-0.014 in. (0.25-0.36 mm)
100700	0.006-0.010 in. (0.15-0.25 mm)
110000, 111000, 112000, 113000, 114000	0.006-0.010 in. (0.15-0.25 mm)
121000, 122000, 124000, 126000	0.006-0.010 in. (0.15-0.25 mm)
130000, 131000, 132000	0.010-0.014 in. (0.25-0.36 mm)

(continued)

Table 2 TWO-LEG ARMATURE AIR GAP (continued)

Model	Armature air gap
140000	0.010-0.014 in. (0.25-0.36 mm)
170000 & 171000	0.010-0.014 in. (0.25-0.36 mm)
190000, 191000, 192000, 193000, 194000, 195000, 196000	0.010-0.014 in. (0.25-0.36 mm)
220000, 221000, 222000	0.010-0.014 in. (0.25-0.36 mm)
250000, 251000, 252000, 253000, 254000, 255000, 256000, 257000, 258000, 259000	0.010-0.014 in. (0.25-0.36 mm)
280000, 281000, 282000, 283000, 285000, 286000, 289000	0.010-0.014 in. (0.25-0.36 mm)

FUEL AND GOVERNOR SYSTEMS

The fuel system consists of the carburetor, fuel pump, if so equipped, and operating linkage. If carburetor mixture and idle speed adjustments are required, refer to Chapter Five.

OPERATING LINKAGE

The engine control linkage may consist of engine-mounted operating levers or remote control linkage. In either case, the apparatus should move without binding (although some friction may be desirable to maintain a set position) and operate as designed, which includes controlling the choke, engine speed and stop switch on some models.

Remote Engine Speed Control—Except Choke-A-Matic

Some engines are controlled by a remote control that controls engine speed while the choke is operated separately. The engine throttle may be controlled either by the governor or directly. No adjustment should be required other than to check for a full range of movement from idle to full throttle.

Choke-A-Matic Engine Control

Some engines are equipped with a Choke-A-Matic mechanism that controls engine speed, oper-

ates the choke and engages a stop switch when the remote control is moved to the appropriate position.

To check the operation of Choke-A-Matic engine control, proceed as follows:

1. Move the speed control lever to the "CHOKE" or "START" position.

2. Remove the air cleaner and verify that the choke slide or plate is completely closed.

3. Move the speed control lever to "RUN," "FAST" and "SLOW" positions; the choke should be open.

4. Reinstall the air cleaner.

5. Start the engine.

6. Move the control lever to the "STOP" position. The engine should stop running.

Inspection/Adjustment

If the unit does not perform properly, check the following items.

If equipped with a control cable between the remote control and engine, the remote control cable must move a certain distance for the remote control and carburetor to be synchronized. At full extension, the control wire must extend 2-1/8 in. (54 mm) from the cable housing as shown in **Figure 1**. The wire must travel at least 1-3/8 in. (34.9 mm) from "CHOKE" or "START" to "STOP" positions.

If equipped with a dial type control (**Figure 2**), adjust the mechanism as follows:

1. Move the dial control to "START" position.

2. Loosen the ferrule screw shown in **Figure 2**.

3. Move the carburetor lever fully clockwise.

4. Position the remote control arm so it is 1/8 in. (3.2 mm) from the bracket.

5. With the carburetor lever and remote control arm in positions previously specified, tighten the ferrule screw.

6. Start the engine.

7. Move the control lever to the "STOP" position. The engine should stop running.

Several Choke-A-Matic configurations have been used on Briggs & Stratton engines. Refer to **Figures 3-7** for some typical setups and the following list for adjustment points.

1. **Figures 3-5**—On these units, lever (A) should just contact link or arm (B) when the control is in "FAST" position. If not, loosen screw (C) and move control wire housing (D) as required, then tighten the screw.

2. **Figure 6**—On these units, adjustment is performed by bending the choke link at the point indicated by the arrow.

3. **Figure 7**—On these units, lever (A) should just contact choke lever (B) when lever (C) is in "FAST" detent. If not, loosen screws (D) and move the control plate as required, then tighten the screws.

CARBURETORS

Two types of carburetors are used on Briggs & Stratton engines, suction type and float type. The suction type carburetor is identified by its location on top of the fuel tank (**Figure 8**), while float type carburetors are identified by the fuel bowl that surrounds the internal float (**Figure 9**).

Suction Type Carburetors Except Pulsa-Prime

Suction type carburetors are mounted on the fuel tank and called either Pulsa-Jet or Vacu-Jet. The carburetors are differentiated by the presence of one fuel tube on Vacu-Jet carburetors and two fuel tubes on Pulsa-Jet carburetors. See **Figure 10**. If the carburetor has a primer bulb, it is a Pulsa-Prime carburetor, which is covered in the following section.

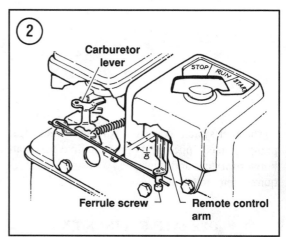

2-1/8 in. min. (54 mm)

1-3/8 in. (34.9 mm) min. travel

Choke or start position   Stop position

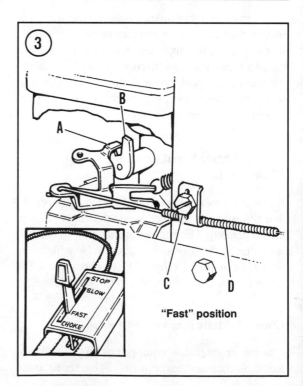

Carburetor lever

Ferrule screw   Remote control arm

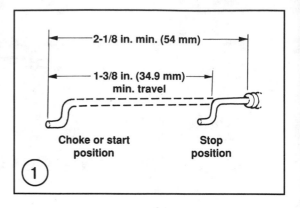

"Fast" position

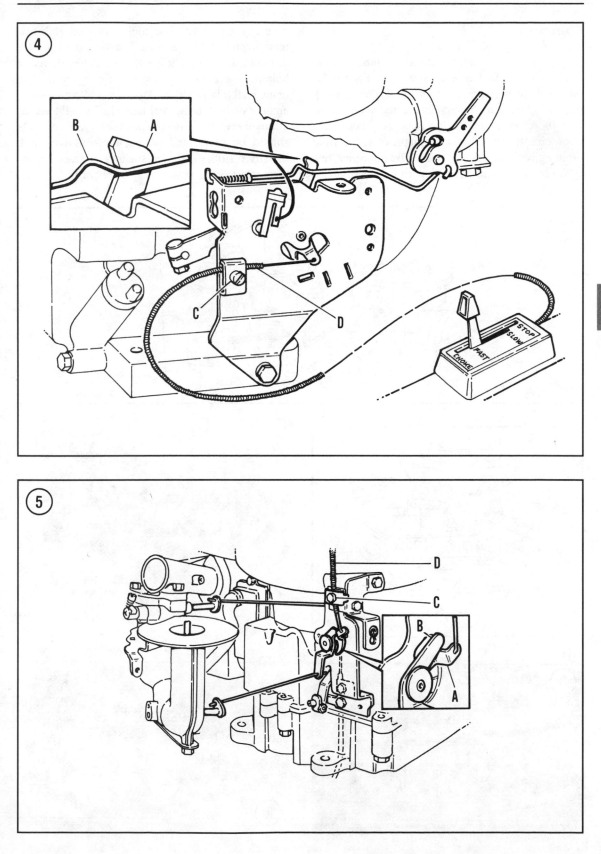

Operation

The Vacu-Jet carburetor has a fuel tube that extends into the fuel tank as shown in **Figure 11**. Atmospheric pressure against the fuel forces fuel up the fuel tube due to the vacuum created in the carburetor bore when the engine runs. A check valve allows fuel to flow up the tube but prevents fuel from draining back into the fuel tank. The mixture screw controls the amount of fuel entering the carburetor bore at high speed. The fuel passes through two metering holes into the bore. The metering holes are different sizes and at idle only the smaller diameter hole passes fuel due to the position of the throttle plate. Fuel mixture in the Vacu-Jet is affected by the amount of fuel in the fuel tank (fuel weight versus atmospheric pressure). Carburetor adjustments should be performed with a half-full fuel tank thereby resulting in a satisfactory mixture adjustment whether the tank is near empty or full.

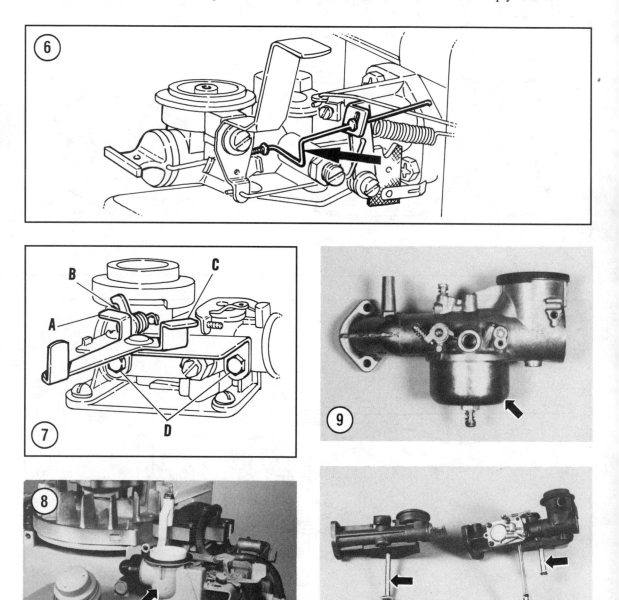

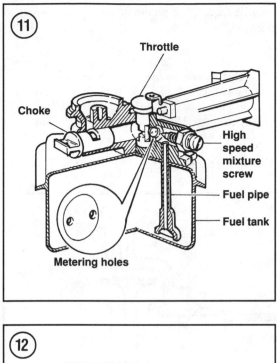

⑪

Throttle

Choke

High speed mixture screw

Fuel pipe

Fuel tank

Metering holes

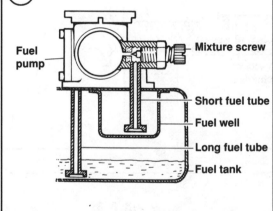

⑫

Fuel pump

Mixture screw

Short fuel tube

Fuel well

Long fuel tube

Fuel tank

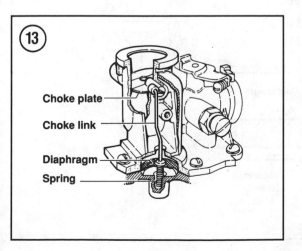

⑬

Choke plate

Choke link

Diaphragm

Spring

The Pulsa-Jet carburetor operates similarly to the Vacu-Jet except in delivery of the fuel to the carburetor. The fuel tank for a Pulsa-jet carburetor has a fuel well (**Figure 12**) that always contains a constant amount of fuel. The short fuel tube passes fuel from the fuel well to the mixture screw. With a constant amount of fuel present in the fuel well, the fuel mixture in the carburetor remains the same regardless of the amount of fuel in the tank, unlike the Vacu-Jet. Fuel passes through the long fuel tube to a diaphragm type pump located either on the side of the carburetor or between the carburetor and fuel tank. The pump transfers fuel from the fuel tank to the fuel well.

Most Pulsa-Jet and Vacu-Jet carburetors are equipped with a plate type choke valve (see Chapter Two). Some models are equipped with an automatic choke plate that is actuated by a link attached to a diaphragm between the carburetor and fuel tank. See **Figure 13**. A compression spring works against the diaphragm holding the choke plate in closed position when the engine is not running. See **Figure 14**. A vacuum passage leads from the carburetor to a chamber under the diaphragm. When the engine starts, increased vacuum pulls down the diaphragm with the choke link, thereby opening the choke plate. See **Figure 15**. This type automatic choke also operates if the engine loses engine speed under heavy load. The resulting loss of intake vacuum results in the choke plate closing, which provides a rich mixture so the engine will not stall. When engine speed increases, the increased vacuum returns the choke plate to the open position.

The automatic choke on some Pulsa-Jet and Vacu-Jet carburetors may be controlled by a bimetallic spring (**Figure 16**) that is connected to the choke plate shaft. Air in the breather tube is directed to the bimetallic spring cavity on the carburetor. The air activates the spring which turns the choke shaft and plate. When the engine is cold, the bimetallic spring is fully contracted, which turns the choke shaft so the choke plate is in the closed position. When the engine warms after starting, heated air causes the bimetallic spring to expand thereby moving the choke plate to the open position.

Some Pulsa-Jet and Vacu-Jet carburetors may be equipped with the slide type choke shown in **Figure 17**. When the choke slide is in running position, a slot in the tube allows incoming air to flow into the carburetor (**Figure 18**). When the choke slide is out,

6

incoming air is blocked and the mixture is richened to enhance starting.

Removal

The fuel tank and carburetor should be removed and installed as a unit. After the fuel tank and carburetor are removed, the carburetor can be separated from the fuel tank. Proceed as follows (note that the following procedure is typical and additional steps may be required to accommodate specific applications):

NOTE
Before removal, note position of springs, linkage and other pieces so they can be reinstalled in their original positions. Make a diagram rather than trusting memory.

1. Remove the air cleaner.

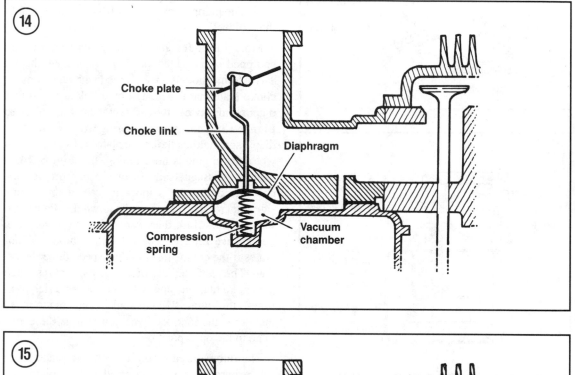

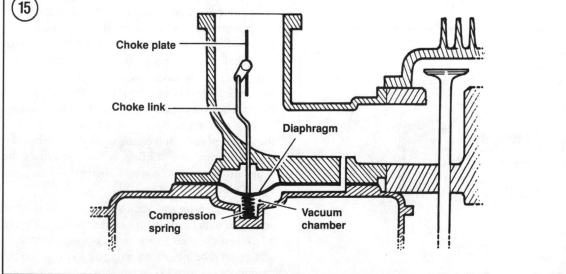

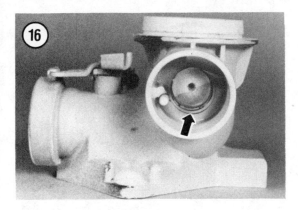

2. Remove any metalwork, such as the blower shroud or engine control panel, that will prevent removal of the fuel tank and carburetor.

3. On models so equipped, disconnect the wire from the stop switch (**Figure 19**).

4. Note the location of the fuel tank mounting screws and, if so equipped, the carburetor mounting screws, then determine if the governor spring must be disconnected to remove the fuel tank and carburetor, and if so, disconnect the governor spring.

NOTE
When attaching or detaching a governor spring end with a closed loop, use a twisting motion at the spring end. Do not pull spring end with pliers or other tools as spring end may be deformed, which can affect governor operation.

5. Unscrew fuel tank mounting screws (**Figure 20**) and, if so equipped, the carburetor mounting screws.

6. Pull the carburetor free of the intake and breather tubes, and if necessary, rotate the carburetor so the bend in the throttle link will disengage from the throttle lever on the carburetor.

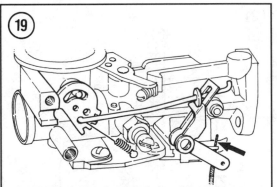

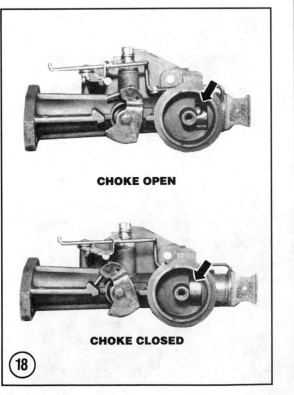

CHOKE OPEN

CHOKE CLOSED

7. Look into the carburetor bore for a screw (**Figure 21**) that is used on some units to secure carburetor to fuel tank and, if so equipped, remove screw.

8. Unscrew the carburetor-to-fuel tank screws and separate the carburetor from the fuel tank while noting any pieces located between the carburetor and the fuel tank. Be especially careful not to damage a diaphragm as it may be reused if undamaged.

Disassembly

To properly clean the carburetor for inspection, all components that cover orifices must be removed. Depending on the type of carburetor cleaning solvent, nonmetallic parts should be removed to prevent damage. Remove only the parts described in the following list as some parts are installed permanently which will result in damage to the carburetor if removal is attempted.

1. If equipped with an automatic choke, remove the cover (**Figure 22**), detach choke link and remove the choke actuating diaphragm and spring (**Figure 23**).

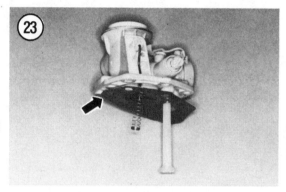

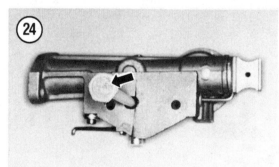

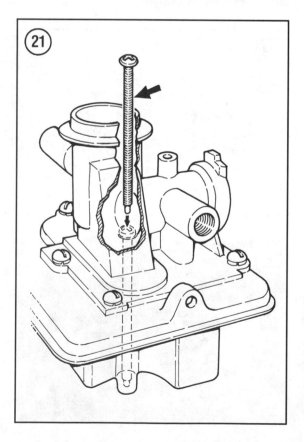

2. Remove the plastic fuel feed tube(s); *do not* remove the metal fuel feed tubes. Fuel feed tubes with a hex end (**Figure 24**) can be removed with a suitable socket by unscrewing. Fuel feed tubes with a round end can be removed by grasping the tube with pliers and pulling the tube from the carburetor body (**Figure 25**).

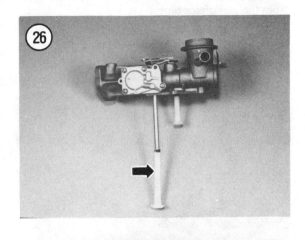

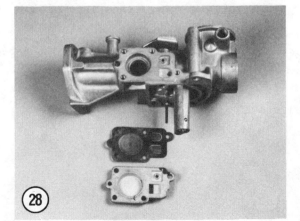

NOTE
A new fuel feed tube must be the same length as the original tube. When ordering parts, measure and compare the old tube with the new tube.

3. If equipped with a brass fuel feed tube, the plastic pickup should be replaced if it cannot be cleaned in place with aerosol carburetor cleaner. If equipped with a long tube (**Figure 26**), detach the retainer clip then pull the plastic tube off the brass tube. If equipped with a plastic pickup on the brass tube, drive the pickup off of the brass tube.

4. On Pulsa-Jet carburetors with a side-mounted fuel pump, unscrew and remove the pump cover (**Figure 27**), then remove the diaphragm, spring and spring cup (**Figure 28**).

5. If equipped with an all-temperature choke, remove the cover shown in **Figure 29**, then force out the choke shaft with the bimetal spring by pushing against the inner end of the shaft (**Figure 30**). Note that the spring post is flared on some carburetors (**Figure 31**) and must be dressed down to release the spring end.

6

6. Pull out the choke shaft and remove the choke plate. Note that on some models with a plastic choke plate and choke shaft that the shaft is bonded to the plate. Use a tool with a sharp edge to cut through the bond along the edge of the shaft (**Figure 32**) to separate the shaft from the plate.

7. Unscrew and remove the fuel mixture screw assembly (**Figure 33**), including the nut, if so equipped. Note that there is a removable valve seat on some models that should be removed with a screwdriver (**Figure 34**).

NOTE
*Some carburetors are equipped with a fuel mixture screw assembly that has a plastic seat (**Figure 35**). Unscrew the adjustment screw four or five turns, then pull the assembly out of the carburetor.*

8. If the carburetor is equipped with Welch plugs (**Figure 36**), pierce the plug with a sharp-pointed punch, then pry out the plug.

CAUTION
Insert the punch into the plug only far enough to pierce the plug, otherwise, underlying metal may be damaged.

9. If so equipped, remove O-ring (**Figure 37**) from the carburetor bore.

10. If so equipped, pull the spiral insert (**Figure 38**) from the carburetor bore.

11. Fully back out the idle speed screw, unscrew the screw securing the throttle plate on the throttle shaft, then remove the plate and shaft.

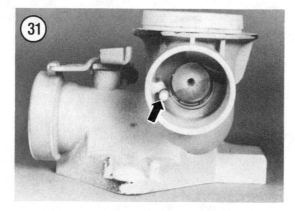

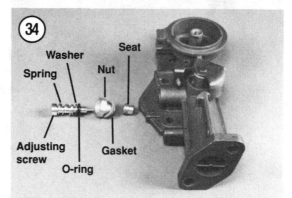

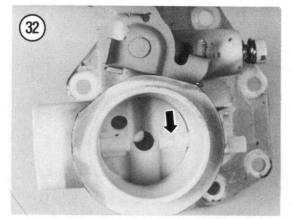

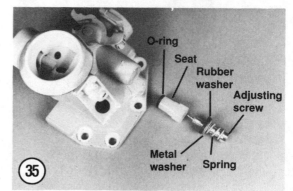

12. The carburetor should now be ready for soaking in carburetor cleaner. Follow the directions of the cleaner manufacturer. Spray the carburetor with aerosol carburetor cleaner to remove any residue, then use compressed air to blow out passages and dry the carburetor.

CAUTION
Some carburetor bodies are made of plastic. They must not be soaked in carburetor cleaner for longer than 15 minutes.

CAUTION
*The metering holes in the mixture screw cavity (**Figure 39**) are calibrated and should be cleaned with compressed air only. Do not enlarge or damage holes.*

Inspection

1. Inspect the carburetor and components. Discard any diaphragms that are torn, creased or otherwise damaged.

2. The fuel pump diaphragm has "flaps" that act as valves (**Figure 40**). The flap valves must be undamaged.

3. Inspect the tip of the fuel mixture needle (**Figure 41**) and replace if the tip is bent or grooved.

4. Install the throttle shaft in the carburetor body and check for excessive play between the shaft and body. The body must be replaced if there is excessive play as bushings are not available.

5. All gaskets and seals should be replaced.

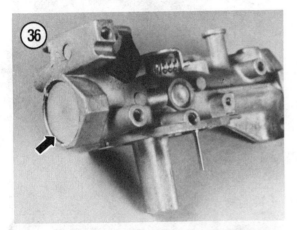

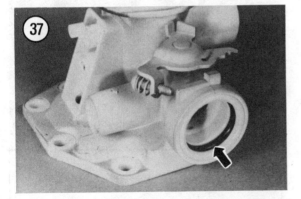

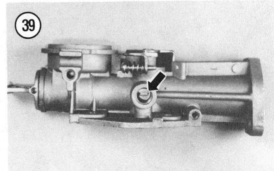

6. Check the flatness of the carburetor mounting surface on the fuel tank. Place a straightedge (be sure the straightedge is perfectly straight) and attempt to slide a 0.002 in. (0.05 mm) feeler gauge between the straightedge and the fuel tank surface as shown in **Figure 42**. If the feeler gauge slides under the straightedge, discard the fuel tank, or if the carburetor is not equipped with an automatic choke, Briggs & Stratton repair kit 391413 can be used.

> *CAUTION*
> *Do not attempt to flatten the surface of the fuel tank by filing.*

7. Note the color of the choke actuating diaphragm spring (**Figure 43**) and measure the spring length. Replace the spring and diaphragm if colored red and length is not 1-1/8 to 1-7/32 in. (28.6-30.9 mm), if colored blue and length is not 1-5/16 to 1-3/8 in. (33.3-34.9 mm), or if colored green and length is not 1-7/64 to 1-3/8 in. (28.2-34.9 mm).

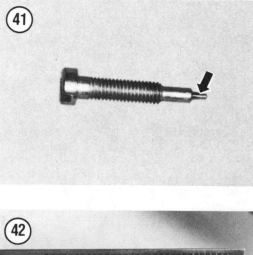

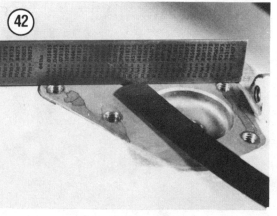

Assembly

1. If so equipped, install the throttle shaft seal so the lip is positioned outward (**Figure 44**).

2. If the throttle plate has a raised edge (**Figure 45**), install the throttle plate with the raised edge towards the mixture screw side of the carburetor. If the throt-

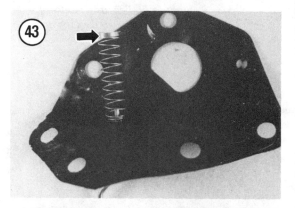

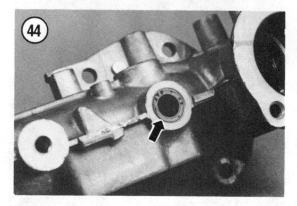

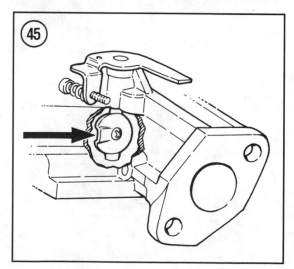

tle plate is flat, install the throttle plate so the mark is on the fuel pump side of the bore (**Figure 46**).

3. If so equipped, install the spiral insert so the end is parallel with the fuel tank mounting surface (**Figure 47**). Insert end should be flush or just below mounting face of carburetor.

4. If the carburetor is equipped with Welch plugs (**Figure 36**), apply a nonhardening sealer to the outer edge of the plug and drive the plug into the hole with the concave side towards the carburetor. The welch plug will be flat when correctly installed.

5. Refer to **Figures 34-35** for exploded views of typical fuel mixture screw assemblies.

6. If equipped with a choke plate that has dimples (**Figure 48**), the choke plate must be installed on the choke shaft so that the dimples are up and the hole in the plate is towards the throttle when the choke is closed. Be sure to install the felt washer on the choke shaft before insertion into the carburetor. If equipped with a spring on the choke shaft, install the spring as shown in **Figure 49** so the spring closes the choke plate.

7. If equipped with a spring-loaded valve on the choke plate (**Figure 50**), install the choke plate so the spring is visible when the choke plate is closed.

8. If equipped with a manual choke using sector gears to rotate the choke (**Figure 51**), note that when the choke is in open position the teeth are engaged as shown when properly assembled.

6

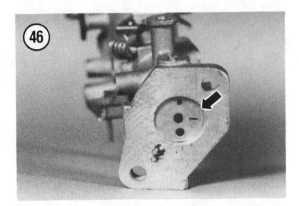

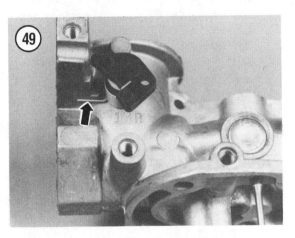

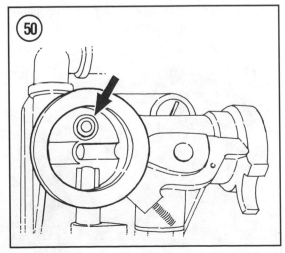

9. If equipped with an automatic choke, install the choke spring, if so equipped, so the spring holds the choke plate in the open position.

10. If equipped with an all-temperature choke, position the choke plate in the closed position, then install the choke shaft with the bimetallic spring so the outer spring end is above the anchor pin (**Figure 52**). Rotate the spring end counterclockwise and attach to the pin. If the carburetor is plastic, use a warm soldering iron to flare the end of the spring anchor pin so the spring end cannot slide off the pin.

11. If equipped with a side-mounted fuel pump, install the spring cup so the smooth side (**Figure 53**) is towards the diaphragm. Tighten the fuel pump cover retaining screws evenly in a crossing pattern.

12. If equipped with a brass fuel feed tube that has a plastic extension tube (B, **Figure 54**) and retainer clip (A), install the plastic tube as follows:

    a. Place the retainer clip (A) on the brass tube.

    b. Hold the small end of the plastic tube in hot water, then push the plastic tube onto the brass tube until the small end engages the groove on the brass tube.

    c. Fit the retainer clip around the small end of the plastic tube as shown in **Figure 54**.

Installation

1. Using a new gasket between the fuel tank and carburetor, install the carburetor on the fuel tank. If equipped with an all-temperature choke, use the following procedure when installing the carburetor on the fuel tank:

    a. Invert the carburetor as shown in **Figure 55** with the choke diaphragm and spring in place. If equipped with a fuel pump, the fuel pump spring and spring cup (smooth side towards

diaphragm) must be installed as well. The choke link should not be attached to the choke lever.

    b. Place the fuel tank on the carburetor while guiding the choke diaphragm spring into the well of the fuel tank (**Figure 56**).

    c. Install the carburetor mounting screws, but do not tighten.

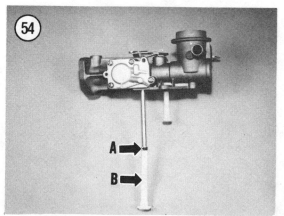

d. Attach the choke link to the choke lever (**Figure 57**), hold the choke plate in the closed position and tighten the carburetor mounting screws.

e. Check choke operation. Hold the choke plate in the open position, then release the choke plate. The choke should return to the closed position when released. If not, the choke spring may not be attached to the diaphragm or it may not be located in the fuel tank well.

2. On carburetors so equipped, be sure to install the screw (**Figure 58**) located in the carburetor bore that is used to secure the carburetor to the fuel tank.

3. If equipped with an O-ring (**Figure 59**) in the carburetor mounting boss, apply a light coat of oil to the O-ring before installing the carburetor on the intake tube.

4. Attach the carburetor and fuel tank to the engine. It may be necessary to hold the carburetor at an angle so the linkage can be attached to the carburetor.

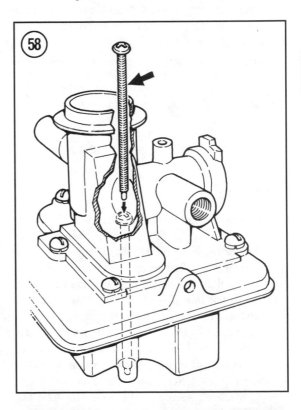

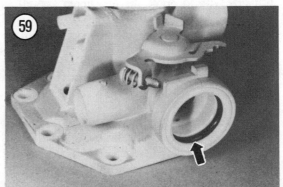

5. Attach the control and governor linkage.

NOTE
When attaching or detaching a governor spring end with a closed loop, use a twisting motion at the spring end. Do not pull the spring end with pliers or other tools as the spring end may be deformed, which can affect governor operation.

6. After installation, check the operation of all control linkage and adjust as required. Be sure the stop switch wire is connected, if so equipped.

7. Install any metalwork, such as the blower shroud or engine control panel, that was removed.

8. Install the air cleaner.

9. Adjust the carburetor as outlined in Chapter Five.

Pulsa-Prime Suction Type Carburetor

The Pulsa-Prime carburetor is mounted on the fuel tank (**Figure 60**) and is equipped with a primer bulb.

Operation

The Pulsa-Prime carburetor has two fuel tubes (**Figure 61**). A screen (B) covers the short fuel tube. The longer fuel tube (C) extends into the fuel tank. A diaphragm type fuel pump between the carburetor and fuel tank transfers fuel from the fuel tank into a fuel well that is a part of the fuel tank under the carburetor. The short fuel tube has a jet at the bottom. The tube extends into the fuel well and passes fuel from the fuel well to the carburetor bore. There are no provisions for mixture adjustment on the Pulsa-Prime carburetor. Actuating the primer bulb forces fuel past check valves in the long fuel tube and primer cavity to prime the fuel pump as well as providing additional fuel for engine starting. Several pushes against the primer bulb are required to fill the fuel system if it is dry.

Removal

The fuel tank and carburetor should be removed and installed as a unit. After the fuel tank and carburetor are removed, the carburetor can be separated from the fuel tank. Proceed as follows (note that the following procedure is typical and additional steps may be required to accommodate specific applications):

NOTE
Before removal, note the position of springs, linkage and other pieces so they can be reinstalled in their original positions. Make a diagram rather than trusting memory.

1. Remove the air cleaner.

2. Remove any metalwork, such as the blower shroud or engine control panel, that will prevent removal of the fuel tank and carburetor.

3. Unscrew the fuel tank mounting screws.

4. Pull the carburetor free of the intake and breather tubes, and if necessary, rotate the carburetor so the bend in the throttle link will disengage from the throttle lever on the carburetor.

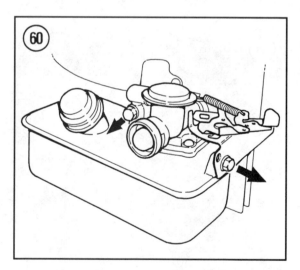

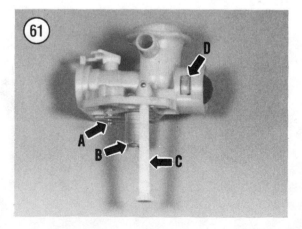

5. Unscrew the carburetor-to-fuel tank screws and carefully separate the carburetor from the fuel tank. Be especially careful not to damage the diaphragm as it may be reused if undamaged.

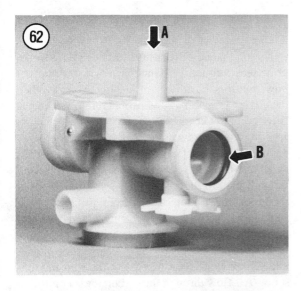

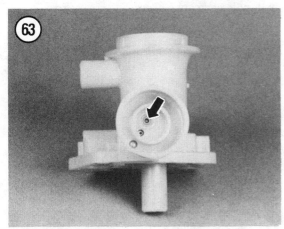

Disassembly

1. Remove the fuel pump spring (A, **Figure 61**) and the screen (B) surrounding the short fuel tube.

2. Grasp the long fuel tube (C, **Figure 61**) with pliers and pull the tube out of the carburetor.

> *NOTE*
> *The main jet (A, **Figure 62**) in the bottom of the short fuel tube is permanently installed and should not be removed. Do not enlarge or damage the main jet hole. Replacement jets are not available.*

3. Remove the O-ring (B, **Figure 62**) from the carburetor bore.

4. Press in the tabs (D, **Figure 61**) on primer bulb retainer ring and remove retainer ring and primer bulb.

5. Using a suitable tool, extract the check valve seat (**Figure 63**) in the primer cavity, then remove the check ball and spring. Do not deform the spring.

6. Use needlenose pliers and pull the throttle plate out of the throttle shaft, then remove the throttle shaft with its dust seal.

7. The carburetor should now be ready for soaking in carburetor cleaner. Follow the directions of the cleaner manufacturer. Spray the carburetor with aerosol carburetor cleaner to remove any residue, then use compressed air to blow out passages and dry the carburetor.

> *CAUTION*
> *The carburetor body is made of plastic. It must not be soaked in carburetor cleaner for longer than 15 minutes.*

Inspection

1. Inspect the carburetor and components. Discard the diaphragm if torn, creased or otherwise damaged, also note the condition of the flap valves (**Figure 64**) which must be undamaged.

2. Install the throttle shaft in the carburetor body and check for excessive play between the shaft and body. The body must be replaced if there is excessive play as bushings are not available.

3. The fuel tank gasket and throttle shaft seal should be replaced.

4. Replace the long fuel tube or the screen around the short fuel tube if the screen is clogged or damaged.

5. Replace the primer bulb if it is cracked or torn.

Assembly

1. Install the throttle shaft with the dust seal. Use needlenose pliers and insert the throttle plate in the throttle shaft so the hole in the plate is out (**Figure 65**). The convex side of the dimples in the throttle plate should be towards the breather tube side of the carburetor. Insert the throttle plate until the two dimples contact the throttle shaft. Rotate the throttle and check for binding. The throttle plate should fit in the bore evenly around the edge when closed.

2. Install the spring and check ball in the primer cavity, then install the ball seat so the groove on the seat is out (**Figure 63**).

3. Moisten the inside of the primer cavity, then install the primer bulb and retainer ring. Push in the retainer ring until the locking tabs engage the slots on the body.

4. Install the O-ring in the carburetor bore.

5. Push the long fuel tube into the carburetor.

6. Install the screen (B, **Figure 61**) surrounding the short fuel tube and install the fuel pump spring (A).

Installation

1. Place the diaphragm on the fuel tank, then place the gasket on the diaphragm. Install the carburetor on the fuel tank and evenly tighten the screws in a crossing pattern.

2. Apply a light coat of oil to the O-ring in the carburetor bore, then install the carburetor and fuel tank on the engine. Rotate the carburetor so the bend in the throttle link will engage the throttle lever on the carburetor.

3. Install the fuel tank mounting screws.

4. Install any metalwork that was removed.

5. Install the air cleaner.

One-Piece Flo-Jet Carburetors

The one-piece Flo-Jet carburetor (**Figures 66** and **67**) is a float type carburetor. The carburetor shown is a "large" version of the one-piece Flo-Jet carburetor. A "small" version is similar except the high

speed mixture screw is located on the top of the carburetor next to the idle mixture screw. Operation and service for the carburetors is similar except as noted.

Operation

The one-piece Flo-Jet operates according to the principles outlined in Chapter Two. A float in the fuel bowl controls the amount of fuel in the bowl. When the engine is running, fuel is drawn into the nozzle (**Figure 66**). On large one-piece Flo-Jets, a high speed mixture screw at the bottom of the fuel bowl controls the amount of fuel entering the nozzle. On small one-piece Flo-Jets, the amount of fuel passing through the nozzle is controlled by the high speed mixture screw on top of the carburetor. Fuel in the nozzle travels into the discharge tube then exits into the carburetor bore through discharge holes. A portion of the fuel travels up the discharge tube into an idle circuit that is controlled by the idle mixture screw. Air flow through the carburetor is controlled by throttle and choke plates.

Removal and installation

1. Remove the air cleaner assembly.

2. Remove any metalwork, such as the blower housing or engine control panel, that will prevent removal of the carburetor.

3. Disconnect the fuel line from the carburetor. Close fuel tank shut-off valve or drain the fuel to prevent fuel leakage.

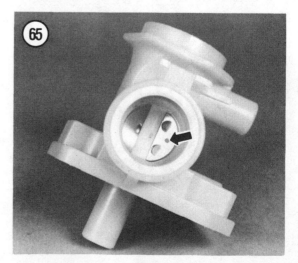

4. If carburetor is secured by a brace, remove the brace.

5. Remove the carburetor mounting screws, disconnect control linkage and remove the carburetor from the engine.

6. To install the carburetor, reverse the removal Steps 1 through 5. Note that on some engines it may be necessary to tilt the carburetor so that the linkage can be reconnected, in which case the carburetor mounting screws must not yet be installed. If the carburetor is secured by a brace, be sure that the brace is reinstalled.

After installation, check the operation of all control linkage and adjust as reqired. Be sure the stop switch wire is connected, if so equipped. Adjust the carburetor as outlined in Chapter Five.

Disassembly

To disassemble the carburetor for cleaning and inspection, proceed as follows:

1. Detach any linkage or brackets from the carburetor.

2. Unscrew the idle mixture screw (A, **Figure 67**).

3. On small one-piece Flo-Jet, unscrew the high speed mixture screw on the top of the carburetor.

4. On large one-piece Flo-Jet, unscrew the discharge tube screw (**Figure 68**).

5. On large one-piece Flo-Jet, unscrew the high speed mixture screw (B, **Figure 67**).

6. Unscrew the fuel bowl retaining nut, which is also the high speed mixture screw nut on large one-piece Flo-Jet carburetors, and remove the fuel bowl and gasket.

7. Dislodge the float pin (**Figure 69**) and remove the float and fuel valve.

8. Unscrew the nozzle (**Figure 70**).

9. Insert a suitable tool through the carburetor intake and drive out the Welch plug (**Figure 71**) in the end of the carburetor.

6

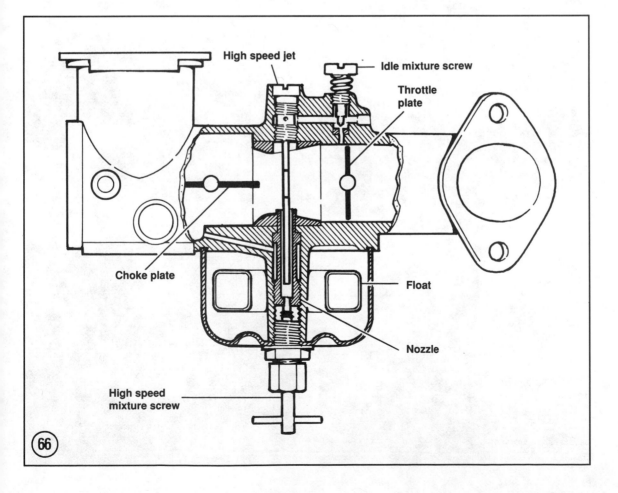

High speed jet

Idle mixture screw

Throttle plate

Choke plate

Float

Nozzle

High speed mixture screw

66

10. If equipped with a metal choke, unscrew the choke plate retaining screws and remove the choke plate and choke shaft (**Figure 72**).

11. If equipped with a plastic choke, insert a sharp tool between the choke shaft and the choke plate and pull out the choke plate, then remove the choke shaft.

12. Extract the venturi from the carburetor bore (**Figure 73**). On some carburetors there may be a plate stop pin (**Figure 74**) that must be removed before removing the venturi. Press or drive the pin into the bore.

13. Unscrew the throttle plate retaining screws and remove the throttle plate.

14. Check the throttle shaft and bushing wear before removal. Play in bushings should not exceed 0.010 in. (0.25 mm), otherwise, the throttle shaft and/or bushings must be replaced.

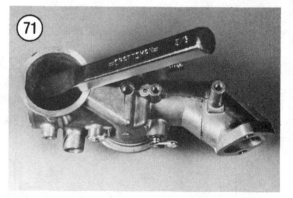

15. Drive out the roll pin (**Figure 75**) in the idle speed arm and throttle shaft, then withdraw the throttle shaft.

16. Remove the throttle shaft seals in the carburetor.

17. If replacement of the fuel inlet valve is required, thread a 1/4-20 self-tapping screw or screw extractor into the fuel inlet valve seat (**Figure 76**) and remove the valve seat.

18. The carburetor should now be ready for soaking in carburetor cleaner. Follow the directions of the cleaner manufacturer. Spray the carburetor with aerosol carburetor cleaner to remove any residue, then use compressed air to blow out passages and dry the carburetor.

CAUTION
Some carburetor parts may be made of plastic and should not be soaked in carburetor cleaner.

Inspection

1. Inspect the carburetor and components for wear or damage.

2. Inspect the tip of the idle mixture and high speed mixture needles (**Figure 77**) and replace if the tip is bent or grooved.

3. Inspect the fuel inlet valve (**Figure 78**) and replace if the tip is grooved.

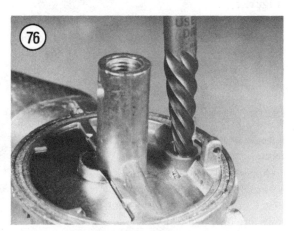

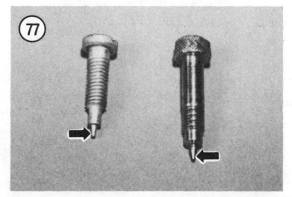

4. If the throttle shaft bushings are worn and must be replaced, proceed as follows:

    a. Thread a 1/4 in. tap or screw extractor into the bushing, clamp the tap or screw extractor into a vise, then pull the bushing out of the carburetor.

    b. Using a vise or other suitable tool, push a new bushing into the carburetor.

    c. Insert the throttle shaft and check for free shaft rotation.

    d. If binding occurs, use a 7/32 in. drill bit as a line reamer by passing the drill through both bushings.

Assembly

1. Install the fuel inlet valve seat so it is flush with the carburetor body (**Figure 79**).

2. Install the throttle shaft seals so the lip is out (**Figure 80**).

3. Install the throttle plate so the dimple is up and convex side is towards intake end of carburetor (**Figure 81**).

4. Install the venturi with the groove (**Figure 82**) towards the fuel bowl, then install the nozzle and discharge tube screw (large Flo-Jet) or the high speed mixture screw (small Flo-Jet) to hold the venturi in place.

5. Drive in the venturi retaining pin (**Figure 74**).

6. Install the choke plate so the cutout is down and the concave side of the dimple is towards intake end of carburetor (**Figure 83**).

7. Apply sealant to the outer edge of the Welch plug before installation, then swage the carburetor body metal around the edge of the plug in several places to secure the plug.

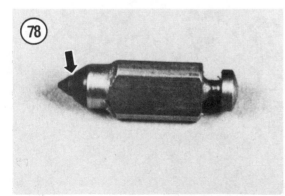

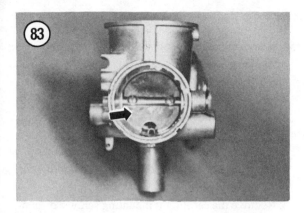

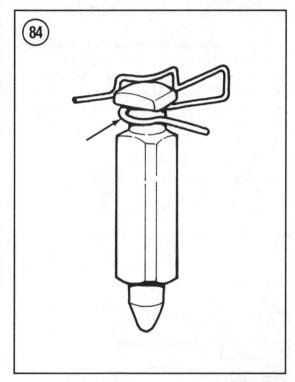

8. When installing the float and fuel inlet valve, be sure the retainer clip fits around the valve stem and the float tang as shown in **Figure 84**.

9. After assembly, check the float level. The float should be parallel with the fuel bowl mating surface on the carburetor (**Figure 85**). To adjust the float level, bend the tang that contacts the fuel inlet valve (**Figure 86**). Do not bend the float.

> *CAUTION*
> *Do not press on float to adjust. Be extremely careful not to force the fuel inlet needle onto its seat as the tip of the inlet valve is easily damaged.*

Two-Piece Flo-Jet Carburetors

The two-piece Flo-Jet carburetor (**Figures 87-88**) is a float type carburetor. The carburetor is identified by the fuel bowl that is integral with the carburetor body. Two castings make up the carburetor. The idle mixture screw (A, **Figure 87**) and fuel inlet valve are located in the cover, which also serves as the attachment point for the float. The high speed mix-

ture screw (B) and nozzle are located in the body, although the nozzle protrudes into the cover to provide fuel for the idle circuit.

The two-piece Flo-Jet has been produced in three versions, small, medium and large. On medium versions, the air inlet is at the end of the carburetor body as shown in **Figure 87**. On small and large versions, the air inlet is at right angles to the carburetor body as shown in **Figure 88** and a Welch plug is located at the end of the body. Carburetor operation and servicing is similar except as noted.

Operation

The two-piece Flo-Jet operates according to the principles outlined in Chapter Two. A float in the fuel bowl controls the amount of fuel in the bowl. When the engine is running, fuel is drawn into the nozzle (**Figure 88**). A high speed mixture screw below the fuel bowl controls the amount of fuel entering the nozzle. Fuel in the nozzle then exits into the carburetor bore through discharge holes. A portion of the fuel travels up the nozzle tube into an idle circuit that is controlled by the idle mixture screw. Air flow through the carburetor is controlled by throttle and choke plates.

Removal and installation

1. Remove the air cleaner assembly.

2. Remove any metalwork, such as the blower housing or engine control panel, that will prevent removal of the carburetor.

3. Disconnect the fuel line from the carburetor. Close fuel tank shut-off valve or drain the fuel to prevent fuel leakage.

4. If carburetor is secured by a brace, remove the brace.

5. Remove the carburetor mounting screws, disconnect control linkage and remove the carburetor from the engine.

6. To install the carburetor, reverse the removal Steps 1 through 5. Note that on some engines it may be necessary to tilt the carburetor so that the linkage can be reconnected, in which case the carburetor mounting screws must not yet be installed. If the carburetor is secured by a brace, be sure that the brace is reinstalled.

7. After installation, check the operation of all control linkage and adjust as required. Be sure the stop switch wire is connected, if so equipped. Adjust the carburetor as outlined in Chapter Five.

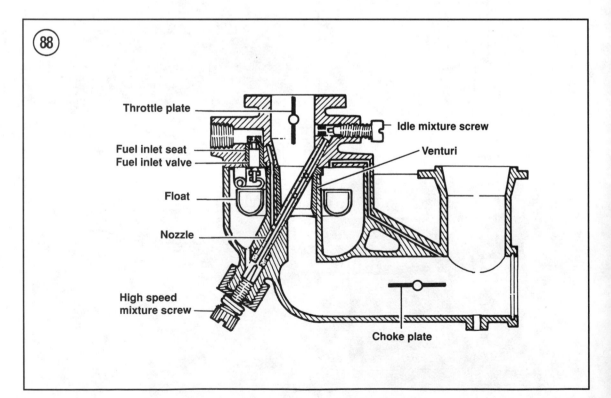

88

- Throttle plate
- Fuel inlet seat
- Fuel inlet valve
- Float
- Nozzle
- High speed mixture screw
- Idle mixture screw
- Venturi
- Choke plate

Disassembly

Before servicing the carburetor, check the cover for flatness. Attempt to insert a 0.002 in. (0.05 mm) feeler gauge between the cover and body as shown in **Figure 89A**. If the feeler gauge can be inserted, then the body is warped or damaged and must be replaced.

To disassemble the carburetor for cleaning and inspection, proceed as follows:

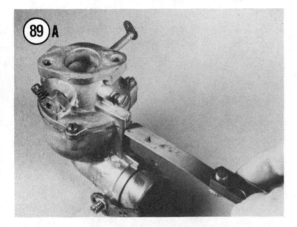

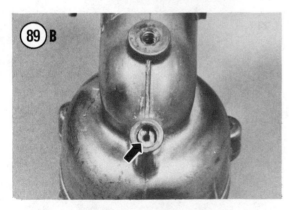

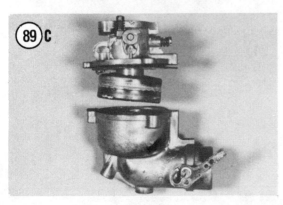

CAUTION
The nozzle is angled between the body and cover. The nozzle must be removed before the cover is removed, otherwise, the nozzle will be damaged.

1. Detach any linkage or brackets from the carburetor.

2. Unscrew the idle mixture screw (A, **Figure 87**).

3. Unscrew the high speed mixture screw (B, **Figure 87**) assembly, as well as the packing nut, if so equipped.

4. Unscrew the nozzle (**Figure 89B**).

5. Unscrew the cover retaining screws and separate the cover assembly from the body (**Figure 89C**).

6. Dislodge the float pin (**Figure 90**) and remove the float, fuel valve and gasket.

7. On models so equipped, extract the removable venturi.

8. If equipped with a Welch plug in the end of the carburetor, drive or pry out the Welch plug.

9. If equipped with a metal choke, unscrew the choke plate retaining screws and remove the choke plate and choke shaft (**Figure 91**).

10. If equipped with a plastic choke, insert a sharp tool between the choke shaft and the choke plate and pull out the choke plate, then remove the choke shaft.

11. Unscrew the throttle plate retaining screws and remove the throttle plate.

12. Check the throttle shaft and bushing wear before removal. Play in bushings should not exceed 0.010 in. (0.25 mm), otherwise, the throttle shaft and/or bushings must be replaced.

6

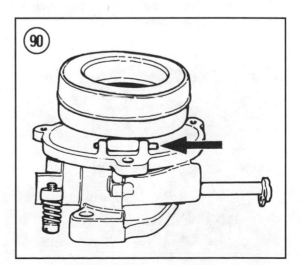

13. Drive out the roll pin (**Figure 92**) in the idle speed arm and throttle shaft, then withdraw the throttle shaft.

14. Remove the throttle shaft seals from the carburetor body.

15. The fuel inlet valve seat may be a threaded or press-in type. If a threaded type, a screwdriver can be used to unscrew the valve seat. If the valve seat is a press-in type (identified by absence of a screwdriver slot) and replacement is required, thread a 1/4-20 self-tapping screw or screw extractor into the fuel inlet valve seat (**Figure 93**) and remove the valve seat.

16. The carburetor should now be ready for soaking in carburetor cleaner. Follow the directions of the cleaner manufacturer. Spray the carburetor with aerosol carburetor cleaner to remove any residue, then use compressed air to blow out passages and dry the carburetor.

> *CAUTION*
> *Some carburetor parts may be made of plastic and should not be soaked in carburetor cleaner.*

Inspection

1. Inspect the carburetor and components for wear and damage.

2. Inspect the tip of the idle mixture and high speed mixture needles (**Figure 94**) and replace if the tip is bent or grooved.

3. Inspect the fuel inlet valve (**Figure 95**) and replace if the tip is grooved.

4. If the throttle shaft bushings are worn and must be replaced, proceed as follows:

a. Thread a 1/4 in. tap or screw extractor into the bushing (**Figure 96**), clamp the tap or screw extractor into a vise, then pull the bushing out of the carburetor.

b. Using a vise or other suitable tool, push a new bushing into the carburetor.

c. Insert the throttle shaft and check for free shaft rotation.

d. If binding occurs, use a 7/32 in. drill bit as a line reamer by passing the drill through both bushings (**Figure 97**).

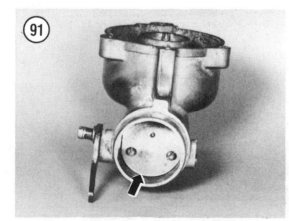

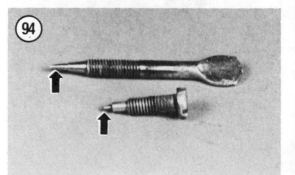

Assembly

1. If equipped with a pressed-in fuel inlet valve seat, install the valve seat so it is flush with the carburetor body.

2. Install the throttle plate so the dimples are up (**Figure 98**).

3. If the carburetor is equipped with a removable venturi, be sure to align the holes in the venturi and gasket during assembly.

4. When installing the float and fuel inlet valve, be sure the retainer clip properly fits around the valve stem and the float tang.

5. After installing the float on the cover, check the float level. The float should be parallel with the fuel bowl mating surface on the carburetor (**Figure 99**). To adjust the float level, bend the tang that contacts the fuel inlet valve (**Figure 100**). Do not bend the float.

> *CAUTION*
> *Do not press on the float to adjust. Be careful not to force the fuel inlet needle onto its seat as the tip of the needle valve is easily damaged.*

6. Apply sealant to the edge of the Welch plug before installation, then swage the carburetor body metal around the edge of the plug in several places to secure the plug.

6

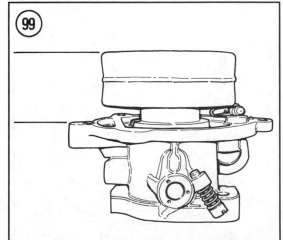

Walbro LMS Carburetor

The Walbro LMS carburetor is a float type carburetor. The carburetor can be identified by the letters "LMS" embossed on the carburetor mounting flange (**Figure 101**). Three versions of the LMS carburetor have been used. Some carburetors have both idle mixture and high speed mixture screws (**Figure 102**), some carburetors have a fixed jet (**Figure 103**) instead of a high speed mixture screw, and some carburetors with fixed jet use a primer system in place of the choke plate.

Operation

The Walbro LMS carburetor operates according to the principles outlined in Chapter Two. A float in the fuel bowl controls the amount of fuel in the bowl. When the engine is running, fuel is drawn past the high speed mixture screw or fixed jet into the nozzle. Fuel in the nozzle then exits into the carburetor bore through a discharge hole. A portion of the fuel travels up the nozzle tube into an idle circuit that is controlled by the idle mixture screw. Air flow through the carburetor is controlled by throttle and choke plates.

Air for the main fuel circuit and idle circuit is introduced through three holes in the carburetor bore (**Figure 104**): left main air bleed (A), right main air bleed (B) and idle air bleed (C).

> *NOTE*
> *If the engine is operated at high altitudes, improved engine performance may be obtained by removing the metal jet in the right main air bleed hole, however, the air jet should be installed if engine is operated at lower altitudes.*

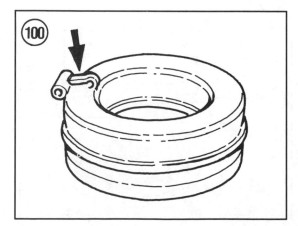

Removing the air jet leans the high speed mixture.

Removal and installation

1. Remove the air cleaner assembly.

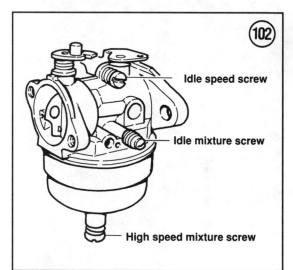

Idle speed screw

Idle mixture screw

High speed mixture screw

2. Remove any metalwork, such as the blower housing or engine control panel, that will prevent removal of the carburetor.

3. Disconnect the fuel line from the carburetor. Close fuel tank shut-off valve or drain the fuel to prevent fuel leakage.

4. Remove the carburetor mounting screws, disconnect control linkage and remove the carburetor from the engine.

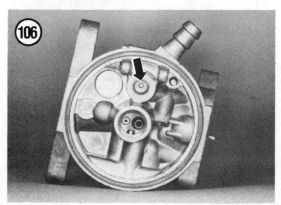

5. To install the carburetor, reverse the removal Steps 1 through 4. Note that on some engines it may be necessary to tilt the carburetor so that the linkage can be reconnected.

6. Tighten carburetor mounting screws to 75 in.-lb. (8.5 N•m) torque.

7. After installation, check the operation of all control linkage and adjust as required. Adjust the carburetor as outlined in Chapter Five.

Disassembly

To disassemble the carburetor for cleaning and inspection, proceed as follows:

1. Unscrew the idle mixture screw (**Figure 102**).

2. Unscrew the fuel bowl retaining screw or, if so equipped, the high speed mixture screw and remove the fuel bowl and gasket.

3. Remove the float pin (**Figure 105**), float and fuel inlet valve.

4. If replacement of the fuel inlet valve seat (**Figure 106**) is required, thread a screw extractor or a self-threading screw into the seat and pull the seat from the carburetor body.

5. Insert a sharp tool between the choke shaft and the choke plate and pull out the choke plate, then remove the choke shaft.

6. Unscrew the throttle plate retaining screw and remove the throttle plate and throttle shaft.

7. The Welch plugs (**Figure 107**) should be removed from the carburetor body to ensure that the fuel passageways are thoroughly cleaned. To remove the Welch plugs, pierce the plug with a shart-pointed punch, then pry out the plug.

6

> *CAUTION*
> *Insert the punch into the plug only far enough to pierce the plug, otherwise, underlying metal may be damaged.*

8. The carburetor should now be ready for soaking in carburetor cleaner. Follow the directions of the cleaner manufacturer. Spray the carburetor with aerosol carburetor cleaner to remove any residue, then use compressed air to blow out passages and dry the carburetor.

> *CAUTION*
> *Some carburetor parts may be made of plastic and should not be soaked in carburetor cleaner.*

Inspection

1. Inspect the carburetor and components for wear and damage.

2. Inspect the tip of the idle mixture and high speed mixture needles (**Figure 108**) and replace if tip is bent or grooved.

3. Inspect the fuel inlet valve (**Figure 109**) and replace if the tip is grooved.

4. Install the throttle shaft in the carburetor body and check for excessive play between the shaft and body. The body must be replaced if there is excessive play as bushings are not available.

Assembly

1. Install the Welch plugs while being careful not to indent the plug; the plug should be flat after installation. Apply a nonhardening sealant around the outer edge of the plug.

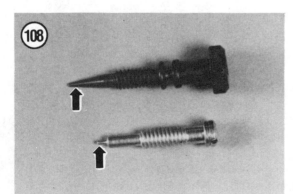

2. Use a 3/16 in. rod to install the fuel inlet valve seat. The groove on the seat must be down (towards carburetor bore). Push in the seat until it bottoms.

3. Install the choke shaft, and if so equipped, the choke return spring.

4. Install the choke plate so the numbers are visible when the choke is closed (**Figure 110**). The plate should be centered on the choke shaft.

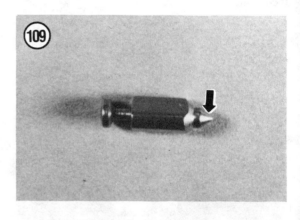

5. Position the choke return spring ends as shown in **Figure 111** so the choke plate is held open.

6. Install the throttle plate so the numbers are visible and towards the idle mixture screw when the throttle is closed (**Figure 112**).

7. Install fuel inlet valve in slot on float (**Figure 113**). The float level is not adjustable. If the float is not approximately parallel with the body when the car-

buretor is inverted, then the float, fuel valve and/or valve seat must be replaced.

8. Tighten the fuel bowl retaining screw or high speed mixture nut to 50 in.-lb. (5.6 N•m) torque.

Walbro LMT Carburetor

The Walbro LMT carburetor is a float type carburetor. The carburetor can be identified by the letters "LMT" embossed on the side of the carburetor (**Figure 114**).

Operation

The Walbro LMT carburetor operates according to the principles outlined in Chapter Two. A float in the fuel bowl controls the amount of fuel in the bowl. When the engine is running, fuel is drawn into the nozzle through the integral main jet. Fuel in the nozzle then exits into the carburetor bore through a discharge hole. Fuel is also drawn into the idle circuit to the idle fuel jet (A, **Figure 115**) and then to the idle mixture screw (B). Air flow through the carburetor is controlled by throttle and choke plates.

Air for the main fuel circuit and idle circuit is introduced through three bleed holes in the carburetor bore (**Figure 116**).

If the engine does not perform well at high altitude, a kit is available that leans the fuel mixture by replacing the standard idle fuel jet and nozzle.

Removal and installation

1. Remove the air cleaner assembly.

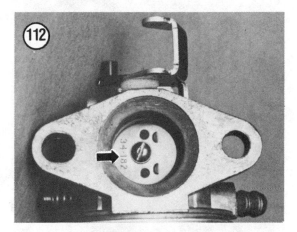

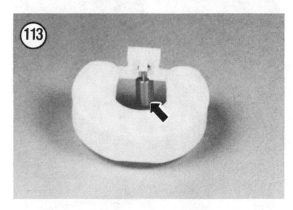

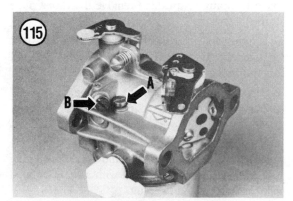

2. Remove any metalwork, such as the blower housing or engine control panel, that will prevent removal of the carburetor.

3. Disconnect the fuel line from the carburetor. Close fuel tank shut-off valve or drain the fuel to prevent fuel leakage.

4. Remove the carburetor mounting nuts, disconnect control linkage and remove the carburetor from the engine.

5. To install the carburetor, reverse the removal Steps 1 through 4. Note that on some engines it may be necessary to tilt the carburetor so that the linkage can be reconnected.

6. Tighten carburetor stud nuts to 65 in.-lb. (7.3 N•m) torque.

7. After installation, check the operation of all control linkage and adjust as required. Adjust the carburetor as outlined in Chapter Five.

Disassembly

To disassemble the carburetor for cleaning and inspection, proceed as follows:

1. Unscrew the idle fuel jet (A, **Figure 115**) and idle mixture screw (B).

2. Unscrew the fuel bowl retaining screw and remove the fuel bowl and gasket.

3. Remove the float pin (**Figure 117**), float and fuel inlet valve.

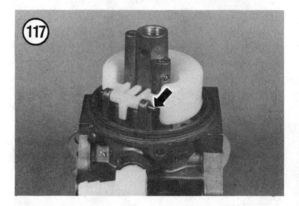

4. If replacement of the fuel inlet valve seat (**Figure 118**) is required, thread a screw extractor or a self-threading screw into the seat and pull the seat from the carburetor body.

5. Unscrew the nozzle (**Figure 119**).

6. If equipped with a metal choke, unscrew the choke plate retaining screws and remove the choke plate and choke shaft.

7. If equipped with a plastic choke, insert a sharp tool between the choke shaft and the choke plate and pull out the choke plate, then remove the choke shaft.

8. Unscrew the throttle plate retaining screws and remove the throttle plate and throttle shaft.

9. The Welch plug should be removed from the carburetor body in order to thoroughly clean the internal fuel passageway. To remove the Welch plug (**Figure 120**), pierce the plug with a sharp-pointed punch, then pry out the plug.

10. The carburetor should now be ready for soaking in carburetor cleaner. Follow the directions of the cleaner manufacturer. Spray the carburetor with aerosol carburetor cleaner to remove any residue, then use compressed air to blow out passages and dry the carburetor.

Inspection

1. Inspect the carburetor and components for wear and damage.
2. Inspect the tip of the idle mixture needle (**Figure 121**) and replace if the tip is bent or grooved.
3. Inspect the fuel inlet valve (**Figure 122**) and replace if the tip is grooved.
4. Install the throttle shaft in the carburetor body and check for excessive play between the shaft and body. The body must be replaced if there is excessive play as bushings are not available.

Assembly

1. Install the Welch plug while being careful not to indent the plug; the plug should be flat after installation. Apply a nonhardening sealant around the outer edge of the plug.
2. Use a 3/16 in. (5 mm) diameter rod to install the fuel inlet valve seat. The groove on the seat must be down (towards carburetor bore). Push in the seat until it bottoms.
3. If equipped with a choke return spring, install the spring as shown in **Figure 123** so spring tension tries to open the choke.
4. Install the choke plate so the edge with a single notch is on the fuel inlet side of the carburetor (**Figure 124**). The plate should be centered on the choke shaft.
5. Install the throttle plate so the numbers are visible and towards the idle mixture screw when the throttle is closed (**Figure 125**).
6. Install the fuel inlet valve in the slot on the float (**Figure 126**). The float level is not adjustable. If the float is not approximately parallel with the body

120

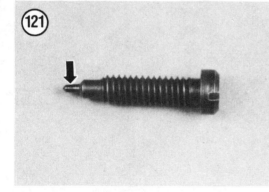

121

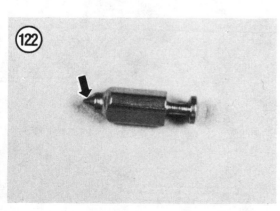

122

6

when the carburetor is inverted, then the float, fuel valve and/or valve seat must be replaced.

7. Tighten the fuel bowl retaining screw to 40 in.-lb. (4.5 N•m).

Cross-Over Flo-Jet

The Cross-Over Flo-Jet is a float type carburetor with a diaphragm type fuel pump located on the side of the carburetor.

Operation

The Cross-Over Flo-Jet carburetor operates according to the principles outlined in Chapter Two. The fuel pump on the side of the carburetor transfers fuel from the fuel tank to the carburetor fuel bowl. A float in the fuel bowl controls the amount of fuel in the bowl. When the engine is running, fuel is drawn into the nozzle. A high speed mixture screw (**Figure 127**) on top of the carburetor controls the amount of fuel discharged from the nozzle into the carburetor bore. Fuel is also drawn up the nozzle into the idle circuit and then to the idle mixture screw. Air flow through the carburetor is controlled by throttle and choke plates.

Removal and installation

1. Remove the air cleaner assembly.

2. Remove any metalwork, such as the blower housing or engine control panel, that will prevent removal of the carburetor.

3. Disconnect the fuel line from the carburetor. Close fuel tank shut-off valve or drain the fuel to prevent fuel leakage.

4. Remove the carburetor mounting screws, disconnect control linkage and remove the carburetor from the engine.

5. To install the carburetor, reverse the removal Steps 1 through 4. Note that on some engines, it may be necessary to tilt the carburetor so that the linkage can be reconnected.

6. After installation, check the operation of all control linkage and adjust as required. Adjust the carburetor as outlined in Chapter Five.

Disassembly

To disassemble the carburetor for cleaning and inspection, refer to **Figure 128** and proceed as follows:

1. Unscrew the fuel pump cover and remove the fuel pump components while being careful not to damage the diaphragm or flapper valves.

2. Unscrew the idle and high speed mixture screws.

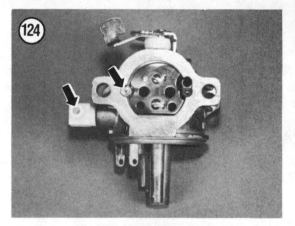

3. Unscrew the fuel bowl retaining screw and remove the fuel bowl and gasket.

4. Remove the float pin, float and fuel inlet valve.

5. Unscrew the nozzle.

6. Unscrew choke plate retaining screws and remove choke plate and choke shaft.

7. Unscrew throttle plate retaining screws and remove throttle plate and throttle shaft.

8. If fuel inlet valve seat replacement is required, thread a suitable self-tapping screw or screw extractor into the fuel inlet valve seat and remove the valve seat.

9. The carburetor should now be ready for soaking in carburetor cleaner. Follow the directions of the cleaner manufacturer. Spray the carburetor with aerosol carburetor cleaner to remove any residue, then use compressed air to blow out passages and dry the carburetor.

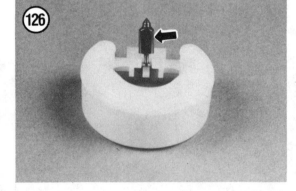

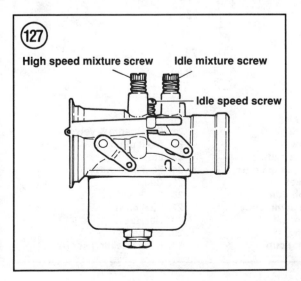

CAUTION
Some carburetor parts may be made of plastic and should not be soaked in carburetor cleaner.

Inspection

1. Inspect the carburetor and components for wear and damage.

2. Inspect the tip of the idle mixture needle and replace if the tip is bent or grooved.

3. Inspect the fuel inlet valve and replace if the tip is grooved.

4. Install the throttle shaft in the carburetor body and check for excessive play between the shaft and body. The body must be replaced if there is excessive play as bushings are not available.

Assembly

1. Install the fuel inlet valve seat so it is flush with the carburetor body surface.

2. Install the throttle plate so the dimples are out as shown in **Figure 129** when the throttle plate is in the closed position.

3. Install the choke plate so the dimple is in as shown in **Figure 130** when the choke plate is in the closed position.

4. To check the float level, invert the carburetor body and float assembly. The float should be parallel to the carburetor body. Adjust the float level by bending the float lever tang that contacts the inlet valve.

CAUTION
Do not press on float to adjust. Be careful not to force the fuel inlet valve needle onto its seat as the valve is easily damaged.

5. When assembling the fuel pump, install the springs (**Figure 131**) on the pegs on the pump body and carburetor body.

GOVERNOR SYSTEM

Briggs & Stratton engines are equipped with either a pneumatic (air vane) or mechanical (flyweight) type governor system. Refer to Chapter Two for a discussion of the operating principles of the governor system.

Refer to **Figure 132** for a view of a typical air vane governor and speed control linkage used on vertical crankshaft lawn mower engines. A view of a typical governor and speed control linkage used on vertical crankshaft engines with a mechanical governor system is shown in **Figure 133**. A view of a typical governor and speed control linkage used on horizontal crankshaft engines with a mechanical governor system is shown in **Figure 134**.

Observe the following when working on the governor or speed control linkage.

1. Before disconnecting the linkage, mark the linkage so it can be reassembled in its original configuration.

2. Do not stretch the governor spring during removal or installation.

3. When attaching or detaching a governor spring end with a closed loop, use a twisting motion at the

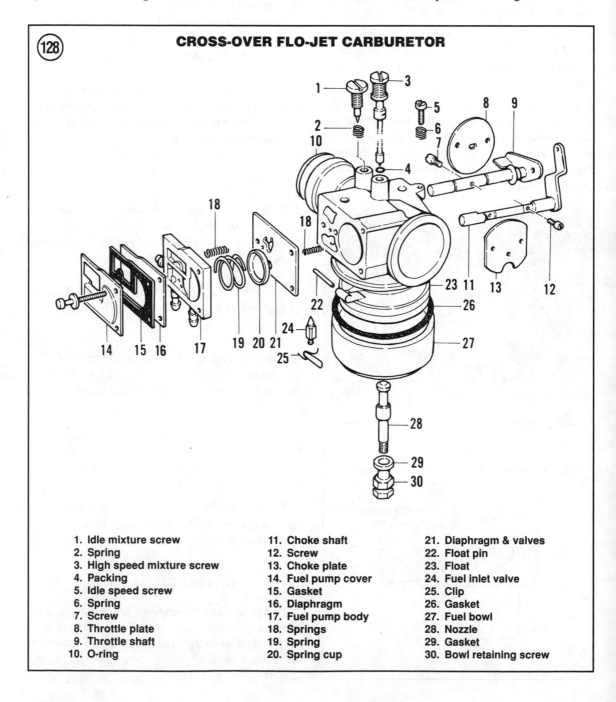

128

CROSS-OVER FLO-JET CARBURETOR

1. Idle mixture screw	11. Choke shaft	21. Diaphragm & valves
2. Spring	12. Screw	22. Float pin
3. High speed mixture screw	13. Choke plate	23. Float
4. Packing	14. Fuel pump cover	24. Fuel inlet valve
5. Idle speed screw	15. Gasket	25. Clip
6. Spring	16. Diaphragm	26. Gasket
7. Screw	17. Fuel pump body	27. Fuel bowl
8. Throttle plate	18. Springs	28. Nozzle
9. Throttle shaft	19. Spring	29. Gasket
10. O-ring	20. Spring cup	30. Bowl retaining screw

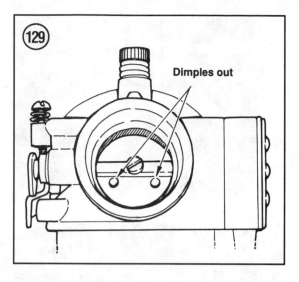

129 Dimples out

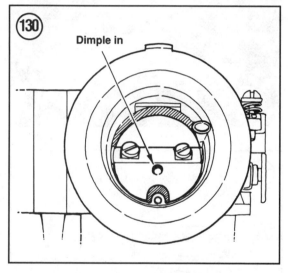

130 Dimple in

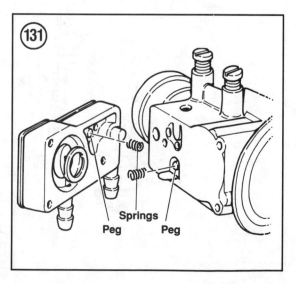

131 Springs Peg Peg

spring end. Do not pull the spring end with pliers or other tools as the spring end may be deformed, which can affect governor operation.

Air Vane Governor Adjustment

Other than checking for disconnected or binding linkage, the air vane governor system does not require adjustment.

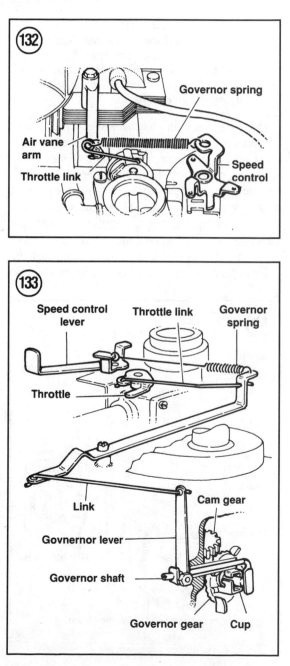

132 Governor spring
Air vane arm
Throttle link
Speed control

133 Speed control lever   Throttle link   Governor spring
Throttle
Link
Cam gear
Govnernor lever
Governor shaft
Governor gear   Cup

6

Mechanical Governor Adjustment

On some engines with a mechanical governor, the idle speed is governed. Refer to the previous sections in this chapter for adjustment of the governed idle speed screw or tang.

On some engines, the maximum governed speed is adjustable. The maximum governed speed is determined by the engine's application and specified by the equipment manufacturer.

> *CAUTION*
> *Adjusting maximum governed engine speed in excess of the engine speed specified by the manufacturer can cause engine damage as well as damage to engine-driven equipment.*

On all engines with a mechanical governor, it may be necessary to adjust the position of the governor lever on the governor shaft. This provides a full range of movement from the internal governor mechanism to the governor lever. Adjust the position of the governor lever assembly as follows:

1. On Quantum 121000, 122000, 124000 and 126000, move the speed control lever to "FAST" position and place an 1/8 in. (3 mm) rod through the holes in the governor control lever (**Figure 135**) and

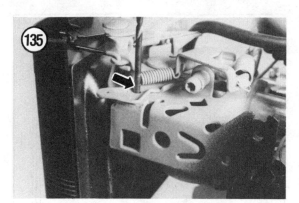

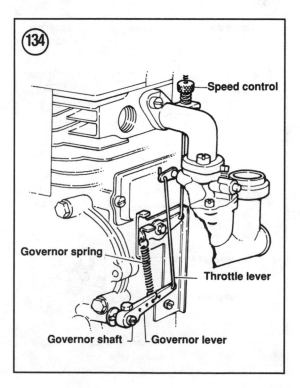

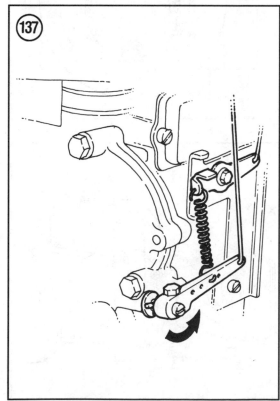

the bracket. Loosen the clamp bolt (**Figure 136**) then rotate the governor shaft counterclockwise until it stops. Hold the shaft and tighten the clamp bolt to 35-45 in.-lb. (4-5 N•m).

2. If the governor shaft is mounted on the crankcase cover as shown in **Figure 137**, loosen the governor lever clamp screw and move the governor lever so the carburetor throttle plate is in wide open position. Turn the governor shaft as far as possible counterclockwise, then tighten the clamp bolt.

3. On engines with less than 13 cubic in. displacement (except 80000, 83000, 100200, 100900 and engines previously specified), loosen the clamp bolt on the governor lever (**Figure 138**). Move the governor lever so the carburetor throttle plate is in wide open position. Using a screwdriver, rotate the governor shaft counterclockwise as far as possible and tighten the clamp bolt.

4. On engines with greater than 13 cu. in. displacement, as well as models 80000, 83000, 100200 and 100900, loosen the clamp bolt on the governor lever (**Figure 139**). Move the governor lever so the carburetor throttle plate is in wide open position. Using a screwdriver, rotate the governor shaft clockwise as far as possible and tighten the clamp bolt.

Troubleshooting

Most governor related problems are caused by incorrect adjustment, misconnected linkage, a stretched governor spring or damaged components.

A simple test can be performed to determine if faulty engine operation is due to the governor system and related linkage. Move the throttle arm or lever on the carburetor through a full range of movement. If the engine operates satisfactorily, then a problem exists in the governor system or speed control linkage. If the engine continues to malfunction, then the problem lies in another area.

When analyzing a suspected problem in the governor system, first check that all linkage is properly connected and no components are damaged. Be sure the governor spring is not stretched. The spring can be easily stretched during removal and installation, resulting in abnormal engine operation. A stretched or damaged governor spring should be replaced.

Refer to Chapter Eleven for overhaul information on the internal governor mechanism of mechanical governors.

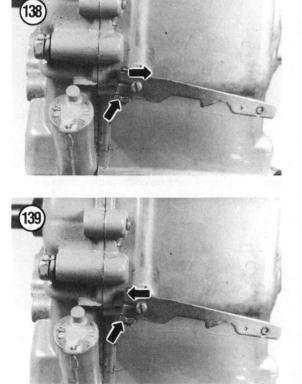

CHAPTER SEVEN

IGNITION SYSTEM AND FLYWHEEL BRAKE

This chapter covers components in the ignition system except the ignition breaker points and the spark plug, which are covered in Chapter Five. Also covered is the flywheel brake used on some later models.

IGNITION COIL

The ignition coil on all models is located outside the flywheel. The ignition coil is similar on all models except an ignition module (**Figure 1** or **Figure 2**) is mounted on the ignition coil of engines equipped with a breakerless, solid-state ignition (Magnetron).

To remove the ignition coil on models equipped with breaker points, the flywheel must be removed so the primary coil wire can be disconnected from the breaker points. See Chapter Eleven for flywheel removal and installation.

Flywheel removal is not required to remove the ignition coil on engines equipped with an ignition module. The ignition module may be separated from the coil on some engines as outlined in following section.

No test procedures are available for the ignition coil, although some professional shops are equipped with coil testers that can be used to dynamically test ignition coils. In most cases, the ignition coil is replaced after tests rule out other components as the cause for an ignition malfunction.

Whenever the ignition coil armature retaining screws are loosened, the armature air gap must be adjusted. Follow the procedure outlined in Chapter Five.

NOTE
The ignition coil primary circuit is designed to operate on small electrical current. The ignition coil may be damaged if a large current, such as current from a battery, is connected to the igni-

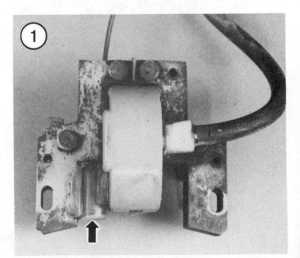

tion coil. This can happen due to improperly connected wires or a faulty ignition switch.

The high tension wire (spark plug lead) is not available separately from the ignition coil. The spark plug terminal is available separately and can be attached to the end of the high tension wire.

IGNITION MODULE

Engines equipped with a breakerless, solid-state ignition system (Magnetron), have an ignition module that is attached to the ignition coil (**Figure 1** or **Figure 2**). The ignition module serves the same function as breaker points in making and breaking the primary current. The ignition module contains electrical components that sense the position of magnets in the flywheel. When the flywheel is in the proper position, the module breaks the primary cir-

cuit in the ignition coil and a spark is generated at the spark plug electrodes.

The ignition module cannot be tested. If the ignition module is suspected of faulty operation, then a new or serviceable module should be installed and the ignition system rechecked.

Removal/Installation

The ignition module cannot be separated from the ignition coil on models with a one-piece coil and module (**Figure 2**). The module and ignition coil are available only as a unit assembly.

Some models are equipped with a removable ignition module (**Figure 1**) that is mounted on the ignition coil. To separate the ignition module from the ignition coil, proceed as follows:
1. Unscrew the module wire lead from the ignition coil armature.
2. Using a 3/16 in. (5 mm) diameter rod, push in as shown in **Figure 3** to release the primary and stop switch wires from the retainer hook.
3. Unsolder the wires while being careful not to overheat the ignition module.
4. Pull back the module retainer (**Figure 3**) and dislodge the module from the ignition coil.
5. When installing the ignition module, note that the armature has a front and back side identified by large rivet heads on the front side and small rivet ends on back side. The module is installed on the back side.
6. Use a 3/16 in. (5 mm) diameter rod to compress the wire retainer spring, then insert the primary and stop switch wires under the retainer hook (**Figure 3**).
7. Solder the wire ends using 60/40 rosin core solder while being careful not to overheat the module.
8. To prevent wire movement due to vibration, cement the wires to the igntion coil armature with Permatex #2 or RTV sealant.

STOP SWITCH

The engine may be equipped with a stop switch mounted on the engine, or a remotely mounted switch may be located elsewhere on the equipment. The stop switch (often called an ignition switch when mounted on equipment) must stop ignition when activated. Because a magneto is used on Briggs & Stratton engines, the ignition system is defeated by grounding the primary circuit.

7

A stop wire runs from the ignition circuit to a variety of stop switches. Some models are equipped with a tab that is mechanically forced against a metal bracket on the engine thereby grounding the ignition. If the engine is mounted on a large piece of equipment, a remote-mounted switch may be used in the grounding circuit to stop the engine. If the engine is equipped with a flywheel brake, the stop switch may be a part of the brake mechanism.

Testing a stop switch designed for use with a magneto type ignition system involves using a continuity checker or ohmmeter. The tests determine if the ignition circuit is grounded when the stop switch is actuated. In all cases, the stop switch should show continuity (zero ohms) to engine ground when the switch is in the STOP position and no continuity (infinity) when the switch is in the RUN position. Also check wiring for loose or bad connections.

NOTE
Automotive type ignition switches should not be used with a magneto type ignition system as battery voltage (if machine is so equipped) may be routed to the ignition circuit, which may damage ignition components.

FLYWHEEL BRAKE

Some later models are equipped with a flywheel brake that simultaneously stops the flywheel and grounds the ignition. The brake should stop the engine within three seconds when the operator releases the mower safety control and the speed control is in high speed position. On Quantum engines (model series 100700, 121000, 122000, 124000 and 126000), a pad type brake contacts the flywheel to stop rotation. The flywheel brake used on model 100700 contacts the inner surface of the flywheel while the flywheel brake used on model series 121000, 122000, 124000 and 126000 contacts the outer surface of the flywheel. On all other models a band type brake stops rotation by gripping the outside of the flywheel.

Adjustment

Adjustment is not required on model series 100700, 121000, 122000, 124000 and 126000. To check the brake band adjustment on all other models, remove the rewind starter and properly ground the

spark plug lead to prevent accidental starting. On electric start models, remove the battery. Turn the starter clutch using a torque wrench with the brake engaged as shown in **Figure 4**. Rotating the flywheel at a steady rate in a clockwise direction should require at least 45 in.-lb. (5.08 N•m) torque. An insufficient torque reading may indicate misadjust-

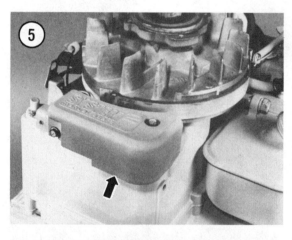

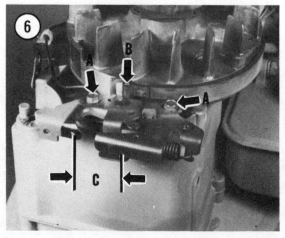

ment or damaged components. When the flywheel brake is disengaged, the flywheel should rotate without the brake dragging, otherwise the brake components are damaged or misaligned.

To adjust the flywheel brake, proceed as follows:
1. Remove switch housing cover (**Figure 5**).
2. Loosen the control bracket screws (A, **Figure 6**) so they are finger tight.
3. Using a suitable tool, turn the control lever tang (B, **Figure 6**) clockwise so the distance (C) between

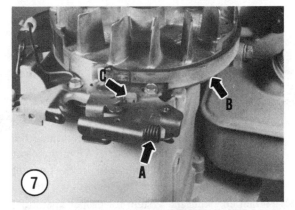

the closest edges of the bracket hole and lever hole is 1.80 in. (46 mm). Hold the tool and tighten the bracket screws to 25-30 in.-lb. (2.82-3.39 N•m).

NOTE
A suitable tool can be made by cutting a slot in the short end of a 1/4-in. Allen wrench.

NOTE
If a pop rivet secures the cable bracket, do not remove the rivet, but measure to the hole in the pop rivet.

Service Brake Band on Models So Equipped

1. Remove the blower housing for access to the flywheel brake mechanism.
2. Detach the outer end of the brake spring (A, **Figure 7**) from its anchor.
3. Remove the brake band (B, **Figure 7**). On older models, the tang (C) that retains the brake band loop on the movable post must be bent back.
4. Replace the brake band if the friction material thickness is less than 0.030 in. (0.76 mm). Replace the brake band if it is contaminated with oil or if it is damaged.
5. If a new brake band is installed, perform the adjustment procedure previously outlined.
6. If detached, be sure the ignition wire is properly connected to the stop switch on the control bracket.

Service Brake Pad on Model 100700

The flywheel must be removed for access to the flywheel brake mechanism. Refer to Chapter Eleven.
1. Detach the ignition stop wire from the stop switch (A, **Figure 8**).
2. Use a suitable tool, such as a valve spring compressor, and remove the brake spring (B, **Figure 8**).
3. Unscrew the shoulder screw (A, **Figure 9**).
4. Detach the E-ring (B, **Figure 9**) on the pivot post and lift out the brake arm while unhooking the link to the control lever.
5. Replace the brake pad and arm (C, **Figure 9**) if the pad is damaged, contaminated by oil, or worn to a thickness less than 0.030 in. (0.76 mm).
6. Attach the control lever link to the brake pad and arm while positioning the arm on the pivot post.

7

7. Install the E-ring retainer (B, **Figure 9**) and shoulder screw (A).

8. Compress and install the brake spring (B, **Figure 8**).

9. Route the ignition stop wire under the breather tube and brake arm as shown in **Figure 10**. Attach the wire to the stop switch (A, **Figure 8**).

Service Brake Pad on Model Series 121000, 122000, 124000 and 126000

For access to the flywheel brake mechanism, remove the rewind starter and blower housing as outlined in Chapter Eight.

1. Disconnect brake spring (A, **Figure 11**) from spring anchor.

2. Disconnect stop wire from stop switch (B, **Figure 11**).

3. If equipped with an electric starter, disconnect the two wires (C, **Figure 11**) from starter safety interlock switch.

4. Remove two mounting screws from brake bracket (D, **Figure 11**) and remove the bracket and brake pad assembly.

5. Replace the brake assembly if brake pad (E, **Figure 11**) is damaged, contaminated by oil or worn to a thickness less than 0.090 in. (2.3 mm). The brake pad is available only as a part of the bracket assembly.

6. When installing the brake bracket, tighten the mounting screws to 40 in.-lb. (4.5 N•m).

7. Connect ignition stop wire to the stop switch (B, **Figure 11**) on the brake bracket. The stop wire must be routed under the breather tube.

8. If the engine is equipped with an electric starter motor, be sure the safety interlock wires (C, **Figure 11**) are connected to the interlock switch on the bracket.

LOW-OIL SHUT-OFF SYSTEM

Some engines may be equipped with a low-oil shut-off system (Oil Gard) that grounds the ignition system and flashes a warning light if the oil level in the crankcase is low. A float is located in the crankcase to detect the engine oil level. A wire lead connects the ignition to the warning light and the warning light to the float mount. When the float lowers sufficiently, the wire lead to the float mount is grounded and the engine stops or will not start.

When checking the system for proper operation, be sure that the wires are properly connected, the lamp is good and the float ground switch operates properly.

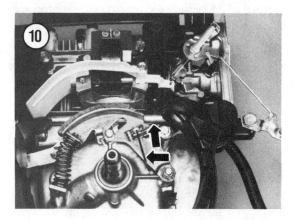

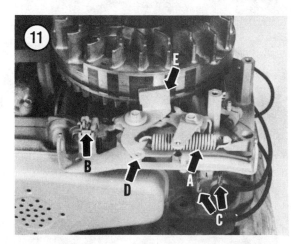

CHAPTER EIGHT

REWIND STARTERS

The rewind starters included in this chapter are divided into sections that cover starters mounted on the blower housing (except Quantum engines), vertical-pull starters and starters used on Quantum engines (model series 100700, 121000, 122000, 124000 and 126000). Refer to the following sections for service information.

NOTE
The starter mounting fasteners must be tight for proper starter operation, including the fasteners securing the blower housing if the starter is attached to the blower housing. Loose fasteners can cause starter drive mechanism damage.

REWIND STARTERS MOUNTED ON BLOWER HOUSING (EXCEPT QUANTUM ENGINES)

Most "L" head Briggs & Stratton engines are equipped with a rewind starter that is mounted on the blower housing (**Figure 1**). In some cases, a detachable plastic ring surrounds the starter housing. The rope pulley drives a ball-type sprag clutch (**Figure 2**) that is mounted on the flywheel. When the rewind starter is operated, the flywheel rotates and one of the balls will engage a sprag. When the engine runs, the balls are thrown out by centrifugal force to a disengaged position.

Major starter problems usually involve a severed rope or a broken rewind spring. The rope can usually be replaced without completely disassembling the starter, while a broken rewind spring requires disassembling the starter. The following procedures will apply to most Briggs & Stratton starters, but some variations may occur.

Replace Unbroken Starter Rope

Do not discard the rope before measuring its length and diameter. The same length and diameter of rope must be installed, which is determined by either measuring the old rope or consulting a parts manual.

8

To replace an unbroken rope, the blower housing must be removed. This usually only requires removing the blower housing retaining screws, but in some cases, a cable retainer or bracket may also require removal. Proceed as follows to replace the rope.

1. Pull out the rope to its full extended length so the rope end in the pulley is towards the housing rope outlet as shown in **Figure 3**.

2. Hold the pulley by clamping the pulley with lock pliers or a C-clamp (**Figure 3**).

3. Pull out the rope knot in the pulley, untie or cut off the knot, then pull the rope out of the pulley.

4. Detach the rope from the rope handle. On early models the rope is knotted around a pin (**Figure 4**), while on later models the rope is retained in the handle by a plastic insert (**Figure 5**).

5. Measure the rope and obtain a replacement rope of the same length and diameter.

6. If the new rope is made of nylon, melt each rope end with a match to prevent the ends from unraveling.

7. Thread the new rope into the rope handle, then attach the rope to the retaining pin or insert as shown in **Figure 4** or **Figure 5**. Pull the rope into the rope handle.

8. Thread the rope through the housing rope outlet into the pulley and out the pulley rope hole. If the pulley is metal, the rope must be inside the internal lug.

> *NOTE*
> *It may be helpful to hook a thin wire into the rope end so the wire can be used to guide and pull the rope into the pulley hole.*

9. Tie a knot in the inner end of the rope.

10. Hold the rope at the handle end, release the pliers or clamp on the rope pulley and slowly allow the rope to wind onto the pulley.

11. Check starter operation. If the rope handle does not rest snugly against the housing when released, shorten the rope in small increments until it does so.

Replace Broken Starter Rope

Do not discard the rope before measuring its total length. The same length of rope must be installed, which is determined by either measuring the old rope or consulting a parts manual.

To replace a broken rope, the blower housing must be removed. This usually only requires removing the

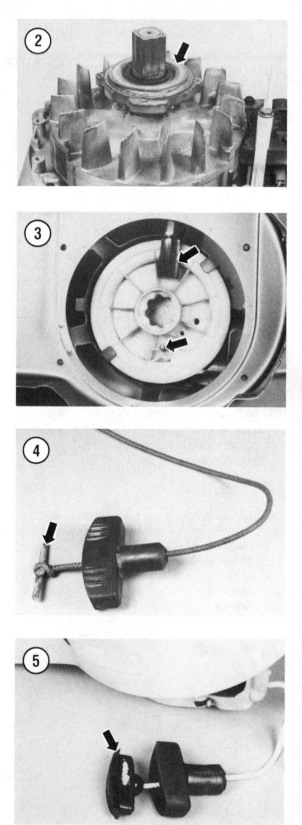

blower housing retaining screws, but in some cases, a cable retainer or bracket may also require removal. Proceed as follows to replace the rope.

1. If the rope is broken, pull the rope out of the hole in the rope pulley. If the rope pulley must be removed for access to the rope, remove the rope pulley as outlined in the following procedure for rewind spring removal.

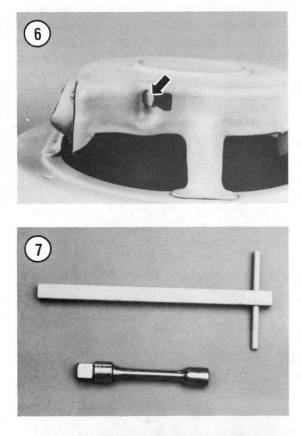

2. Detach the rope from the rope handle. On early models the rope is knotted around a pin (**Figure 4**), while on later models the rope is retained in the handle by a plastic insert (**Figure 5**).

3. Measure the rope and obtain a replacement rope of the same length and diameter.

4. If the new rope is made of nylon, melt each rope end with a match to prevent the ends from unraveling.

5. Thread the new rope into the rope handle, then attach the rope to the retaining pin or insert as shown in **Figure 4** or **Figure 5**. Pull the rope into the rope handle.

6. Use a suitable tool inserted in the rope pulley hub and turn the pulley counterclockwise until the rewind spring is tight. When the rewind spring is wound tight, the outer spring end should be pulled into the narrow end of the spring slot in the housing (**Figure 6**).

NOTE:
*A tool can be constructed from 3/4 in. square metal or wooden stock (**Figure 7**), or a 1/2 in. × 3/4 in. socket drive adapter can also be used.*

7. Let the pulley unwind one turn or until the rope hole in the pulley is aligned with the rope outlet in the housing as shown in **Figure 8**.

8. Hold the pulley by clamping the pulley with lock pliers or a C-clamp (**Figure 8**).

9. Thread the rope through the housing rope outlet into the pulley and out the pulley rope hole. If the pulley is metal, the rope must be inside the internal lug.

NOTE
It may be necessary to hook a thin wire into the rope end so the wire can be used to guide and pull the rope into the pulley hole.

10. Tie a knot in the end of the rope.

11. Hold the rope at the handle end, release the pliers or clamp on the rope pulley and slowly allow the rope to wind onto the pulley.

12. Check starter operation. If the rope handle does not rest snugly against the housing when released, shorten the rope in small increments until it does so.

8

Replace Rewind Spring or Rope Pulley

To remove the rope pulley or rewind spring, proceed as follows:

1. If the rewind spring is under tension, detach the rope from the rope handle. Slowly release the rope and allow it to wind onto the pulley.

2. If the rewind spring is broken, detach the rope from the rope handle. Turn the pulley so the rope is wound onto the pulley.

3. Disengage the outer end of the rewind spring from the slot in the side of the starter housing (**Figure 6**).

4. Bend back the pulley retaining tabs (**Figure 9**). Be careful not to break the plastic bumpers on the retaining tabs of models so equipped. Note that spare tabs may be located on the housing in the event a tab breaks off.

> *WARNING*
> *The rewind spring is sharp and can uncoil uncontrolled. Safety eyewear and gloves should be worn when working on or around the rewind spring.*

5. Lift up the pulley and disconnect the rewind spring.

6. Remove the rewind spring from the starter housing, then clean the housing. Replace the plastic bumpers, on models so equipped, if the bumpers are broken or worn excessively.

7. Apply a light coat of oil to the rewind spring and a small amount of grease to the spring side of the pulley.

8. Insert either end of the spring through the spring hole in the housing (**Figure 10**).

9. Connect the inner end of the spring into the pulley slot (**Figure 11**) and install the pulley in the starter housing.

10. Bend the pulley retainer tabs (**Figure 9**) towards the pulley so that the gap between the tab or plastic bumper, if so equipped, and the pulley is 1/16 in. (1.6 mm).

11. Rotate the pulley counterclockwise so that the spring winds into the housing.

> *NOTE*
> *A tool to turn the pulley hub can be constructed from 3/4 in. square metal or wooden stock (**Figure 7**), or a 1/2 in. × 3/4 in. socket drive adapter can also be used.*

12. Turn the pulley until the rewind spring is tight. When the rewind spring is wound tight, the outer spring end should be pulled into the narrow end of the spring slot in the housing (**Figure 6**).

13. Let the pulley unwind one turn or until the rope hole in the pulley is aligned with the rope outlet in the housing as shown in **Figure 8**. Hold the pulley in this position by clamping the pulley with lock pliers or a C-clamp.

14. If installing a new rope, measure the length and diameter of the old rope and obtain a replacement rope of the same size. If the new rope is made of nylon, melt each rope end with a match to prevent the ends from unraveling. Thread the new rope into the rope handle, then attach the rope to the retaining pin or insert as shown in **Figure 4** or **Figure 5**. Pull the rope into the rope handle.

15. Thread the rope through the housing rope outlet into the pulley and out the pulley rope hole. If the pulley is metal, the rope must be inside the internal lug.

> *NOTE*
> *It may be helpful to hook a thin wire into the rope end so the wire can be used to*

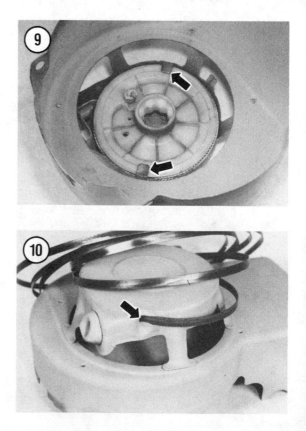

guide and pull the rope into the pulley hole.

16. Tie a knot in the end of the rope.

17. Hold the rope at the handle end, release the pliers or clamp on the rope pulley and slowly allow the rope to wind onto the pulley.

18. Check starter operation. If the rope handle does not rest snugly against the housing when released, shorten the rope in small increments until it does so.

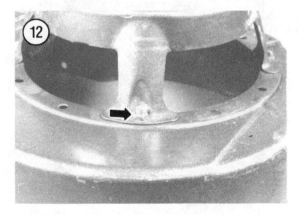

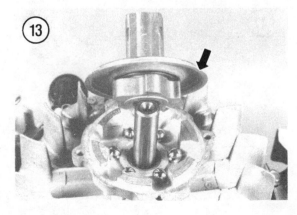

Replace Starter Housing

The welded starter housing on engines larger than 4 horsepower (3 kW) can be separated from the blower housing and replaced using bolts. The spot welds that secure the starter housing must be drilled out using a 3/16 in. drill bit. The drill must remove metal only from the welded portion. Install new bolts so the nuts are on the outside of the housing as shown in **Figure 12**.

Replace Starter Clutch

The starter clutch may not engage properly, which may require cleaning or replacement. To service the starter clutch, proceed as follows.

1. Remove the rewind starter/blower housing for access to the starter clutch.

2. Unscrew and remove the screen attached to the clutch housing.

NOTE
The screen must be installed before running the engine.

3. Use a suitable tool and pry the cover (**Figure 13**) off the clutch unit, then lift off the cover with the ratchet.

4. Remove the clutch balls and clean the housing and balls.

NOTE
Do not lubricate the clutch balls or the housing.

5. Inspect the balls and replace if damaged.

6. If necessary, replace the felt seal in the cover.

NOTE
The starter clutch housing serves as the flywheel retaining nut. Refer to Chapter Eleven for removal procedure.

7. To reassemble the clutch, place a drop of oil on the end of the crankshaft and install the ratchet.

8. Place the balls in the pockets of the clutch housing.

9. Install the cover.

VERTICAL-PULL REWIND STARTER

A typical vertical-pull rewind starter is shown in **Figure 14**. When the starter rope is pulled, the starter

8

gear inside the starter housing travels up a helix to engage the ring gear on the flywheel.

Replacing the rope or rewind spring will require complete or partial disassembly, depending on the service required, using the following procedure. Do not discard the old rope before measuring its length and diameter. The same length and diameter of rope must be installed, which is determined by either measuring the old rope or consulting a parts manual.

1. Remove the starter from the engine.

NOTE
If the rope or spring is broken, proceed to Step 4.

2. If the rope is unbroken, pull the rope so approximately 12 in. (30 cm) of rope is exposed, and if there is spring tension, hold the spring cover (**Figure 15**) so the rope can't rewind.

WARNING
The rope must not be pulled when the spring cover is removed as a rewind spring under tension can uncoil uncontrolled.

3. Pull out a loop of rope as shown in **Figure 15**, then unwind the rope around the outside of the spring cover in a counterclockwise direction approximately four turns to relieve spring tension.

4. Pry off the spring cover.

WARNING
The rewind spring is sharp and can uncoil uncontrolled. Safety eyewear and gloves should be worn when working on or around the rewind spring.

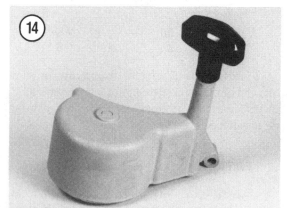

5. Unscrew the center screw (A, **Figure 16**).

6. If the rewind spring must be replaced, disengage the anchor from the inner spring end (C, **Figure 16**), then carefully extract the spring. If only the spring requires replacement, proceed to Step 19 for spring installation procedure.

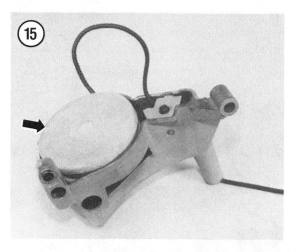

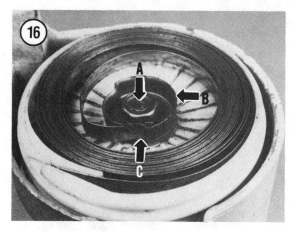

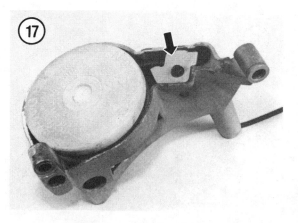

7. If the spring does not require replacement, reinstall the cover to hold the spring in place.

8. Detach the rope from the rope handle.

9. Unscrew and remove the rope guide (**Figure 17**).

10. While noting the position of the wire linkage, lift out the rope pulley, helix and gear assembly (**Figure 18**).

11. Remove the rope from the pulley.

12. If necessary, drive out the rope guide pulley shaft and remove the guide pulley (**Figure 19**).

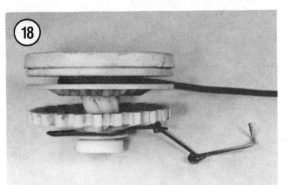

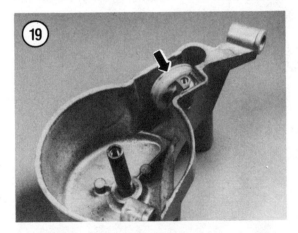

13. Clean and inspect starter components. The wire linkage should move the gear on the helix through full travel range. The pulley, helix and gear are available only as a unit assembly.

14. If installing a new rope, measure the length and diameter of the old rope and obtain a replacement rope of the same size. If the new rope is made of nylon, melt each rope end with a match to prevent the ends from unraveling. Thread the new rope into the pulley and tie a small knot. Cut off the rope end so no more than 3/16 in. (4.8 mm) rope extends past knot. Pull the rope into the pulley and be sure the rope does not interfere with gear movement.

15. If removed, install the rope guide pulley and shaft (**Figure 19**).

16. Install the rope pulley and gear assembly with the wire linkage in the starter housing.

17. Pass the rope over the rope guide pulley and out the rope outlet of the housing. Attach the rope handle.

18. Be sure the wire end is located in the groove (**Figure 20**) and install the rope guide (**Figure 17**).

19. Install the rewind spring so the spring is coiled in a counterclockwise direction from the outer end (**Figure 21**) and install the spring cover.

20. Rotate the spring cover counterclockwise so the rope is wrapped on the pulley.

21. Remove the spring cover and carefully attach the anchor (B, **Figure 16**) to the inner spring end (C).

22. Install the center screw (A, **Figure 16**) and tighten it to 75-90 in.-lb. (8.5-10.2 N•m).

23. Lightly lubricate the spring with oil then install the spring cover.

24. Pull the rope handle so approximately 12 in. (30 cm) of rope is exposed, hold the spring cover so the rope can't rewind.

25. Pull out a loop of rope as shown in **Figure 22**, then wind the rope around the outside of the spring

8

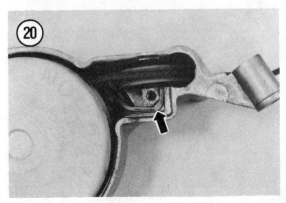

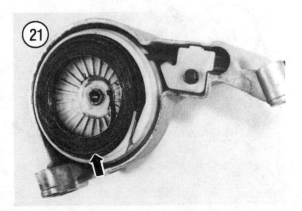

cover in a clockwise direction two or three turns to increase spring tension.

26. Check starter operation.

QUANTUM 100000 SERIES REWIND STARTER

When the starter rope is pulled on the Quantum series 100000 starter, the starter gear on the starter travels laterally on the helix to engage the gear teeth on the underside of the flywheel.

Do not discard the old rope before measuring its length and diameter. The same length and diameter of rope must be installed, which is determined by either measuring the old rope or consulting a parts manual.

Removal

1. Be sure the fuel valve is in the closed position, then detach the fuel line (**Figure 23**) from the fuel valve.

2. Unscrew and remove the cover plate (**Figure 24**) on top of the engine.

3. Unscrew the fuel tank retaining screw shown in **Figure 25** and lift off the fuel tank.

4. Detach the rope handle from the rope.

5. Loosen the starter shaft retaining screw (**Figure 26**) as far as necessary and pull the starter off the engine.

Replace Rope

1. Turn the metal cover (A, **Figure 27**) clockwise while unwinding the rope from the pulley, then hold

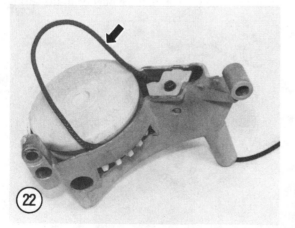

the cover and pull the inner rope end and rope out of the pulley. Slowly release the metal cover.

2. Tie a knot in the end of the new rope.

3. Turn the metal cover clockwise until the rewind spring is wrapped tight.

4. Turn the metal cover counterclockwise so the rope outlet segment of the metal cover is over the rope

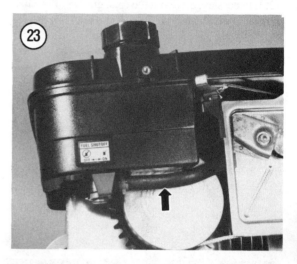

hole in the pulley as shown in **Figure 28** and hold the cover in this position.

5. Insert the rope through the rope pulley and pull the rope through the pulley so the knot is seated in the pulley (**Figure 29**).

6. Slowly release the metal cover so the rope winds onto the pulley.

7. Install the starter.

Install New Rewind Spring

1. Remove and save the sticker (B, **Figure 27**) on the side of the metal cover (A).

2. Mount the starter shaft in a vise with soft jaws and unscrew the center screw (A, **Figure 30**).

NOTE
The center screw has left-hand threads and must be turned clockwise to un-screw.

3. Bend the cover tang that traps the inner end (B, **Figure 30**) of the rewind spring in or out as necessary, then push the inner spring end into the cover.

4. While holding the cover and starter assembly, lift the assembly off the starter shaft.

5. Separate the gear from the helix.

WARNING
The rewind spring is sharp and can uncoil uncontrolled. Safety eyewear and gloves should be worn when working on or around the rewind spring.

8

6. Lift off the cover to expose the rewind spring (**Figure 31**).

7. Invert the pulley so the spring side is down and place the pulley in a towel or rags on the floor. Tap the end of the helix to dislodge the spring.

8. Clean and inspect the starter.

9. Mount the starter shaft in a vise with soft jaws.

10. If removed, place the plastic washer (A, **Figure 32**) and steel washer (B) on the starter shaft.

11. Install the gear on the helix.

12. Apply a small amount of grease on the starter shaft.

13. Place the pulley and gear assembly on the starter shaft so the brake spring on the gear hub is located between the posts on the starter shaft as shown in **Figure 33**.

14. Place the plastic washer in the center of the spring case (**Figure 34**).

15. Apply grease to the ribs of the case that contact the side of the rewind spring.

16. Install the rewind spring so the coils are wound in a clockwise direction from the outer end (**Figure 34**).

NOTE
A new spring is held in a retainer that can be used to guide the spring into the spring case. Align the outer hook end with the notch in the spring case and push the spring into the case.

17. Apply grease to the upper side of the rewind spring.

18. Push the tang on the metal cover towards the screw hole and place the metal cover over the spring.

19. Engage the inner end of the spring in the slot of the metal cover by turning the cover clockwise.

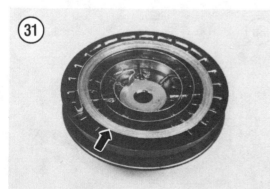

20. If the starter rope handle is located on the top of the engine, position the cover so the arrow or "O" embossed on the cover is aligned with the starter shaft cam as shown in **Figure 35**. If the starter rope handle is located near the cylinder head, position the cover so the arrow or "O" embossed on the cover is 90° to the left of the starter cam when viewed from the top of the cover (**Figure 36**).

21. Install the center screw and tighten it to 55 in.-lb. (6.2 N•m).

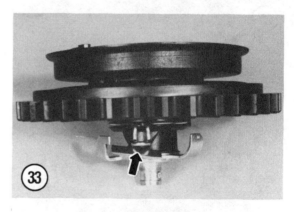

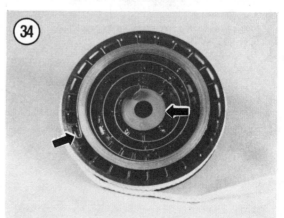

NOTE
The center screw has left-hand threads and must be turned counterclockwise to install.

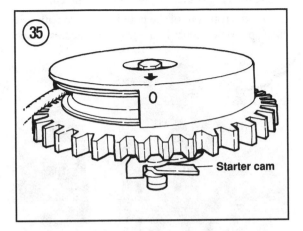

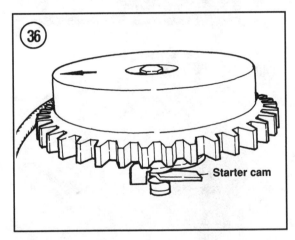

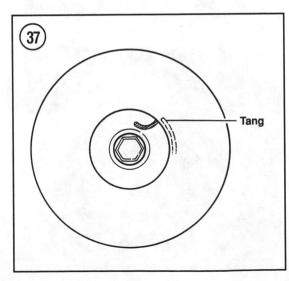

22. Use a screwdriver and push the spring retaining tang on the metal cover inward so the tang is inside the metal cover (**Figure 37**).

23. Install the rope as previously outlined.

Installation

1. Install the starter on the engine with "O" or "Arrow" on the starter cover pointing at the rope eyelet.

2. Install starter retaining screw (**Figure 26**). Note that the starter retaining screw has a pointed end that must engage a depression on the sarter shaft (**Figure 38**). Tighten screw to 80 in.-lb. (9.0 N•m).

3. Thread starter rope through the eyelet, handle and handle insert. Tie a knot in the end of the rope, then pull the knot into the insert and handle.

4. Install the fuel tank and cover plate.

5. Connect the fuel line and open the fuel shut-off valve.

QUANTUM 121000, 122000, 124000 AND 126000 SERIES REWIND STARTERS

The rewind starter used on Quantum 121000, 122000, 124000 and 126000 series engines is a pawl type starter. When the rope is pulled, two pawls extend outward to engage notches in the starter cup that is attached to the flywheel.

Removal

To remove the rewind starter, proceed as follows:

1. Unscrew or unsnap and remove the plastic guard over the starter.

2. Detach the fuel line from the fuel tank (**Figure 39**).

3. Unscrew the upper fuel tank retaining screws and the lower fuel tank retaining screw (**Figure 39**). Note the spacer on the lower screw.

4. Remove the fuel tank.

5. Unscrew the oil fill tube retaining screw (**Figure 40**) and relocate the oil fill tube outward so the flange will not interfere with removal of the blower housing.

6. Remove blower housing mounting screws and remove the blower housing and starter assembly.

Replace Unbroken Starter Rope

NOTE
Do not discard the rope before measuring its length and diameter. The same length and diameter of rope must be installed, which is determined by either measuring the old rope or consulting a parts manual.

1. Remove the rewind starter as previously outlined.

2. Pull out the rope to its full extended length so the rope end in the pulley is towards the housing rope outlet, then hold the pulley by installing a restraining device (such as a tie-wrap) around the starter housing and a strut (**Figure 41**) on the rope pulley so the spring cannot rewind.

3. Pull out the rope knot in the pulley, untie or cut off the knot, then pull the rope out of the pulley.

4. Detach the rope from the rope handle.

5. Measure the rope and obtain a replacement rope of the same length and diameter. If the new rope is made of nylon, melt each rope end with a match to prevent the ends from unraveling.

6. Tie a knot in one end of the rope.

7. Thread the rope through the pulley rope hole and out the rope outlet in the housing.

8. Attach the rope handle to the rope.

9. Hold the pulley, release the restraining device on the rope pulley and slowly allow the rope to wind onto the pulley.

10. Check starter operation.

Replace a Broken Starter Rope

NOTE
Do not discard the rope before measuring its total length. The same length of

rope must be installed, which is determined by either measuring the old rope or consulting a parts manual.

1. Remove the starter as previously outlined.

2. Pull the rope out of the hole in the rope pulley. If the rope pulley must be removed for access to the

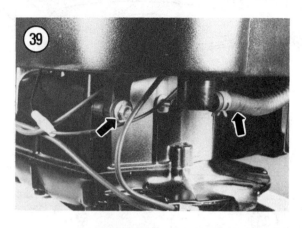

rope, remove the rope pulley as outlined in the following procedure for rewind spring removal.

3. Detach the rope from the rope handle.

4. Measure the rope and obtain a replacement rope of the same length and diameter. If the new rope is made of nylon, melt each rope end with a match to prevent the ends from unraveling.

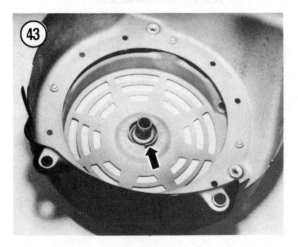

5. Rotate the rope pulley counterclockwise as far as possible, then allow the pulley to turn clockwise so the rope hole in the pulley and the rope outlet in the housing are aligned. Hold the pulley by installing a restraining device (such as a tie-wrap) around the starter housing and a strut (**Figure 41**) on the rope pulley so the spring cannot rewind.

6. Tie a knot in one end of the rope.

7. Thread the rope through the pulley rope hole and out the rope outlet in the housing.

8. Attach the rope handle to the rope.

9. Hold the pulley, release the restraining device on the rope pulley and slowly allow the rope to wind onto the pulley.

10. Check starter operation.

Service Drive Mechanism or Replace Rewind Spring

1. Remove the starter from the engine as previously outlined.

2. Detach the rope handle and allow the rope to wind slowly into the starter.

3. Place a round support such as a piece of pipe under the retainer and drive out the center pin using a 5/16 in. (8 mm) diameter rod or punch as shown in **Figure 42**. Note that the drive components will be loose when the center pin is removed.

4. Remove the drive mechanism components.

5. Lift out the rope pulley. The rewind spring is housed on the rope pulley. Remove the rope from the pulley.

> *NOTE*
> *The rewind spring is available only as a unit assembly with the rope pulley. Do not attempt to separate the spring cover or rewind spring from the pulley.*

6. Inspect the drive mechanism and replace any parts which are damaged or excessively worn. Inspect the starter cup on the flywheel for wear or damage that may cause faulty starter engagement. Inspect the pulley for cracks and other damage as well as excessive wear.

7. Note the location of the end of the spring retainer flange in the starter housing (**Figure 43**) and the location of the inner end of the rewind spring in the rope pulley (**Figure 44**). Place the rope pulley in the starter housing so the spring inner end is aligned with the end of the retainer flange.

8. Rotate the rope pulley counterclockwise so the inner end of the spring engages the spring retainer flange.

9. Install the pawl return springs in the wells in the pulley hub. Note that the straight spring end fits in a slot while the angled end points up as shown in **Figure 45**.

10. Install the pawls as shown in **Figure 46** so the angled spring end forces the pawl towards the center of the pulley.

11. Place the gray plastic washer on the pulley hub (**Figure 47**).

12. Place the retainer on the pulley hub so the stamped bosses are adjacent to the pawls (**Figure 48**).

13. Place the spring and steel washer on the retainer.

14. Insert the center pin in the starter (**Figure 49**), then drive the pin into the starter until the pin is flush with the flat surface of the retainer (**Figure 50**).

15. Rotate the rope pulley counterclockwise as far as possible, then allow the pulley to turn clockwise so the rope hole in the pulley and the rope outlet in the housing are aligned. Hold the pulley by installing a restraining device (such as a tie-wrap) around the starter housing and a strut (**Figure 41**) on the rope pulley so the spring cannot rewind.

16. Tie a knot in one end of the rope.

17. Thread the rope through the pulley rope hole and out the rope outlet in the housing.

18. Attach the rope handle to the rope.

19. Hold the pulley, release the restraining device on the rope pulley and slowly allow the rope to wind onto the pulley.

20. Check starter operation.

Replace Starter Housing

The starter housing may be riveted to the blower housing. The rivets can be drilled out and replaced using bolts. Service replacement starters include the hardware required for installation.

8

ELECTRICAL SYSTEM

The electrical system on Briggs & Stratton engines uses an alternator adjacent to the flywheel to provide electrical energy. Current from the alternator may be used to power lights or directed to a battery and other electrical components.

TESTING

Before testing any components, isolate the problem as much as possible. For instance, if the electric starter is inoperable, check the battery's condition, and if satisfactory, check for voltage at the starter to be sure the switch is operating properly. The electrical systems on Briggs & Stratton engines are relatively simple. Common sense troubleshooting will reduce testing time and prevent the purchase of unnecessary parts.

Most of the following test procedures can be accomplished using a volt-ohmmeter and an ammeter. In some cases, a simple continuity tester or voltage tester will suffice, on the other hand, it may be necessary to have the component tested in a shop if expensive test equipment is not available.

WARNING
Some of the test procedures involve working with high voltages. All safety precautions related to working with or around harmful electrical circuits and devices must be followed.

BATTERY

A 6- or 12-volt battery is used on electrical systems requiring a battery. The battery's negative terminal must be grounded to the engine or equipment. The size of the battery depends on the application and should meet the specifications of the equipment manufacturer.

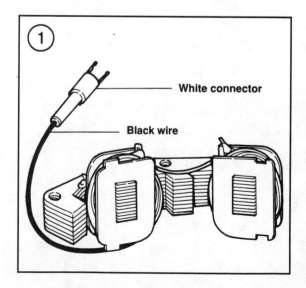
White connector
Black wire

System 3 and System 4 engines have a 6- or 12-volt battery that is rechargeable using 110-volt house current. The engine charging system also charges the battery during engine operation. The battery and 110-volt charger must be tested using special equipment according to the manufacturer's procedure.

Except on System 3 and System 4 engines, service and testing procedures applicable for wet-cell type batteries as found in automobiles and other vehicles also apply to batteries used with Briggs & Stratton engines.

Be sure to follow all safety precautions associated with working on or around batteries.

NOTE
*Recycle your old battery. When you replace the old battery, be sure to turn in the old battery at that time. The lead plates and the plastic case can be recycled. Most motorcycle dealers will accept your old battery in trade when you purchase a new one, but if they will not, many automotive supply stores certainly will. **Never** place an old battery in your household trash since it is illegal, in most states, to place any acid or lead (heavy metal) contents in landfills. There is also the danger of the battery being crushed in the trash truck and spraying acid on the truck operator.*

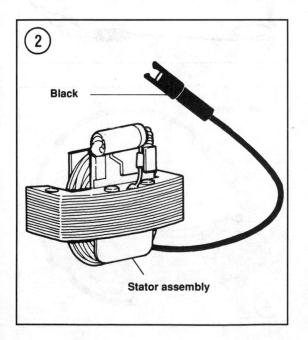
Black

Stator assembly

WARNING
Protect your eyes, skin and clothing. If electrolyte gets into your eyes, flush your eyes thoroughly with clean water and get prompt medical attention.

CAUTION
Be careful not to spill battery electrolyte on painted or polished surfaces. The liquid is highly corrosive and will damage the finish. If it is spilled, wash it off immediately with soapy water and thoroughly rinse with clean water.

CHARGING/LIGHTING SYSTEM

The charging system consists of the alternator, rectifier and regulator. The alternator produces alternating current, the rectifier converts the alternating current to direct current and the regulator maintains a specific voltage level. In low-amperage systems, a regulator may not be used as maximum engine speed limits the charging system to a safe output level.

A lighting system consists of just the alternator. The alternating current produced by the alternator is used to power lights on the equipment.

Some systems are designed to use alternator output for both a charging system and a lighting system. The charging system provides direct current for battery charging as well as powering accessories. The lighting system powers the lights.

Note that current for lights may be either alternating current (no rectifier) or direct current (rectified) depending on the system.

Stator Air Gap
Model Series 90000, 100000 and 120700

The alternator stator on model series 90000, 100000 (**Figure 1**) and 120700 (**Figure 2**) can be moved to adjust the air gap between the flywheel and the alternator stator legs. Turn the flywheel so the magnets in the flywheel rim are away from the alternator stator. Loosen the stator mounting screws. On model series 90000 and 100000 insert a 0.010 in. (0.25 mm) shim between the stator legs and flywheel. On model series 120700 insert a 0.007 in. (0.18 mm) shim. Rotate the flywheel so the magnets are aligned with the stator legs, tighten the stator mounting screws to 25 in.-lb. (2.8 N•m), then remove the shim. Rotate the flywheel and check for

9

any interference between the flywheel and stator legs.

Testing

The charging/lighting system can be tested using conventional electrical test equipment such as a volt-ohmmeter and ammeter. Be sure the ammeter is capable of measuring the maximum amperage the system is capable of producing.

Some systems are equipped with a rectifier diode that allows current to flow in one direction only. The diode is tested with an ohmmeter. The rectifier diode may be contained in a wire. To test the diode, insert a pin into the wire (**Figure 3**) behind the diode. With the wiring connector disconnected, attach ohmmeter test leads as shown in **Figure 3** and note ohmmeter reading, then reverse the tester leads and again note the ohmmeter reading. With the ohmmeter set on R × 1, the meter should read low resistance then infinity, or vice versa, when the ohmmeter leads are reversed for two readings. If the ohmmeter readings are both low or both infinity, then the diode is faulty.

Identification

The alternator must be identified before testing the system. Model series 90000, 91000, 92000, 93000, 94000, 110000, 111000, 112000, 113000 and 114000 may be equipped with a System 3 or System 4 alternator as shown in **Figure 1**. Model series 121000, 122000, 124000 and 126000 may be equipped with the 1/2 amp alternator shown in **Figure 2**. Model series 130000, 131000 and 132000 may be equipped with the 1.2 amp alternator shown in **Figure 4** or the 1-1/2 amp alternator shown in **Figure 5**. A variety of alternators have been used on all larger engines. Refer to **Figures 6-35** for identification. Note the color of the wires and connectors as well as the configuration of the stator. Refer to the following sections for testing procedures.

System 3 and System 4

Refer to **Figure 1**.

To test alternator output, disconnect black stator lead at white connector. Connect red lead of a DC ammeter to stator lead and black ammeter lead to engine. With engine running, alternator output

should be at least 0.5 amps DC at 2800 rpm. If alternator output is zero or low and stator air gap is correct, replace stator.

1/2 amp alternator

Refer to **Figure 2**.

To test alternator output, disconnect stator lead at black connector. Connect red lead of a DC ammeter to stator lead and black ammeter lead to engine. With engine running, alternator output should be at least 0.5 amps DC at 2800 rpm. If alternator output is zero or low and stator air gap is correct, replace stator.

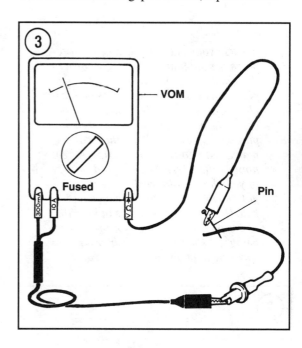

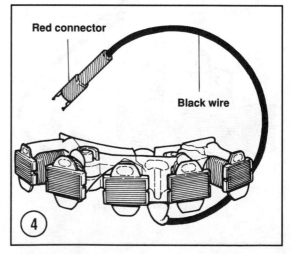

1.2 amp alternator

Refer to **Figure 4**.

The 1.2 amp alternator provides battery charging current. The stator is located under the flywheel. A 12 ampere hour battery should be used for warm temperature operation and a 24 ampere hour battery should be used for cold temperatures.

To test alternator output, disconnect black stator lead at red connector. Connect red lead of a DC ammeter to stator lead and black ammeter lead to engine. With engine running, alternator output should be at least 1.0 amps DC at 3600 rpm. If alternator output is zero or low, replace stator.

1-1/2 amp alternator

Refer to **Figure 5**.

The 1-1/2 amp alternator provides battery charging current. The stator is located under the flywheel. A 12 ampere hour battery should be used for warm temperature operation and a 24 ampere hour battery should be used for cold temperatures.

The solid-state rectifier on early models is adjacent to starter drive housing, while on later models the rectifier diodes are contained in the stator wire near the connector. Only later inline type rectifier is available and may be substituted for early type.

To test alternator output, disconnect charging lead from charging terminal on early models, or disconnect stator lead at connector on later models. Connect red lead of a DC ammeter to charging terminal

or stator lead and black ammeter lead to engine. With engine running, alternator output should be least 1.2 amps DC at 3600 rpm. Test rectifier if output is low or zero.

Check for a faulty rectifier as follows:
1. With engine stopped, disconnect lead from output terminal on early models, or disconnect stator connector on later models.
2. Insert a pin in one of the stator wires and connect one ohmmeter lead to pin and other ohmmeter lead to output terminal on early models or to end of connector on later models.
3. Check for continuity.
4. Reverse ohmmeter leads and again check for continuity. Ohmmeter should show a continuity reading (low ohms) for one direction only.
5. Repeat test on other stator wire. If tests show no continuity in either direction or continuity in both directions, rectifier is faulty and must be replaced.
6. With a pin inserted in one of the stator wires, connect one ohmmeter lead to pin and other ohmmeter lead to engine.
7. Check for continuity.
8. Reverse ohmmeter leads and again check for continuity. Ohmmeter should show a continuity reading (low ohms) for one direction only.
9. Repeat test on other stator wire.
10. Replace stator lead if tests indicate rectifier diodes are faulty.
11. The old stator leads must be cut and the new stator leads must be attached using rosin core solder. Mechanical fasteners must not be used to splice the old and new stator leads together.
12. If rectifier tests satisfactorily, replace stator.

3 amp DC alternator

Refer to **Figure 6**.

The 3 amp DC alternator is regulated only by engine speed and provides 2 to 3 amp charging current to maintain battery state of charge. A 30 ampere hour battery should be used for warm temperature operation and a 50 ampere hour battery should be used for cold temperatures. The stator is located under the flywheel.

To check output, connect red lead of a DC ammeter to red stator lead and black ammeter lead to positive terminal of battery. Run engine at 3600 rpm. Ammeter should indicate 2-4 amps charging current, depending on state of charge of battery (amme-

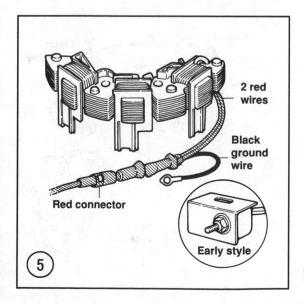

2 red wires

Black ground wire

Red connector

Early style

⑤

9

ter reading will be higher if battery charge is low). Test rectifier diode if output is low or zero.

Check for a faulty rectifier diode as follows:

1. With engine stopped and stator lead disconnected, insert a pin in the stator wire and connect one ohmmeter lead to pin and other ohmmeter lead to end of connector.

2. Check for continuity.

3. Reverse ohmmeter leads and again check for continuity. Ohmmeter should show a continuity reading (low ohms) for one test and infinity for other test.

4. Replace the stator lead if tests indicate diode is faulty.

5. The old stator lead must be cut and the new stator lead must be attached using rosin core solder. Mechanical fasteners must not be used to splice the old and new stator leads together.

6. If rectifier diode tests satisfactorily, replace stator.

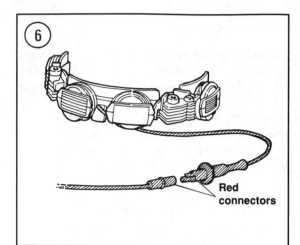

AC alternator

Refer to **Figure 7**.

This AC alternator is used to power 12-volt lights. Output is determined by engine speed. The stator is located under the flywheel.

To check output, connect red lead of a voltmeter to white connector of black stator lead and black voltmeter lead to engine. Run engine at 3600 rpm. Voltmeter should indicate at least 14 volts, otherwise, the stator must be replaced.

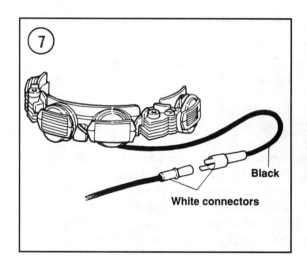

4 amp alternator

Refer to **Figure 8**.

Some engines are equipped with a 4 amp alternator that is regulated only by engine speed. A solid-state rectifier and 7-1/2 amp fuse are used with this alternator. The stator is located under the flywheel.

1. If the battery is run down and no output from alternator is suspected, first check the 7-1/2 amp fuse. If the fuse is good, clean and tighten all connections.

2. To check alternator output, disconnect alternator charging lead and connect an ammeter as shown in **Figure 9**. Start engine and check for alternator output. Ammeter should indicate at least 2.5 amps at 3600 rpm.

3. If ammeter shows no charge, stop engine, remove ammeter and install a test lamp as shown in **Figure**

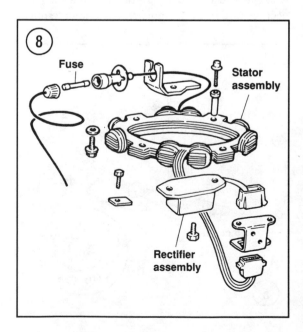

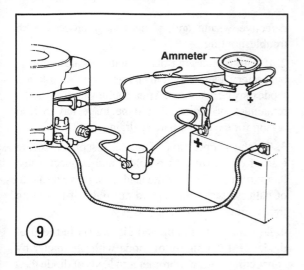

(9)

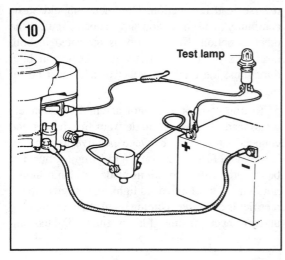

(10)

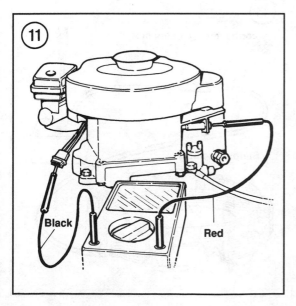

(11)

10. Test lamp should not light. If it does light, stator or rectifier is defective. Unplug rectifier plug under blower housing. If test lamp does not go out, stator is shorted.

4. If a shorted stator is indicated, use an ohmmeter and check for continuity by touching one test lead to lead inside of fuse holder as shown in **Figure 11**. Touch remaining test lead to each of the four pins in rectifier connector. Unless ohmmeter shows continuity at each of the four pins, stator winding is open and stator must be replaced.

5. If a defective rectifier is indicated, unbolt and remove flywheel blower housing with rectifier. Connect one ohmmeter test lead to blower housing and remaining test lead to the single pin connector in rectifier connector. See **Figure 12**. Check for continuity, then reverse leads and again test for continuity. If tests show no continuity in either direction or continuity in both directions, rectifier is faulty and must be replaced.

5 and 9 amp regulated alternators

Refer to **Figure 13**.

The 5 and 9 amp alternators provide regulated charging current. Charging rate is determined by

9

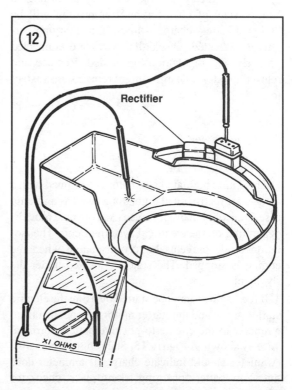

(12)

state of charge in battery. The stator is located under the flywheel.

Alternator output is determined by the size of the flywheel magnets cast into the flywheel. Magnets are 11/16 in. × 7/8 in. (18 mm × 22 mm) on 5 amp flywheels and 15/16 in. × 1-1/16 in. (24 mm × 27 mm) on 16 amp flywheels.

1. To check stator output, disconnect green connector and connect voltmeter leads to stator lead. With engine running at 3600 rpm, voltmeter should indicate at least 28 VAC for 5 amp systems and 40 VAC for 9 amp systems. If not, replace stator.

2. To test regulator, the 12 volt battery must have a minimum charge of 5 volts. Connect red lead of ammeter to regulator-to-battery wire connector (red) lead and black ammeter lead to positive battery terminal.

> *CAUTION*
> *Test leads must be connected before starting engine and must not be disconnected while engine is running as regulator may be damaged.*

3. Run engine at 3600 rpm. Ammeter should indicate 3-5 amps for 5 amp system or 3-9 amps for 9 amp system. Ammeter reading will vary according to battery state of charge (ammeter reading will be higher if battery charge is low). If no charging current is indicated, check that wires are connected properly and regulator is grounded. Replace and retest regulator if charge current remains unsatisfactory.

7 amp alternator

Refer to **Figure 14**.

The 7 amp regulated alternator is equipped with a solid-state rectifier and regulator as well as a 15 amp fuse. An isolation diode is also used on most models, depending on the electrical system circuit. The isolation diode prevents battery discharge when the engine is stopped. The stator is located under the flywheel.

1. If the engine cannot be started by using the electric starter motor and the starter motor is good, install an ammeter in the engine-to-positive battery terminal wire as shown in **Figure 15**. Start engine manually. Ammeter should indicate charge. If ammeter does not show battery charging taking place, check for

defective wiring and, if necessary, proceed with troubleshooting.

2. If battery charging occurs with engine running, but battery does not retain charge, then the isolation diode may be defective. After troubleshooting diode, remainder of circuit should be inspected to find reason for excessive battery drain.

3. To check operation of diode, disconnect white lead of diode from fuse holder and connect a test lamp from the diode white lead to negative terminal of battery. Test lamp should not light. If test lamp lights, diode is defective.

4. Disconnect test lamp and disconnect red lead of diode. Test continuity of diode with ohmmeter by connecting leads of ohmmeter to leads of diode then reverse lead connection. Ohmmeter should show continuity in one direction and an open circuit in the other direction. If continuity is indicated in both directions or if open circuit is indicated in both directions, the diode is defective and must be replaced.

5. To troubleshoot alternator assembly, disconnect white lead of isolation diode from fuse holder and connect a test lamp between positive terminal of battery and fuse holder on engine. Engine must not be started. With connections made, test lamp should not light. If test lamp does light, stator, regulator or rectifier is defective. Unplug regulator-rectifier plug under blower housing. If lamp remains lighted, sta-

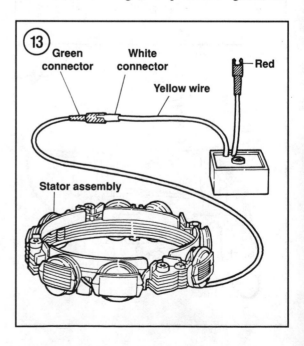

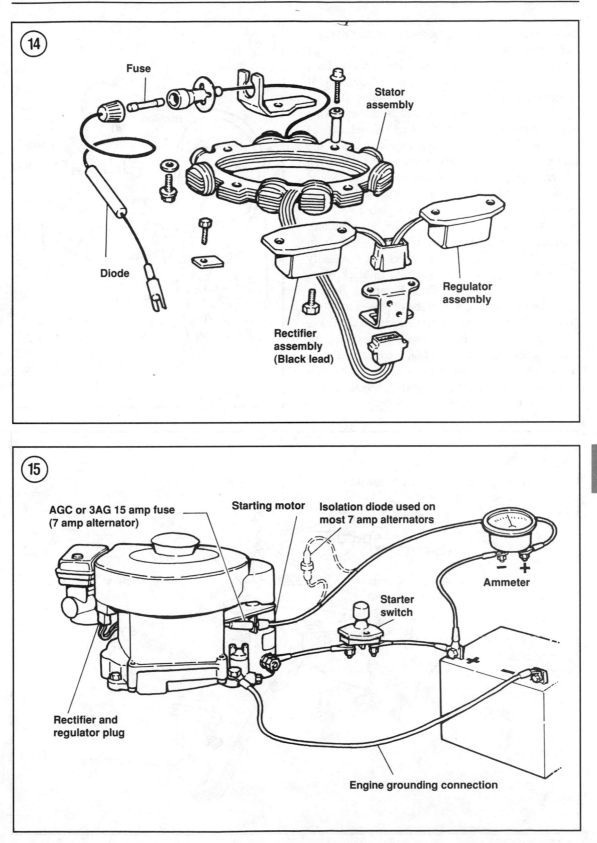

14

Fuse

Stator
assembly

Diode

Rectifier
assembly
(Black lead)

Regulator
assembly

15

AGC or 3AG 15 amp fuse
(7 amp alternator)

Starting motor

Isolation diode used on
most 7 amp alternators

Ammeter

Starter
switch

Rectifier and
regulator plug

Engine grounding connection

9

tor is grounded. If lamp goes out, regulator or rectifier is shorted.

6. If previous test indicated stator is grounded, check stator leads for defects and repair if necessary. If shorted leads are not found, replace stator.

7. Check stator for an open circuit as follows: Using an ohmmeter, connect positive lead to fuse holder as shown in **Figure 11** and negative lead to one of the pins in rectifier and regulator connector. Check each of the four pins in connector. Ohmmeter should show continuity at each pin, if not, then there is an open in stator and stator must be replaced.

8. To test rectifier, unplug rectifier and regulator connector plug and remove blower housing from engine. Using an ohmmeter, check for continuity between connector pins connected to black wires and blower housing as shown in **Figure 16**. Be sure good contact is made with metal of blower housing. Reverse ohmmeter leads and check continuity again. Ohmmeter should show a continuity reading for only one direction on each plug. If either pin shows a continuity reading for both directions, or if either pin shows no continuity for either direction, then rectifier must be replaced.

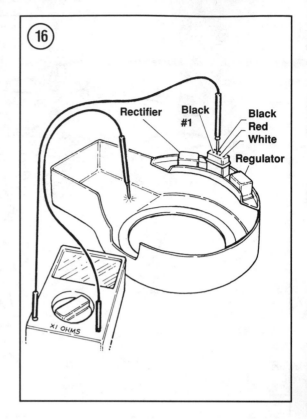

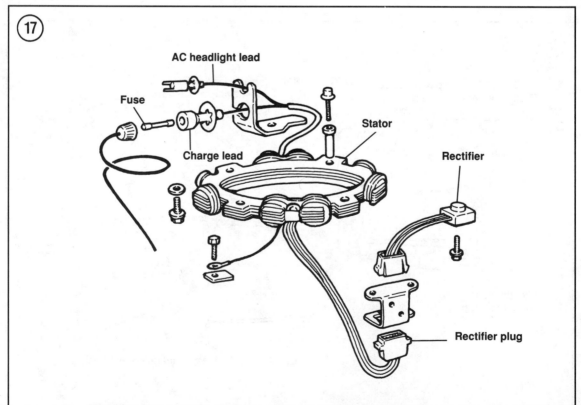

9. To test regulator unit, repeat procedure used to test rectifier unit in Step 8 except connect ohmmeter lead to pins connected to red wire and white wire. If ohmmeter shows continuity in either direction for red lead pin, regulator is defective and must be replaced. White lead pin should read as an open on ohmmeter in one direction and a weak reading in the other direction. Otherwise, regulator is defective and must be replaced.

Early dual circuit alternator

Refer to **Figure 17**.

A dual circuit alternator may be used on some early engines. The early dual circuit system is identified by a fuse in the system. The dual circuit alternator has one circuit to provide charging current to maintain battery state of charge and a separate circuit to provide alternating current for lights (**Figure 18**). The amount of current produced is regulated only by engine speed. A solid-state rectifier in the charging circuit converts the alternating current to direct current. The stator is located under the flywheel.

The total rating for lights (12 volt) connected to the lighting circuit should be 60-100 watts. The lights are powered only when the engine is running.

The charging system is protected by a 7-1/2 amp fuse.

NOTE
The lights must be connected to the lighting circuit, not to the battery.

1. To check charging alternator output, install an ammeter in circuit as shown in **Figure 19**. Start engine and allow it to operate at a speed of 3000 rpm. Ammeter should indicate charging.

2. If no alternator output is indicated in Step 1, and fuse is known to be good, test for a short in stator or rectifier as follows: Disconnect charging lead from battery and connect a small test lamp between battery positive terminal and fuse cap as shown in **Figure 20**. *Do not* start engine. Test lamp should not light. If it does light, stator's charging lead is grounded or rectifier is defective. Unplug rectifier

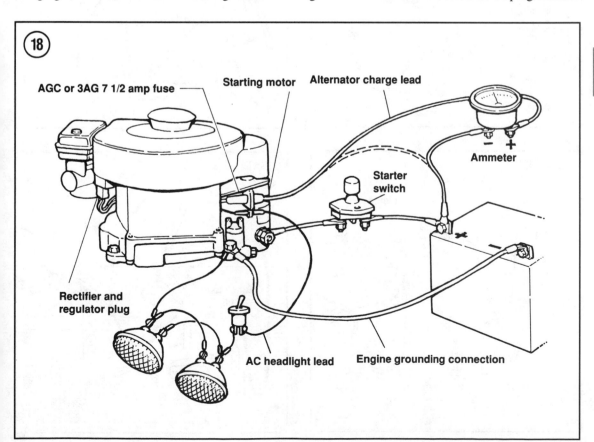

18

AGC or 3AG 7 1/2 amp fuse

Starting motor

Alternator charge lead

Ammeter

Starter switch

Rectifier and regulator plug

AC headlight lead

Engine grounding connection

9

plug under blower housing. If test lamp goes out, rectifier is defective. If test lamp does not go out, stator charging lead is grounded.

3. If test indicates stator charging lead is grounded, remove blower housing, flywheel, starter motor and retaining clamp, then examine length of red lead for damaged insulation or obvious shorts in lead. If bare spots are found, repair with electrical tape and shellac. If short cannot be repaired, replace stator.

4. Charging lead should also be checked for continuity as follows: Touch one lead of an ohmmeter to lead at fuse holder and the other ohmmeter lead to red lead pin in connector as shown in **Figure 21**. If ohmmeter does not show continuity, charging lead is open and stator must be replaced.

5. Charging coils should be checked for continuity as follows: Touch ohmmeter test leads to the two black lead pins as shown in **Figure 22**. If ohmmeter does not show continuity, charging coils are defective and stator must be replaced.

6. Test for grounded charging coils by touching one test lead of ohmmeter to a clean ground surface on the engine and the other test lead to each of the black lead pins as shown in **Figure 23**. If ohmmeter shows continuity, charging coils are grounded and stator must be replaced.

7. To test the rectifier, use an ohmmeter and check for continuity between each of the three lead pin

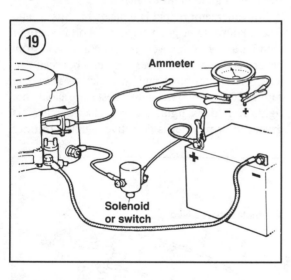

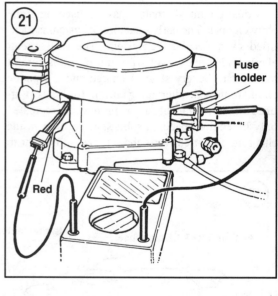

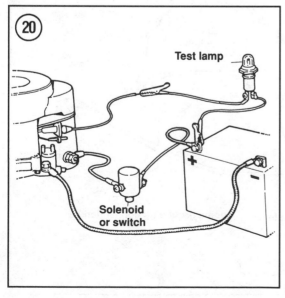

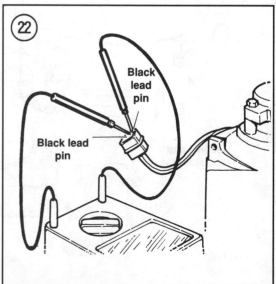

sockets and blower housing. See **Figure 24**. Reverse ohmmeter leads and check continuity again. Ohmmeter should show a continuity reading for one direction only on each lead socket. If any pin socket shows continuity reading in both directions or neither direction, rectifier is defective and must be replaced.

8. To test AC lighting alternator circuit, connect a load lamp (GE 4001 or equivalent) or voltmeter to AC output plug and ground as shown in **Figure 25**. Load lamp should light at full brilliance at medium engine speed. A voltmeter should indicate at least 14 volts when engine is running at 3600 rpm.

9. If lamp does not light or is very dim at medium speeds, or voltage reading is insufficient, remove blower housing and flywheel. Disconnect ground end of AC coil from retaining clamp screw (**Figure 26**). Connect an ohmmeter between ground lead of AC coil and AC output terminal as shown in **Figure 26**. Ohmmeter should show continuity. If not, stator must be replaced.

10. Be sure AC ground lead is not touching a grounded surface, then check continuity from AC output terminal to engine ground. If ohmmeter indicates continuity, lighting coils are grounded and stator must be replaced.

Later dual circuit alternator

Refer to **Figure 27**.

The dual circuit alternator has one circuit to provide charging current to maintain battery state of charge and a separate circuit to provide alternating current for lights. The amount of current produced is regulated only by engine speed (light intensity will vary according to engine speed). A solid-state rectifier in the charging circuit converts the alternating current to direct current. The stator is located under the flywheel.

The total rating for lights (12 volt) connected to the lighting circuit should be 60-100 watts. The lights are powered only when the engine is running.

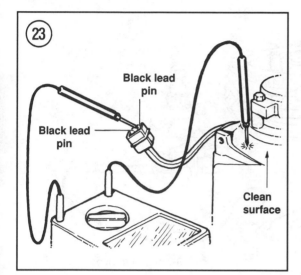

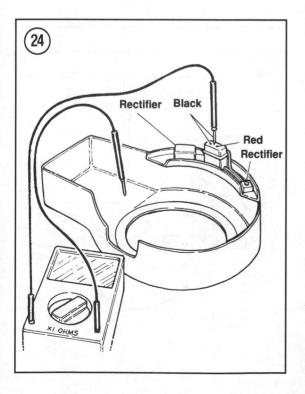

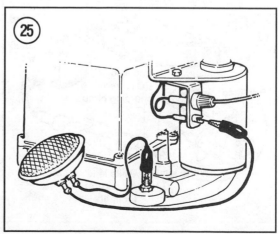

NOTE
The lights must be connected to the lighting circuit, not to the battery.

1. To test charging circuit output, connect an ammeter in series (**Figure 28**) between the charging lead connector and the battery positive terminal. Attach the red ammeter lead to the DC output pin in the connector which is identified by a bump on the connector as shown in **Figure 29**. Run engine at 3600 rpm. Ammeter should indicate 2-4 amp charging current, depending on battery state of charge (ammeter reading will be higher if battery charge is low).

2. If no charging current is indicated in Step 1, check the diode in the connector. Attach an ohmmeter lead to the DC output pin in the charging lead connector

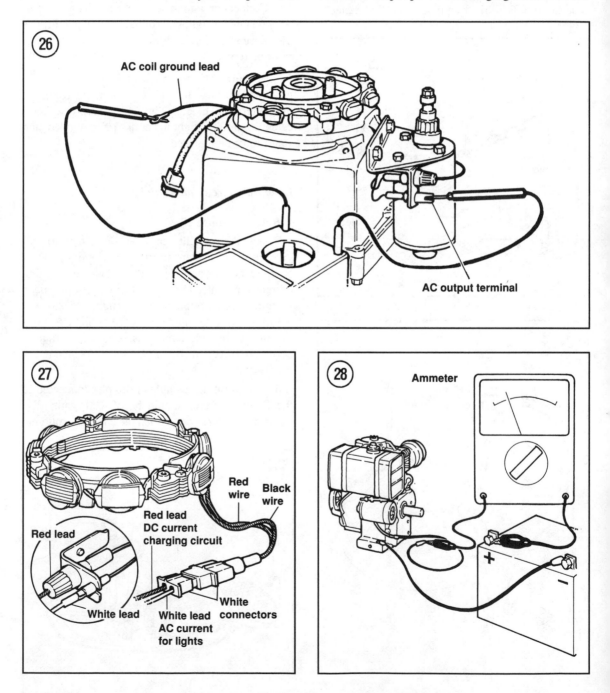

(**Figure 29**). Stick a pin through the red charging circuit wire just behind the plug and connect remaining ohmmeter lead to pin. Note reading then reverse leads. Ohmmeter should indicate continuity in only one position. If not, renew connector and lead assembly. The old stator lead must be cut and the new stator lead must be attached using rosin core solder. Mechanical fasteners must not be used to splice the old and new stator leads together. If diode is good, but system still does not show a charge, replace stator.

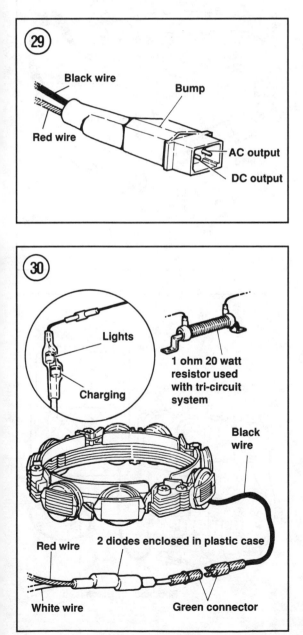

3. To test the lighting circuit, connect an AC voltmeter in series with AC output pin in connector (black wire shown in **Figure 29**) and connect remaining tester lead to engine ground. Run engine at 3600 rpm. Voltmeter reading should be at least 14 volts. Replace stator if there is insufficient voltage.

Tri-circuit alternator

Refer to **Figure 30**.

The tri-circuit alternator stator produces alternating current and has a single output lead. The stator is located under the flywheel. Circuit separation is achieved by the use of a positive (+) diode and a negative (–) diode. The charging lead diode rectifies negative (–) 12 VDC (5 amps at 3600 rpm) for lighting. This same charge lead contains a second diode which rectifies positive (+) 12 VDC (5 amps at 3600 rpm) for battery charging and external loads. Some equipment manufacturers incorporate one or both diodes in the wiring harness. Check wiring diagram for models being serviced for diode location.

1. To test alternator output, connect an AC voltmeter in series between stator output lead (black wire with green connector) and engine ground. Run engine at 3600 rpm. Voltmeter should register 28 volts AC or more. Voltage will vary with engine rpm. If charge current is not indicated, replace stator.

2. To check diodes, disconnect charge lead (red and white wires with a green connector) from stator output lead. Connect an ohmmeter lead to connector pin (**Figure 31**) and connect remaining lead to the red wire (charging circuit) by inserting a pin through the wire. Reverse connections. Ohmmeter should indicate continuity in one position only. If not, replace diode. Repeat the procedure on white wire (lighting circuit).

Quad circuit alternator

Refer to **Figure 32**.

Current from the quad circuit alternator is 8 amp positive (+) DC at the red regulator lead and 8 amp negative (–) DC at the black regulator lead. Note that the black regulator wire changes to a white wire at white connector. Charging rate is determined by the state of charge in the battery. The stator is located under the flywheel and output capacity is determined by the size of magnets cast into the flywheel.

9

NOTE
The regulator-rectifier must be securely attached to engine so unit is grounded, otherwise, it will not function properly.

1. To check stator output, disconnect yellow connector on stator lead and connect voltmeter leads to pins for stator leads. Run engine at 3600 rpm. Voltmeter should indicate at least 30 VAC. If not, replace stator.

2. To test regulator output, the battery must have a minimum charge of 5 volts. Connect the red lead of an ammeter to charging circuit positive (red) lead and connect black lead of ammeter to positive battery terminal (**Figure 33**).

CAUTION
Test leads must be connected before starting engine and must not be disconnected while engine is running as regulator may be damaged.

3. Run engine at 3600 rpm. Ammeter should indicate 3-8 amps. Ammeter reading will vary according to battery state of charge (ammeter reading will be higher if battery charge is low). If no charging current is indicated, check that wires are connected properly and regulator-rectifier is grounded. Re-

place and retest regulator-rectifier if charge current remains unsatisfactory.

4. To check lighting circuit of regulator, obtain a 1 ohm, 20 watt resistor. Use a suitable jumper wire and

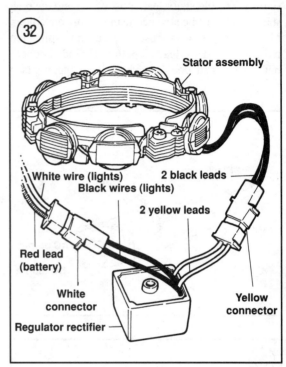

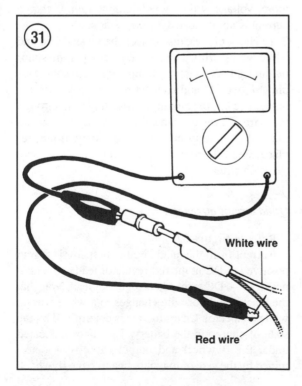

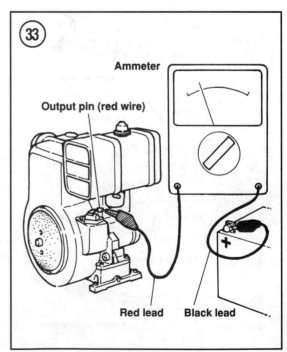

connect to white connector of regulator as shown in **Figure 34**. Connect red lead of an ammeter to the resistor and the black ammeter lead to the positive battery terminal. Run engine at 3600 rpm just long

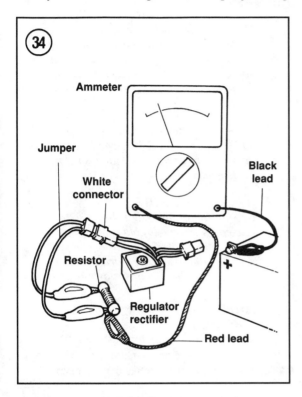

enough to produce test reading. Ammeter should indicate approximately 8 amp, if not replace regulator-rectifier.

> *CAUTION*
> *Resistor will get hot during test. Perform test only as long as necessary.*

Later 10, 13 and 16 amp alternator

Refer to **Figure 35**.

The 10, 13 and 16 amp alternators provide regulated charging current. Charging rate is determined by state of charge in battery. Stator is located under the flywheel and output capacity is determined by the size of magnets cast into the flywheel.

Alternator output is determined by the size of the flywheel magnets. Magnets are 11/16 in. × 7/8 in. (18 mm × 22 mm) on 10 amp flywheels, 11/16 in. × 1-1/16 in. (18 mm × 27 mm) on 13 amp flywheels, and 15/16 in. × 1-1/16-in. (24 mm × 27 mm) on 16 amp flywheels.

> *NOTE*
> *The regulator-rectifier must be securely attached to engine so unit is grounded, otherwise, it will not function properly.*

1. To check stator output, disconnect yellow connector and connect voltmeter leads to pins for stator leads. With engine running at 3600 rpm, voltmeter should indicate at least 20 VAC for 10 and 13 amp systems, and 30 VAC for 16 amp systems. If not, replace stator.

2. To test regulator output, the battery must have a minimum charge of 5 volts. Connect the red lead of an ammeter to charging circuit positive (red) lead and connect black lead of ammeter to positive battery terminal (**Figure 36**).

> *CAUTION*
> *Test leads must be connected before starting engine and must not be disconnected while engine is running as regulator may be damaged.*

3. Run engine at 3600 rpm. Ammeter should indicate 3-10 amps on 10 amp system, 3-10 amps on 13 amp system and 3-13 amps on 16 amp system. Ammeter reading will vary according to battery state of charge (ammeter reading will be higher if battery charge is low). If no charging current is indicated, check that

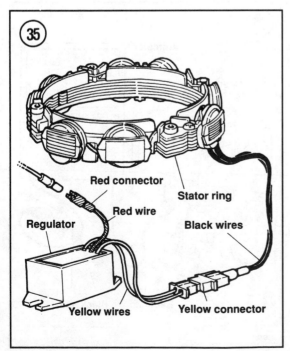

wires are connected properly and regulator-rectifier is grounded. Replace and retest regulator-rectifier if charge current remains unsatisfactory.

ELECTRIC STARTER SYSTEM

This section covers 12-volt starter motors that use current provided by a wet-cell storage battery. A switch located either on the engine or on the equipment is used to energize the starter motor by connecting the wires leading from the positive battery terminal to the starter motor. A pinion gear on the starter motor engages a ring gear on the engine flywheel to rotate the engine crankshaft when the starter motor is energized. When the motor is energized, a helix moves the pinion gear towards the flywheel ring gear, then when the engine is running, the faster moving ring gear "unscrews" the pinion gear so it moves away from the ring gear thereby disengaging the gears.

Troubleshooting

If the starter motor does not rotate the engine when the starter switch is actuated, or the motor turns slowly, isolate the problem before assuming the motor is faulty. Use the following steps.
1. Check for loose, dirty and corroded wiring connections as well as faulty wiring.
2. Be sure the battery is fully charged and proper size.
3. Check for faulty safety interlocks on equipment.
4. Check for a faulty starter switch. A jumper wire can be connected between the battery and starter motor to determine if the starter switch is faulty.
5. Operate manual starter to determine if excessive force is required to start the engine (may be due to excessive load connected to engine, wrong oil viscosity or internal engine damage).

ELECTRIC STARTER MOTORS

The electric starter motors used on Briggs & Stratton engines are classified as either direct drive or gear reduction starter motors. The direct drive starter motor has the drive pinion gear mounted directly on the armature shaft. On gear reduction starter motors, a set of intermediate gears transfers power from the armature shaft to the pinion gear shaft. Refer to the following sections for service information.

CAUTION
Before working on starter motor, disconnect the negative battery terminal lead.

CAUTION
The starter motor field magnets may be made of ceramic material. Do not clamp the starter housing in a vise or hit the housing as the field magnets may be damaged.

CAUTION
Do not run the starter motor continuously for more than 30 seconds. Allow the motor to cool for 10 minutes before further operation.

NOTE
Be sure the proper engine oil viscosity is used. In extremely cold temperatures, oil with the improper viscosity can prevent or inhibit engine starting due to excessive oil drag against moving parts.

Direct Drive Starter Motors

Direct drive starter motors used on Briggs & Stratton engines have been manufactured by Briggs & Stratton, American Bosch and Mitsubishi.

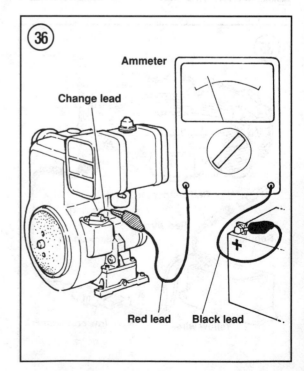

The recommended battery size for use with these starter motors is 30 amp-hour if ambient temperature is higher than 20° F (–7° C), 40 amp-hour if ambient temperature is higher than –5° F (–21° C), and 50 amp-hour or more if ambient temperature is less than –5° F (–21° C).

The correct wire size must be used between the battery and starter motor and between the battery and ground. The recommended wire size is #6 AWG if length is 4 ft. (1.2 m) or less, #5 AWG if length is 5 feet (1.5 m) or less, and #4 AWG if length is 6 feet (1.8 m) or less.

NOTE
Direct drive starter motors may be equipped with a steel or a plastic pinion gear. The flywheel ring gear must be made of the same material as the pinion gear, i.e. a steel pinion gear must be used with a steel flywheel ring gear.

NOTE
To replace a worn or damaged flywheel ring gear, drill out the retaining rivets using a 3/16 in. drill bit. Attach the new ring gear using screws provided with the new ring gear.

Testing

If the starter motor runs, but the engine does not turn, check the starter drive mechanism. The flywheel ring gear teeth may be worn or the starter motor drive may be broken or stuck. The pinion gear (**Figure 37**) should slide freely on the helix.

NOTE
Do not lubricate the drive assembly. The starter drive is designed for dry operation.

If the starter motor will not turn the engine or labors excessively, and the battery and starter switch are good, remove and inspect the starter motor.

Disassembly

Refer to **Figures 38-40** for exploded views of typical direct drive starter motors. Depending on the problem, the starter motor can be either partially or

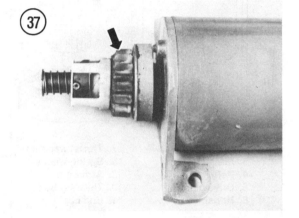

9

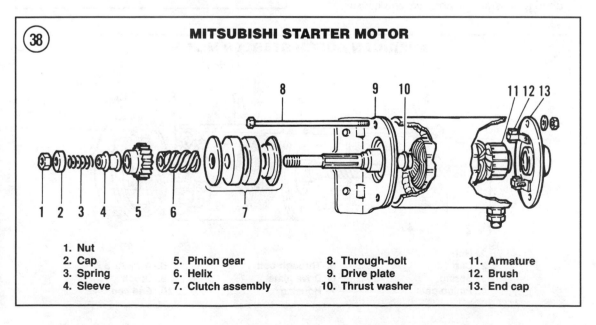

MITSUBISHI STARTER MOTOR

1. Nut
2. Cap
3. Spring
4. Sleeve
5. Pinion gear
6. Helix
7. Clutch assembly
8. Through-bolt
9. Drive plate
10. Thrust washer
11. Armature
12. Brush
13. End cap

completely disassembled. It is not necessary to re-move the drive assembly if the brushes require serv-ice.

1. If the drive assembly is faulty, remove the nut or retaining pin at the end of the armature shaft and remove the drive assembly components. Some mod-els may have a cap over the end of the shaft that must be pried off.

2. If equipped with a nut on the end of the armature shaft, clamp the pinion gear in a vise to prevent shaft rotation.

3. If equipped with a retaining pin, support the end of the shaft while driving out the pin.

4. Some starter drives are equipped with a return spring as shown in **Figure 41** or **Figure 42**.

5. Be aware that individual drive components are available for some models, but on some models the drive assembly is available only as a unit assembly.

6. Before disassembling the motor, make marks on the drive plate, housing and end cap so they can be reassembled in their original positions (**Figure 43**). Note which end of the motor the through-bolts and nuts are located so they can be installed in their original positions.

7. To service the brushes and check the condition of the commutator, unscrew the through-bolts and re-move the end cap (**Figure 44**). Before removing the brushes, note the position of the brushes and wires.

8. To remove the armature, the drive assembly must be removed. Due to the magnetic force of the per-manent field magnets, considerable force may be required to separate the armature and housing.

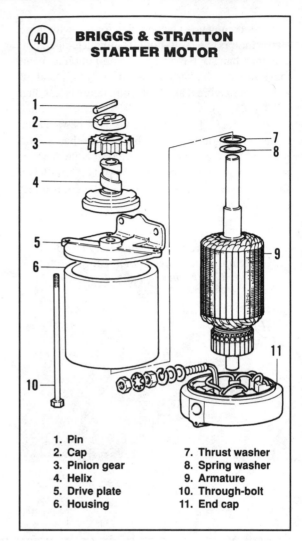

BRIGGS & STRATTON STARTER MOTOR

1. Pin
2. Cap
3. Pinion gear
4. Helix
5. Drive plate
6. Housing
7. Thrust washer
8. Spring washer
9. Armature
10. Through-bolt
11. End cap

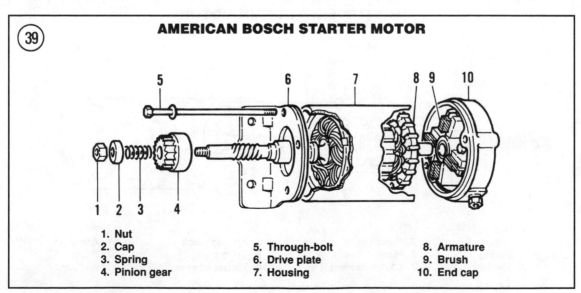

AMERICAN BOSCH STARTER MOTOR

1. Nut
2. Cap
3. Spring
4. Pinion gear
5. Through-bolt
6. Drive plate
7. Housing
8. Armature
9. Brush
10. End cap

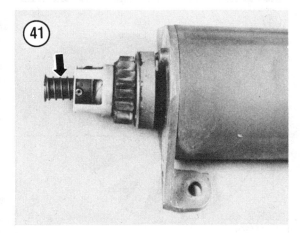

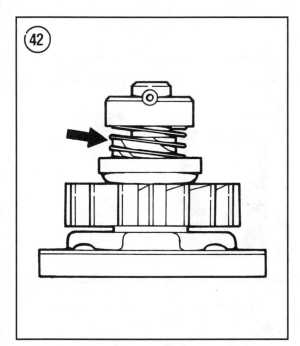

9. Note the position of any spacers on the armature shaft.

Inspection

1. Clean starter components but do not use cleaning solvents that will damage the armature.

2. Measure the length of each brush. On Briggs & Stratton motors, minimum allowable brush length (**Figure 45**) is 1/8 in. (3.2 mm). Minimum brush length is not specified for American Bosch and Mitsubishi motors, however, if the brush is worn so that the wire is exposed, replace the brush.

3. Check strength of the brush springs. The spring must force the brush against the commutator with sufficient pressure to ensure good contact. Be sure brushes do not bind in holders.

4. Inspect the condition of the commutator (**Figure 46**). The mica between the commutator bars should be slightly undercut as shown in **Figure 47**. Undercut the mica or clean the slots between the commutator bars using a piece of hacksaw blade. After undercutting, remove burrs by sanding the commutator lightly with crocus cloth.

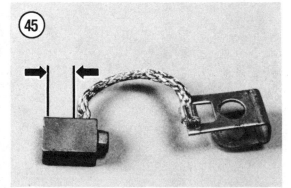

9

5. Inspect the commutator bars for discoloration. If a pair of bars is discolored, grounded armature coils are indicated.

6. If the commutator is worn excessively, the armature should be taken to a shop equipped with a lathe so the commutator can be cut down. Measure the diameter of the commutator. On Briggs & Stratton starter motors, minimum allowable commutator diameter is 1.23 in. (31.24 mm).

7. Use an ohmmeter and check for continuity between the commutator bars (**Figure 48**); there should be continuity between pairs of bars. If there is no continuity between pairs of bars, the armature is open. Replace the armature.

8. Connect an ohmmeter between any commutator bar and the armature shaft (**Figure 49**); there should be no continuity. If there is continuity, the armature is grounded. Replace the armature.

NOTE
If more extensive starter motor testing is required, then the motor should be taken to a professional shop. However, this cost should be compared with the cost of a replacement starter motor.

Inspect the bushings in the drive plate (**Figure 50**) and end cap. If the bushings are damaged or excessively worn, then the drive plate and/or end cap must be replaced; individual bushings are not available.

Reassembly

1. Apply a small amount of SAE 20 oil on bushings.
2. Install the spacers in their original positions on the armature shaft.
3. Install the armature in starter housing.

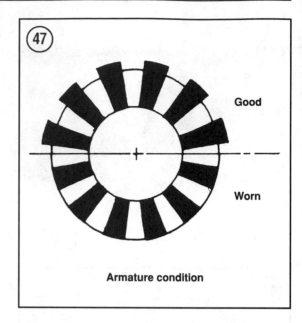

Armature condition

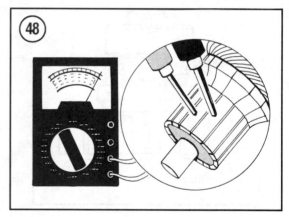

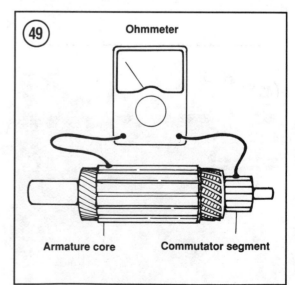

Ohmmeter

Armature core   Commutator segment

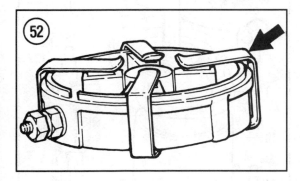

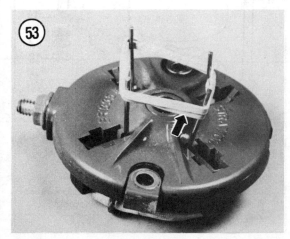

4. Align the marks on the drive plate, housing and end cap. Note that some motors have notches on the housing and end cap that must be aligned during assembly.

5. Some type of brush holder is necessary to retain the brushes and springs during assembly.

    a. If the end cap has two brushes, a piece of manual rewind starter spring can be modified to hold the brushes as shown in **Figure 51**.

    b. On end caps with four brushes that project axially, spring clips may be needed to hold the brushes (**Figure 52**).

    c. On end caps with four brushes that project inward, pins can be inserted into slots in the end cap to hold in the brushes. Hold the pins with a rubber band (**Figure 53**).

    d. Use care when installing the end cap so the commutator and brushes are not damaged.

6. After assembling the motor portion of the starter, rotate the armature. The armature should rotate without binding, although magnetic force will inhibit rotation.

7. Install the starter drive pinion gear so the chamfered side is towards the end of the shaft (**Figure 54**). If equipped with a retaining pin, a new pin should be installed and the split side of the pin must be towards the end of the shaft.

Gear Reduction Starter Motors (Except Model Series 130000)

Gear reduction starter motors are used in 6- and 12-volt systems as well as Ni-Cad battery systems. The following discussion applies to the 6- and 12-

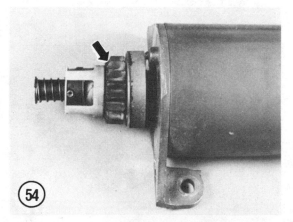

volt starter motors. The starter motor used on Ni-Cad battery systems is similar.

Testing

1. If the starter motor runs, but the engine does not turn, check the starter drive mechanism. The flywheel ring gear teeth may be worn or the starter motor drive may be broken or stuck. The starter gear (C, **Figure 55**) should slide freely on the helix (A).

> *NOTE*
> *Do not lubricate the drive assembly. The starter drive is designed for dry operation.*

> *NOTE*
> *To replace a worn or damaged flywheel ring gear, drill out retaining rivets using a 3/16 in. drill bit. Attach the new ring gear using screws provided with the new ring gear.*

2. If the starter motor will not turn the engine or labors excessively, and the battery and starter switch are good, remove and inspect the starter motor.

Disassembly

Refer to **Figure 56** for an exploded view of the starter motor. Depending on the problem, the starter motor can be either partially or completely disassembled. It is not necessary to remove the drive assembly if the brushes require service.

1. If the drive assembly is faulty, remove the E-ring (B, **Figure 55**) and pull the helix (A) out of the clutch gear, then remove the nylon drive gear from the helix.

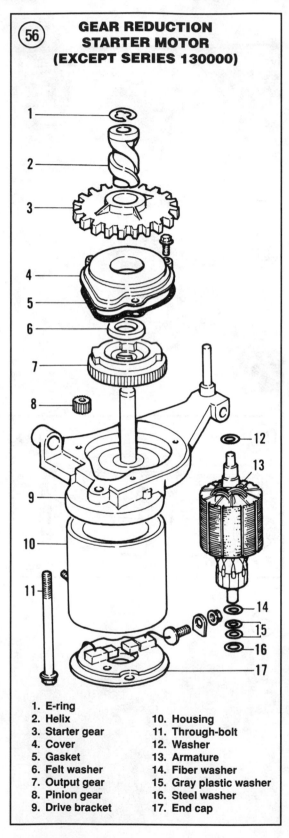

56 GEAR REDUCTION STARTER MOTOR (EXCEPT SERIES 130000)

1. E-ring
2. Helix
3. Starter gear
4. Cover
5. Gasket
6. Felt washer
7. Output gear
8. Pinion gear
9. Drive bracket
10. Housing
11. Through-bolt
12. Washer
13. Armature
14. Fiber washer
15. Gray plastic washer
16. Steel washer
17. End cap

2. Unscrew the gear cover for access to the clutch gear (A, **Figure 57**) and starter motor pinion gear (B). Remove the clutch gear and pinion gear.

3. To service the brushes and check the condition of the commutator, unscrew the through-bolts and remove the end cap. Before removing the brushes, note the position of the brushes and wires.

4. To remove the armature, the drive assembly must be removed. Due to the magnetic force of the permanent field magnets, considerable force may be required to separate the armature and housing.

5. Note the position of any washers on the armature shaft.

Inspection

1. Clean starter components but do not use cleaning solvents that will damage the armature.

2. Measure the length of each brush. Minimum allowable brush length (**Figure 58**) is 5/64 in. (2.0 mm).

3. Check strength of the brush springs. The spring must force the brush against the commutator with sufficient pressure to ensure good contact. Be sure brushes do not bind in holders.

4. Inspect the condition of the commutator (**Figure 59**). The mica between the commutator bars should be slightly undercut as shown in **Figure 47**. Undercut the mica or clean the slots between the commutator bars using a piece of hacksaw blade. After undercutting, remove burrs by sanding the commutator lightly with crocus cloth.

5. Inspect the commutator bars for discoloration. If a pair of bars is discolored, grounded armature coils are indicated.

6. Use an ohmmeter and check for continuity between the commutator bars (**Figure 48**); there should be continuity between pairs of bars. If there is no continuity between pairs of bars, the armature is open. Replace the armature.

7. Connect an ohmmeter between any commutator bar and the armature shaft (**Figure 49**); there should be no continuity. If there is continuity, the armature is grounded. Replace the armature.

NOTE
If more extensive starter motor testing is required, then the motor should be taken to a professional shop. However, this cost should be compared with the cost of a replacement starter motor.

8. Inspect the bushings in the drive plate and end cap (**Figure 60**). If the bushings are damaged or excessively worn, then the drive plate and/or end cap must be replaced; individual bushings are not available.

Reassembly

1. Apply a small amount of SAE 20 oil on bushings.

2. Install the fiber washer (B, **Figure 61**) and the steel washer (C) on the end of armature shaft with

needed number of gray plastic washers (A) between the fiber washer and steel washer so the combined height of the washers is 0.200-0.225 in. (5.08-5.71 mm) as shown in **Figure 62**.

3. Install the armature in the starter housing.

4. Align the notches and bosses on the drive plate, housing and end cap (**Figure 63** and **64**) during assembly.

5. When installing end cap on armature, a piece of manual rewind starter spring can be modified to hold the brushes in as shown in **Figure 65** to fit the brushes on the commutator.

6. Note location of wave washer (B, **Figure 66**), gray plastic washer (A) and steel washer (C) on armature shaft.

7. With the motor assembled, but before installing the starter drive, check the end play of the armature shaft. There should be a slight amount of end play. If end play exceeds 0.025 in. (0.63 mm), disassemble motor and install another plastic washer (A, **Figure 66**) at drive end of armature shaft. If end play is less than 0.005 in. (0.13 mm), remove washer. The armature should rotate without binding, although magnetic force will inhibit rotation.

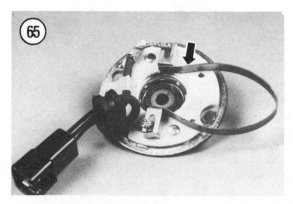

8. When assembling starter drive, place some gear lubricant, such as Lubriplate, on clutch gear contact surface of drive plate (**Figure 67**). Place about 3/4 ounce of gear lubricant in contact area of pinion and clutch gear (**Figure 68**). Apply a small amount of light oil to felt washer (**Figure 68**). The hub side of nylon starter gear (**Figure 69**) must be towards the end of the shaft.

Gear Reduction Starter Motor Used on Model Series 130000

Model series 130000 may be equipped with the gear reduction electric starter motor shown in the exploded view in **Figure 70**.

The recommended battery size for use with these starter motors is 12 amp-hour if ambient temperature is warm and 20 amp-hour or more if ambient temperature is cold.

Testing

1. If the starter motor runs, but the engine does not turn, check the starter drive mechanism. The flywheel ring gear teeth may be worn or the starter motor drive may be broken or stuck. The drive gear should slide freely on the helix.

> *NOTE*
> *Do not lubricate the drive assembly. The starter drive is designed for dry operation.*

> *NOTE*
> *To replace a worn or damaged flywheel ring gear, drill out the retaining rivets using a 3/16 in. drill bit. Attach the new ring gear using screws provided with the new ring gear.*

2. If the starter motor will not turn the engine or labors excessively, and the battery and starter switch are good, remove and inspect the starter motor.

Disassembly

Refer to **Figure 70** for an exploded view of starter motor. Depending on the problem, the starter motor

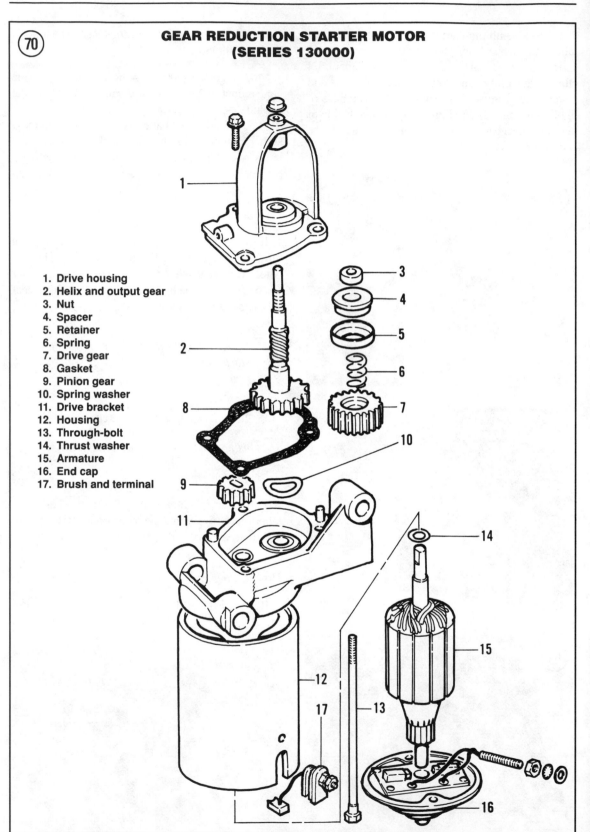

**GEAR REDUCTION STARTER MOTOR
(SERIES 130000)**

1. Drive housing
2. Helix and output gear
3. Nut
4. Spacer
5. Retainer
6. Spring
7. Drive gear
8. Gasket
9. Pinion gear
10. Spring washer
11. Drive bracket
12. Housing
13. Through-bolt
14. Thrust washer
15. Armature
16. End cap
17. Brush and terminal

can be either partially or completely disassembled. It is not necessary to remove the drive assembly if the brushes require service.

1. The drive components (2 through 7, **Figure 70**) are available only as a unit assembly.

2. Secure drive gear (7) and unscrew nut (3) to disassemble drive unit.

3. Unscrew drive housing (1) screws for access to pinion gear (9).

4. Before disassembling the motor, make marks on the drive bracket, housing and end cap so they can be reassembled in their original positions.

5. To service the brushes and check the condition of the commutator, unscrew the through-bolts and remove the end cap. Before removing the brushes, note the position of the brushes and wires.

6. To remove the armature, the drive assembly must be removed. Due to the magnetic force of the permanent field magnets, considerable force may be required to separate the armature and housing.

7. Note the position of any spacers on the armature shaft.

Inspection

1. Clean starter components but do not use cleaning solvents that will damage the armature.

2. Measure the length of each brush. Minimum allowable brush length is 1/4 in. (6.4 mm).

3. Check strength of the brush springs. The spring must force the brush against the commutator with sufficient pressure to ensure good contact. Be sure brushes do not bind in holders.

4. Inspect the condition of the commutator. The mica between the commutator bars should be slightly undercut as shown in **Figure 47**. Undercut the mica or clean the slots between the commutator bars using a piece of hacksaw blade. After undercutting, remove burrs by sanding the commutator lightly with crocus cloth.

5. Inspect the commutator bars for discoloration. If a pair of bars is discolored, grounded armature coils are indicated.

6. Use an ohmmeter and check for continuity between the commutator bars (**Figure 48**); there should be continuity between pairs of bars. If there is no continuity between pairs of bars, the armature is open. Replace the armature.

7. Connect an ohmmeter between any commutator bar and the armature shaft (**Figure 49**); there should be no continuity. If there is continuity, the armature is grounded. Replace the armature.

NOTE
If more extensive starter motor testing is required, then the motor should be taken to a professional shop. However, this cost should be compared with the cost of a replacement starter motor.

8. Inspect the bushings in the drive plate and end cap. If the bushings are damaged or excessively worn, then the drive plate and/or end cap must be replaced; individual bushings are not available.

Reassembly

1. Apply a small amount of SAE 20 oil on bushings.

2. Align the match marks on the drive bracket, housing and end cap during assembly.

3. Install the armature in the starter housing.

4. When installing end cap on armature, a piece of manual rewind starter spring can be modified to hold the brushes in as shown in **Figure 65** to fit the brushes on the commutator.

5. After assembling motor portion of starter, rotate armature. The armature should rotate without binding, although magnetic force will inhibit rotation.

6. When assembling starter drive, place some gear lubricant, such as Lubriplate, on pinion gear (9, **Figure 70**) and output gear (2)—*do not* lubricate the helix.

CHAPTER TEN

GENERAL INSPECTION AND REPAIR TECHNIQUES

FAILURE ANALYSIS

All mechanics hate to repeat a job. To a professional mechanic, repeating a job means lost money and a blemished reputation, either of which hurts business. To a do-it-yourselfer, repeating a job means frustration, money wasted on parts and possibly turning the work over to a professional shop.

The cause for most engine failures is usually easily identified and fixed. The trap that some mechanics fall into is overlooking or misidentifying the primary cause for engine failure or malfunction. It is often easy to merely replace parts rather than taking the time to inspect parts for clues that will identify the cause for failure. Not determining and correcting the primary cause will result in another repair job, often replacing the very parts that were just installed. Failure analysis is detective work that pays off in a long-lasting repair job.

Most small-engine failures are due to abuse and neglect as exemplified by the three leading causes of engine failure: abrasive grit, lack of lubrication and overheating. All of the foregoing are usually caused by improper maintenance. Small engines often operate in a harsh environment and receive minimal service. Knowing the engine's operating conditions as well as its service and repair history can provide clues to the cause for the engine failure and prevent future problems.

NOTE
Be sure any engine-driven equipment is operating properly. Damaged or improperly adjusted equipment that is driven by the engine (such as a loose lawn mower blade) can affect engine operation or cause engine damage.

CAUTION
Exercise caution when operating engine-driven equipment. Safety devices must be operable except as specified by the manufacturer for troubleshooting purposes.

Presuming that troubleshooting has determined that an internal engine problem exists, learn as much

as possible before undertaking engine repair. If possible, operate the engine and note any symptoms such as engine smoke, excessive vibration and abnormal engine noise. Before removing the engine from the equipment, look for loose mounting fasteners. Look for clues during disassembly, such as missing or maladjusted parts. Inspect parts before and after cleaning. Before cleaning, look for and identify any grit or debris in the engine. After cleaning, look for discoloration and scoring, then measure the parts and compare dimensions with the manufacturer's specifications.

Some major problem areas and their effect on engine parts are discussed in the following sections.

Abrasive Grit

Particles that can cause engine wear are defined as abrasive grit. Grit can be made of dirt, sand, coal dust, cement dust or any other abrasive particle. Many small engines operate in environments in which abrasive grit is present, making the engine particularly vulnerable to the entrance of grit. Abrasive grit causes premature wear which results in symptoms of hard starting, loss of power, high oil consumption and oily exhaust smoke.

Grit generally enters the engine either through the intake system or through the oil fill hole. A dirty air cleaner element or poorly fitting air cleaner element is generally responsible for grit entering the intake system. Not cleaning around the oil fill hole before adding oil to the engine or a poorly fitting oil fill tube will allow grit to contaminate the engine oil. Grit can also enter the engine due to poorly fitting oil seals or gaskets.

Because grit can contaminate both the air and oil in an engine, all wear surfaces in an engine can be damaged. Look for signs of wear due to grit on the following components:

1. *Intake system*—grit-blasting produces a dull finish on passages. The carburetor throttle shaft bearing area may be excessively worn.

2. *Valves*—a groove will form on the valve face (**Figure 1**) and the valve guide and valve stem will be worn (**Figure 2**). Excessive valve stem wear creates a ridge that can be detected by running a fingernail along the stem.

3. *Piston and piston rings*—heavily scratched piston and piston rings (**Figure 3**). Worn piston rings will have excessive piston ring end gaps. The oil control ring face will be worn flat. Compare the worn oil control ring shown on the left in **Figure 4**; a new oil control ring is on the right. Dirty oil caused the wear.

4. *Cylinder bore*—the cross-hatch pattern will be worn away and a ridge will form at the top of the cylinder bore.

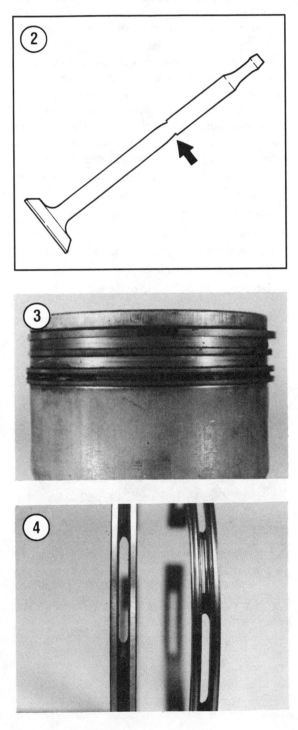

10

5. *Connecting rod*—the big-end bearing surface will have a dull finish.

6. *Crankshaft*—one or more journals will be scored. Note the crankpin journal shown in **Figure 5**.

7. *Camshaft*—the journals and lobes will be scored, as well as the wear surfaces on the tappets.

Note that grit may be embedded in softer metals such as the aluminum of the connecting rod and crankcase bearing surfaces. If the rod or bushing is not replaced, then the new crankshaft will be damaged again.

Another cause of engine damage due to abrasive grit is a poor cleaning procedure during an engine overhaul. Particles produced during machining and not removed before assembling the engine can damage the engine when it runs. Parts can be contaminated if handled with greasy hands or if stored in a dirty environment.

Insufficient Lubrication

Engine oil lubricates and cools engine parts. Insufficient oil in the crankcase or poor quality oil can lead to scoring or discoloration of engine parts. Insufficient lubrication can be a result of:

1. Low oil level.

2. Wrong oil viscosity.

3. Engine running at a high operating angle.

4. Fuel entering crankcase and diluting oil.

5. Overfilling (the splash lubrication device cannot operate effectively).

Insufficient lubrication is characterized by the discoloration and scoring of engine parts. The temperature of rotating parts that touch becomes excessive and aluminum parts often melt. The aluminum is transferred to the contacting part, such as metal transfer from the connecting rod to the crankshaft crankpin (shown in **Figure 5**), or from the main bearing to the crankshaft journal (shown in **Figure 6**). The bearing surface becomes scored and, in some cases, seizure occurs, which can result in broken parts, such as the broken connecting rod shown in **Figure 7**. Burnt oil may also be found in localized areas where excessive heat is generated by moving parts.

> *NOTE*
> *The area near the crankshaft crankpin may be blue due to a heat treating process used during manufacture and should*

not be misidentified as a damaged crankpin.

Overheating

Overheating is a condition that is caused by either insufficient external cooling or excessive temperature in the cylinder. Insufficient external cooling is generally a result of debris in the cylinder fins, missing shrouds or poor ventilation around the engine. Excessive temperature in the cylinder is usually caused by a lean air:fuel carburetor mixture setting. If improperly adjusted, carburetors with adjustable mixture screws may provide a lean mixture that is harmful to engine operation. Nonadjustable carburetors may provide a lean mixture if dirty.

Some characteristics of an overheated engine are:

1. Loss of power.

2. High oil consumption.

3. Hot spots on the cylinder bore.

4. Cylinder head mounting surface discolored.

5. Exhaust valve seat loose.

6. Tar-like oil in the bottom of the engine.

Overspeeding

Engines are designed to operate reliably up to a specified upper engine speed. If the specified engine speed limit is exceeded, physical forces may exceed the design limits of the engine components and failure will result. The most common component failure is breakage of the connecting rod just below the rod small end.

Overspeeding is identified by a lack of other indications for engine failure, such as overheating or scoring. An obvious cause for overspeeding is an altered or malfunctioning governor system.

Breakage

An engine failure may be due to components that have failed due to structural faults. In these instances, attempt to determine the cause for the failure. If the engine had been previously repaired or serviced, did a mistake cause the part to fail. For instance, applying an incorrect bolt torque or cracking the flywheel during removal can cause parts failure. If the engine had not been serviced previously, a manufacturing flaw may have caused failure (check for the availability of a redesigned part).

When checking broken parts, be sure to check the condition of associated parts that may have been struck or otherwise damaged. Check all parts that may have contributed to the breakage. A chain of events may have occurred that caused the broken part, but the prime cause may not be apparent at first.

Another cause of breakage is vibration. Single-cylinder engines are particularly prone to vibrate, but the manufacturer accommodates the effects of vibration in the engine design. If, however, the engine is not securely mounted, excessive vibration

can loosen and possibly break parts. Look for loose mounting bolts, elongated mounting holes and a polished mounting surface, any of which will indicate that the engine was not securely mounted during operation.

PRECISION MEASUREMENTS

This section covers precision measuring tools, how to use them and specific measuring applications. Note that a list of tools that are commonly required for engine service and overhaul is provided in Chapter One.

Precision Measuring Tools

The ability to measure engine components accurately is essential to accomplish successful engine overhauls. Although engine overhauls can be performed by eyeballing and an educated guess, the results are hit-or-miss, and usually a costly miss. Engines are built to close tolerances, and it is essential that the mechanic be equipped with the tools necessary to obtain consistent and accurate measurements to determine which engine components can be reused reliably and which components should be replaced.

Each type of measuring tool is designed to measure a dimension with a certain degree of accuracy. When selecting the measuring tool, be sure it provides the proper degree of accuracy. For instance, a ruler is inappropriate for measuring a crankshaft journal and a micrometer is overkill when measuring rewind starter rope diameter.

Precision measuring tools are available in varying degrees of quality and price, and in this case, the price usually reflects the quality. However, adequate measuring tools are available at a reasonable price for small engine work. A professional mechanic will usually choose high quality tools that will provide the best service life.

As with other tools, precision measuring tools will provide their best service life if cared for properly. Particular attention must be paid to the care of precision measuring tools, in part due to the cost of replacement, but more importantly because the tool may read inaccurately. Dropping, hitting or improper use can damage the tool resulting in measurements that may be as small as one thousand of an inch off, but the inaccuracy may be sufficient to

10

affect the reuse or replacement of expensive parts. A mechanic should keep in mind the condition of the measuring tool and verify any measurement by using another measuring tool if the measurement appears questionable. A standard gauge of a specific dimension is often used to check the accuracy of precision tools.

A key ingredient when measuring an object accurately is the person performing the measurement. Highly accurate measurements are only possible if the mechanic possesses a "feel" for using the measuring tool. The most sensitive portion of the hand is the fingertips. Heavy-handed use of measuring tools will produce less accurate measurements than if the tool is grasped gently by the fingertips so the point at which the tool contacts the object can be readily felt. The feel acquired when using a tool not only produces more accurate measurements, but there is less chance of damaging the tool's measuring surfaces.

Refer to the following sections for information on specific precision measuring tools.

Dial and Vernier Calipers

Precision measurements can be taken using good quality, direct reading calipers. Calipers are useful in that quick measurements are possible for a variety of situations. Inside and outside dimensions can be measured as well as determining depths. Most calipers can measure dimensions of 6 in. or greater.

Direct reading calipers are available either in dial or Vernier versions (**Figure 8**). Dial calipers are equipped with a calibrated dial that reads in thousands of an inch (or metric equivalent) which provides convenient reading. Vernier calipers have scales marked on the fixed and movable pieces that must be compared to determine the reading. For instance, to read the measurement shown in **Figure 9**, note that the scale on the movable piece is graduated in increments of 0.025 in. and the fixed scale is marked in thousandths. The first number established is determined by the location of the "0" line on the fixed scale in relation to the first line to the left on the movable scale. In this case the number is 0.150 in. To determine the next number, note which of the lines on the fixed scale is aligned with a mark on the movable scale (or is most nearly aligned). The number of the mark on the fixed scale is the number of thousandths, in this case 17, that is added to the first

number. In this example, adding 0.017 to 0.150 results in a measurement of 0.167 in. Note that in **Figure 9** the caliper is also calibrated to read metric dimensions; the ability to read both U.S. and metric dimensions is something to consider when purchasing a Vernier caliper.

Vernier and dial calipers are handy, versatile measuring tools, although they are not quite as accurate as a micrometer.

Micrometer

The micrometer is the measuring device most used when precision measurement is required. Micrometers are available in a variety of shapes and sizes to measure both inside and outside dimensions, although outside micrometers are most often used.

The actual measuring device of a micrometer is based on the rotation of a precision-machined screw thread that travels a specified distance (usually 0.025 in.) for each complete rotation. Dividing the distance the screw travels in each rotation into units (thousandths) provides a means to measure a dimension.

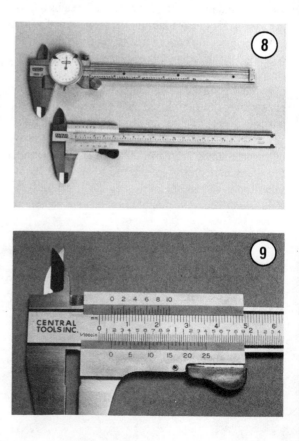

Figure 10 shows the parts of a typical micrometer. The part being measured is placed between the anvil and spindle, then the thimble is rotated so the contact surfaces of the anvil and spindle just contact the part. Acquiring a feel when using the micrometer is essential to obtain an accurate measurement. Depending on the quality of the micrometer and the ability of the user, measurements of ten thousandths inch is possible, although measurements requiring that degree of accuracy are best performed with a Vernier micrometer.

To read a micrometer, note the nearest numbered line to the left of the thimble. The number denotes hundredths. In the example shown in **Figure 11** the nearest tenths line is 4, so the measurement is at least 0.4 in. Then note the number of lines between the numbered line (4) and the edge of the thimble, in this example there are three lines. Each line equals 0.025 in., so 3 × 0.025 in. equals 0.075 in., which added to 0.4 equals 0.475 in. Now note which horizontal line on the thimble is most nearly aligned with the reference line on the sleeve. In this example the 18 line is aligned, so 0.018 in. is added to the previously read 0.475 in. to equal the measured dimension of 0.493 in.

Care should be exercised in using and storing a micrometer. Rough use can affect the accuracy of a micrometer. The micrometer's accuracy should be checked periodically or any time a reading is suspect. Micrometers can be zeroed by adjusting the position of the anvil or sleeve.

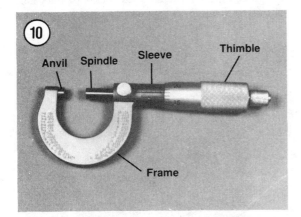

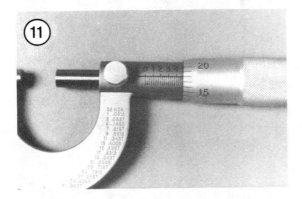

Dial Indicator

A dial indicator or gauge is a precision measuring tool that is generally used to measure the travel or out-of-roundness of a part. Measuring crankshaft or camshaft end play is a typical use for a dial indicator (**Figure 12**). A consideration when purchasing a dial indicator is whether apparatus is included for securing the dial indicator during measuring.

10

> *NOTE*
> *When positioning the dial indicator for a reading, the dial indicator must be securely mounted to prevent any deflection in the set-up apparatus from creating a false reading.*

Dial indicators are available to measure a variety of ranges and in various graduations. A special type of dial indicator is available to measure cylinder bore taper and out-of-roundness, but a cylinder bore dial gauge is expensive and generally used only by a professional shop.

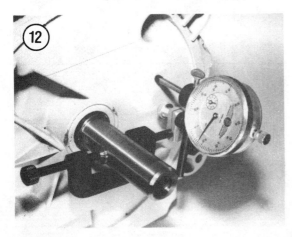

Telescoping Gauges

A telescoping gauge (sometimes called a snap gauge) is used to measure hole diameters. The telescoping gauge (**Figure 13**) does not have a scale gauge for direct reading. Thus an outside micrometer is required in conjunction with the telescoping gauge to determine bore dimensions.

Particular attention must be taken when using a telescoping gauge to make sure the true diameter is measured and the gauge is not off center or cocked. Several measurements should be taken to be sure the true measurement is obtained.

Small Hole Gauges

Small hole gauges are used to measure hole diameters, such as valve guides, or the widths of grooves or slots (**Figure 14**). An outside micrometer must be used together with the small hole gauge to determine the measured dimension.

Go-No Go Gauges

These types of gauges are used to quickly and accurately determine if a given hole is within the specifications specified by the manufacturer. For instance, the manufacturer may state that if the gauge will fit into a particular hole, then the hole is too large and a bushing must be installed to return the hole to the desired specification. Go-no go gauges are generally available only from the engine or equipment manufacturer.

REPAIR TECHNIQUES

Removing Frozen Nuts and Screws

Removing nuts and screws that are frozen due to rust can be frustrating and time consuming. But the problem can be lessened if excessive force is not used when initially trying to turn the nut or screw. A broken screw or damaged threads usually result if more than normal force is placed on the wrench.

Before turning a rusty nut or screw, apply a penetrating oil such as Liquid Wrench or WD-40 (available at hardware or auto supply stores). Apply it liberally and let it penetrate for 10-15 minutes. Tap the fastener several times with a small hammer; do not hit it hard enough to cause damage. Reapply the penetrating oil if necessary.

Particular care should be taken when removing a frozen nut on a stud because removal may break the stud. Observe the end of the stud when attempting

to turn the nut to be sure the nut is turning and the stud is not. If penetrating oil will not loosen the nut, a nut splitter tool (**Figure 15**) can be used to separate the nut from the stud.

For frozen screws, apply penetrating oil as previously described, then insert a screwdriver in the slot and rap the top of the screwdriver with a hammer. This loosens the rust so the screw can be removed in the normal way. If the screw head is disfigured, grip the head with locking pliers and twist the screw out.

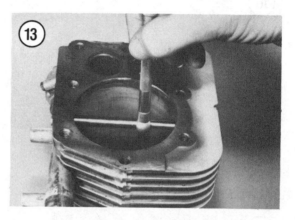

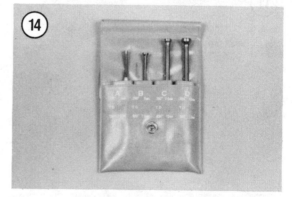

Repairing Damaged Threads

Fastener threads can be damaged for a variety of reasons, and in some cases, restoring the threads is required.

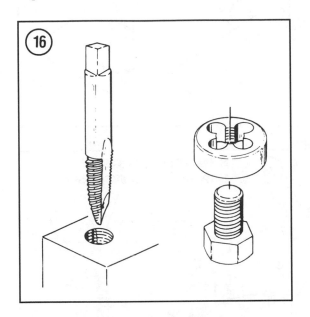

NOTE
Be sure to identify the thread size and type (U.S. or metric) before attempting to restore the threads. The only positive method of identification is to use a screw pitch gauge or known fastener.

Often the threads can be cleaned by running a tap (for internal threads) or die (for external threads) through the threads. See **Figure 16**. To clean or repair spark plug threads, a spark plug tap or thread chaser can be used.

If an internal thread is damaged, it may be necessary to install a thread repair insert (**Figure 17**). Thread repair inserts are available in a wide variety of U.S. and metric thread sizes at auto supply stores and some hardware stores. Note that a specific size drill bit must be used, which must be purchased separately. To install a typical thread repair insert, proceed as follows:

1. Drill out the old threads using the drill bit recommended for the thread size being repaired (**Figure 18**). Be sure the hole is straight and the centerline of the hole is not moved while drilling.

2. Cut new threads in the hole using the tap provided in the kit (**Figure 19**). This is a special tap that cuts threads to fit the outer threads on the thread repair insert.

3. Turn the thread repair insert into the hole (**Figure 20**) using the special tool until the top of the insert is a quarter to one-half turn below the surface (**Figure 21**).

4. Snap off the insert tang by pushing down on the tang; don't attempt to twist off the tang.

10

Removing Broken Screws or Bolts

When the head breaks off of a screw or bolt, several methods are possible for removing the remaining portion.

If a large portion of the screw or bolt projects out, try gripping it with locking pliers. If the projecting portion is too small, file it to fit a wrench or cut a slot in it to fit a screwdriver as shown in **Figure 22**.

If the head breaks off flush, use a screw extractor using the following procedure while referring to **Figure 23**.

1. Center punch the exact center of the remaining portion of the screw or bolt.
2. Drill a small hole in the screw.
3. Tap the screw extractor into the hole.
4. Back the screw out with a wrench on the extractor.

If the preceding procedures are unsuccessful, contact a professional shop. A technique known as electric discharge milling (EDM) is available at some machine shops to remove broken screws and studs, but be sure to get an estimate first.

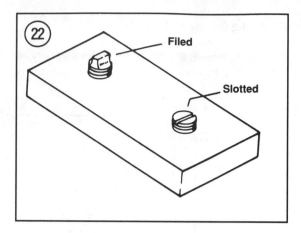

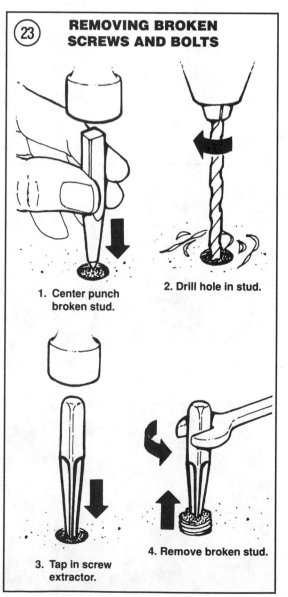

REMOVING BROKEN
SCREWS AND BOLTS

1. Center punch broken stud.

2. Drill hole in stud.

3. Tap in screw extractor.

4. Remove broken stud.

ENGINE OVERHAUL

The following sections provide disassembly, inspection and reassembly information for the major engine components of a basic engine.

Due to the many variations of Briggs & Stratton engines, it is not possible to address all possibilities when outlining disassembly and reassembly steps. The mechanic must take a thoughtful approach and address any additional steps necessary to service a particular engine.

In most cases, the engine must be removed from the equipment before undertaking the procedure. In some cases, however, the job may be performed with the engine mounted on the equipment, such as cylinder head removal. Before removing the engine from the equipment, note the location of any wiring, cables or brackets.

Table 1 provides engine specifications. **Table 2** lists special tightening torques. **Table 3** and **Table 4** list general tightening torques for inch series and metric series bolts and nuts. **Tables 1-4** are located at the end of this chapter.

CAUTION
Be sure to contact the equipment manufacturer for instructions regarding the removal and installation of engine-driven components. Improper service can damage the engine and equipment. Be sure all safety devices operate correctly.

Briggs & Stratton tools, or suitable equivalent tools, may be recommended for some procedures outlined herein. The Briggs & Stratton tools are available as part of Briggs & Stratton Tool Kit 19300 (see Chapter Twelve). Good quality tools are also available from small engine parts suppliers. Be careful when substituting a "home-made" tool for a recommended tool. Although time and money may be saved if an existing or fabricated tool can be made to work, consider the possibilities if the tool does not work properly. If the substitute tool damages the engine, the cost to repair the damage may exceed the cost of the recommended tool.

NOTE
Some procedures may require that work be performed by a professional shop. Be sure to get an estimate, then compare it with the cost of a new or rebuilt engine or shortblock (a basic engine assembly).

MUFFLER

In most cases, the muffler is secured to the engine by screws or it is screwed directly into the engine. In some applications, the muffler is connected to the engine by a pipe.

Mufflers that are secured by screws can be removed after bending back the locking tabs (**Figure 1**) and unscrewing the retaining screws.

11

If the muffler is screwed into the engine (**Figure 2**), grasp the muffler with a suitable tool and unscrew the muffler. Note that a lock ring (**Figure 3**) is used to lock the muffler in place on some engines. The lock ring must be loosened before unscrewing the muffler. If the muffler body collapses due to rust, it may be necessary to cut away the muffler body so the threaded pipe can be grasped.

If the muffler is significantly damaged due to rust, it should be replaced.

CRANKCASE BREATHER

The crankcase breather vents gases in the crankcase to the carburetor or air cleaner, which provides a negative pressure in the crankcase, if the breather is operating properly. Oil may be forced past the piston rings, oil seals and gaskets if the breather malfunctions.

The crankcase breather is located on the side of the engine (**Figure 4**) and covers the valve chamber. Unscrew the retaining screws to remove the breather.

After cleaning the breather in solvent, be sure the holes in the breather body are open. Check the gap between the fiber valve and the breather body as shown in **Figure 5**. If a 0.045 in. (1.14 mm) wire gauge can be inserted, replace the breather. Do not apply pressure against the fiber disc.

Do not attempt to disassemble the breather; it is available only as a unit assembly.

FLYWHEEL
(ALL MODELS EXCEPT QUANTUM MODEL SERIES 100700, 121000, 122000, 124000 AND 126000)

The flywheel is secured to the crankshaft by either a retaining nut or the starter clutch on engines equipped with a rewind starter on the blower housing. The flywheel on later series 280000 engines is secured by a screw. A separate fan is attached to the flywheel on some larger engines.

Removal

1. Disconnect the spark plug wire and properly ground it to the engine.
2. Remove the blower housing and any other components so the flywheel is accessible.

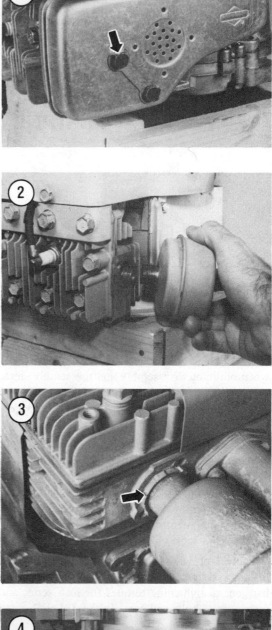

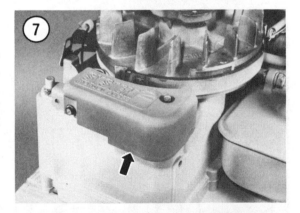

3. Remove the screen from the flywheel or from the starter clutch (**Figure 6**).

4. If equipped with a flywheel brake, remove the cover (**Figure 7**) and disconnect the outer end of the brake spring from its anchor (A, **Figure 8**).

5. Place the Briggs & Stratton or aftermarket flywheel holder on the flywheel (**Figure 9**). The tool should not engage fins above the magnets.

NOTE
*In some instances, particularly on larger engines, a strap wrench that grips the periphery of the flywheel may be needed if a flywheel holder is not available. If the flywheel has fins, **do not** attempt to hold the flywheel by inserting a tool between the fins.*

6. If equipped with a starter clutch, place the Briggs & Stratton or aftermarket starter clutch tool on the starter clutch (**Figure 9**).

7. While holding the flywheel, unscrew the starter clutch or flywheel retaining nut or screw.

NOTE
*If a starter clutch wrench is not available, it is possible to loosen the starter clutch using a large pipe wrench or other suitable tool to grip the ears on the clutch (**Figure 10**).*

8. Remove the fan if the engine is equipped with a separate fan.

9. If the engine is equipped with a flywheel retaining nut, install the nut so it covers the top threads on the crankshaft as shown in **Figure 11**. If equipped with a starter clutch, obtain a suitable size nut and thread it onto the crankshaft so it covers the top threads on

11

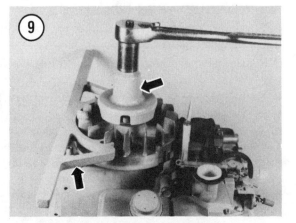

the crankshaft. If a flywheel retaining screw is used, install the screw into the crankshaft, but allow sufficient space so the flywheel can move upwards.

10. Install a flywheel puller as shown in **Figure 11** so the puller screws engage the two holes adjacent to the flywheel hub.

> *NOTE*
> *The puller holes in the flywheel may not be threaded. The flywheel puller screws must be self-tapping or threads must be cut into the holes using a 1/4 × 20 tap.*

> *CAUTION*
> *Briggs & Stratton does not recommend the use of a flywheel knocker to break the flywheel loose from the crankshaft. The tool can damage the crankshaft and internal engine parts.*

> *WARNING*
> *Do not strike the flywheel. The flywheel must be replaced if the flywheel is cracked or any fins are damaged.*

11. Rotate the puller nuts evenly until the flywheel pops free.

12. Remove the flywheel and the flywheel key. If additional engine work is planned, it is a good practice to wrap the crankshaft threads with tape to prevent damage to the threads.

Inspection

1. Inspect the flywheel and the crankshaft. The tapered portion of the flywheel and crankshaft must be clean and smooth with no damage due to movement between the flywheel and crankshaft.

2. Check the fit of the flywheel on the crankshaft. There should be no looseness or wobbling.

3. Replace the flywheel if any cracks are evident or any fins are broken.

4. Be sure the keyways in the crankshaft and flywheel are not damaged or worn.

5. Inspect the flywheel key. If any indications of shearing (**Figure 12**) are apparent, then the key must be replaced. The key is made of aluminum to prevent or lessen the possibility of crankshaft damage if the crankshaft suddenly stops, such as when a lawn mower blade strikes an obstruction.

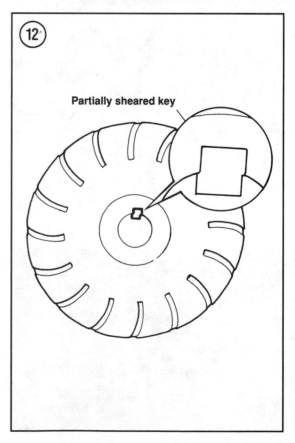

Partially sheared key

CAUTION
A steel key must not be used under any circumstances.

Installation

When installing the flywheel, note that the washer between the flywheel and starter clutch (**Figure 13**)

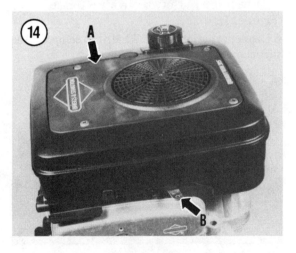

or retaining nut may be either a flat washer or a Belleville washer, which has a rounded cross-section.

1. Install the Belleville washer so the cupped side is towards the flywheel.
2. Install the flywheel and flywheel key.
3. Place the flywheel holder tool on the flywheel (**Figure 9**).
4. Tighten the starter clutch, retaining nut or screw to the torque shown in **Table 2**.
5. Connect the flywheel brake spring (**Figure 8**) if so equipped.
6. Install the screen and blower housing.

FLYWHEEL (QUANTUM MODEL SERIES 100700)

The flywheel is secured to the crankshaft by a retaining nut. A separate fan is attached to the flywheel.

Removal

1. Disconnect the spark plug wire and properly ground it to the engine.
2. Remove the engine top cover (A, **Figure 14**).
3. Remove the screen from the fan.
4. Pull and tie the flywheel brake lever (B, **Figure 14**) so the flywheel brake pad is disengaged from the flywheel.
5. Place the Briggs & Stratton or aftermarket flywheel holder on the flywheel as shown in **Figure 15** (the fuel tank was removed for illustrative purposes).

NOTE
If the flywheel holder tool is not available, a strap wrench that grips the periphery of the flywheel can be used if additional parts are removed so the wrench can be installed.

6. While holding the flywheel, unscrew the flywheel retaining nut.

CAUTION
Briggs & Stratton does not recommend the use of a flywheel knocker to break the flywheel loose from the crankshaft. The tool can damage the crankshaft and internal engine parts.

WARNING
Do not strike the flywheel. The flywheel must be replaced if the flywheel is cracked or any fins are damaged.

7. Remove the washer and fan.

8. Install the flywheel retaining nut (A, **Figure 16**) so it covers the top threads on the crankshaft.

9. Install a flywheel puller (B) as shown in **Figure 16** so the puller screws engage the two holes adjacent to the flywheel hub.

NOTE
The puller holes in the flywheel may not be threaded. The flywheel puller screws must be self-tapping or threads must be cut into the holes using a 1/4 × 20 tap.

10. Rotate the puller nuts evenly until the flywheel pops free.

11. Remove the flywheel and the flywheel key. If additional engine work is planned, it is a good practice to wrap the crankshaft threads with tape to prevent damage to the threads.

Inspection

1. Inspect the flywheel and the crankshaft. The tapered portion of the flywheel and crankshaft must be clean and smooth with no damage due to movement between the flywheel and crankshaft.

2. Check the fit of the flywheel on the crankshaft. There should be no looseness or wobbling. Replace the flywheel if any cracks are evident. Be sure the keyways in the crankshaft and flywheel are not damaged or worn.

3. Inspect the flywheel key. If any indications of shearing (**Figure 12**) are apparent, then the key must be replaced. The key is made of aluminum to prevent or lessen the possibility of crankshaft damage if the crankshaft suddenly stops, such as when a lawn mower blade strikes an obstruction.

CAUTION
A steel key must not be used under any circumstances.

Installation

1. Install the flywheel onto the crankshaft and align keyway.

2. Insert the flywheel key in the keyway.

3. Install the washer and fan onto flywheel.

4. Place the flywheel holder tool on the flywheel.

5. Tighten the flywheel retaining nut to 55 ft.-lb. (75 N•m).

6. Install the fan screen and engine top cover.

FLYWHEEL
(QUANTUM MODEL SERIES 121000, 122000, 124000 AND 126000)

The flywheel is secured to the crankshaft by a retaining nut. A separate fan is attached to the flywheel.

Removal

1. Disconnect the spark plug wire and properly ground it to the engine.

2. Remove the blower housing with the rewind starter as outlined in Chapter Eight.

3. Detach the end of the flywheel brake spring (**Figure 17**).

4. Dismount the ignition coil and, if so equipped, the alternator stator.

5. Hold the flywheel with a flywheel holder tool or a strap wrench and unscrew the flywheel retaining nut (B, **Figure 18**).

NOTE
***Do not** attempt to hold the flywheel by inserting a tool between the fins.*

CAUTION
Briggs & Stratton does not recommend the use of a flywheel knocker to break the flywheel loose from the crankshaft. The tool can damage the crankshaft and internal engine parts.

WARNING
Do not strike the flywheel. The flywheel must be replaced if the flywheel is cracked or any fins are damaged.

6. Remove the starter cup (A, **Figure 18**).

7. Install the nut (A, **Figure 19**) so it covers the top threads on the crankshaft.

8. Install a flywheel puller (B, **Figure 19**) so the puller screws engage the two holes adjacent to the flywheel hub.

NOTE
The puller holes in the flywheel may not be threaded. The flywheel puller screws must be self-tapping or threads must be cut into the holes using a 1/4 × 20 tap.

9. Rotate the puller nuts evenly until the flywheel pops free.

10. Remove the flywheel and the flywheel key. If additional engine work is planned, it is a good practice to wrap the crankshaft threads with tape to prevent damage to the threads.

Inspection

1. Inspect the flywheel and the crankshaft. The tapered portion of the flywheel and crankshaft must be clean and smooth with no damage due to movement between the flywheel and crankshaft.

2. Check the fit of the flywheel on the crankshaft. There should be no looseness or wobbling. Replace the flywheel if any cracks are evident or any fins are broken. Be sure the keyways in the crankshaft and flywheel are not damaged or worn.

3. Inspect the flywheel key. If any indications of shearing (**Figure 12**) are apparent, then the key must be replaced. The key is made of aluminum to prevent or lessen the possibility of crankshaft damage if the crankshaft suddenly stops, such as when a lawn mower blade strikes an obstruction.

CAUTION
A steel key must not be used under any circumstances.

Installation

1. Install the flywheel onto the crankshaft and align keyway.

2. Insert the flywheel key in the keyway.

3. Install the starter cup (A, **Figure 18**) and flywheel retaining nut (B).

4. Place the flywheel holder tool on the flywheel.

5. Tighten the flywheel retaining nut to 55 ft.-lb. (75 N•m).

6. Install the ignition coil and adjust the armature air gap as outlined in Chapter Five.

7. Reconnect the flywheel brake spring (**Figure 17**).

8. Install the blower housing and rewind starter.

11

CYLINDER HEAD

Removal

To remove the cylinder head, the blower housing must be removed on most engines, as well as any brackets that will interfere with removal. On some engines, components attached to the cylinder head with a bracket must also be removed.

1. Unscrew the cylinder head retaining screws (**Figure 20**) and remove the cylinder head.

> *NOTE*
> *Some engines have three cylinder head screws that are longer than the rest of the screws. Note the location of these screws for reference when reinstalling the cylinder head.*

2. It may be necessary to tap the cylinder head to break it free from the gasket. Remove the cylinder head gasket (**Figure 21**).

Inspection/Cleaning

1. Look for black carbon tracks on the cylinder head and the top of the engine which indicate that the gasket was leaking. Evidence of leakage past the gasket may indicate that the cylinder head is warped.

2. Two methods may be used to check for a warped cylinder head and correct it. A large file can be drawn across the cylinder head surface to indicate and remove the high spots. Another method is to place the head on a flat plate, such as glass, that has dabs of valve grinding compound on it, then move the head in a figure-eight pattern on the plate. Either method can be used satisfactorily. Using a file will remove metal more quickly, but care should be used to remove no more metal than is necessary to produce a level surface.

3. Use a wooden or plastic scraper to remove carbon deposits from the cylinder head.

4. Rotate the crankshaft so the piston is at the top of the cylinder and both valves are closed, then remove carbon from the piston, valves and cylinder block. Spray a suitable solvent on hardened deposits to soften them. Be careful not to damage engine surfaces.

Installation

1. Install a new head gasket. Do not apply any type of sealer to the head gasket.

2. Apply graphite grease to the cylinder head screws before installation.

3. Except on Quantum model series 100700, 121000, 122000, 124000 and 126000, three cylinder

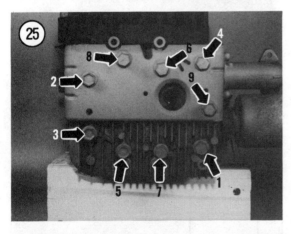

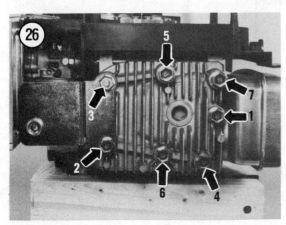

head screws are longer than the rest of the screws. Be sure the correct length screws are installed in the correct holes. Note the position of the three long screws (A, **Figure 22**) for engines with a displacement less than 15 cu. in. or (A, **Figure 23**) for engines with a displacement greater than 15 cu. in.

4. Initially tighten the cylinder head screws finger-tight. Then using a torque wrench, tighten the screws progressively in three steps to the final specified torque as follows:

   a. Tighten the cylinder head screws on engines with a displacement less than 15 cu. in. (246 cc), except Quantum model series 100700, 121000, 122000, 124000 and 126000, in the sequence shown in **Figure 24**.

   b. Tighten the cylinder head screws on engines with a displacement greater than 15 cu. in. (246 cc) in the sequence shown in **Figure 25**.

   c. Tighten the cylinder head screws on Quantum model series 100700 in the sequence shown in **Figure 26**.

   d. Tighten the cylinder head screws on Quantum model series 121000, 122000, 124000 and 126000 in the sequence shown in **Figure 27**.

   e. Tighten the cylinder head screws on engines with less than 15 cu. in. (246 cc) displacement, including Quantum engines, to specified torque of 140 in.-lb. (15.8 N•m).

   f. Tighten the cylinder head screws on engines with a displacement greater than 15 cu. in. (246 cc) to specified torque of 165 in.-lb. (18.6 N•m).

VALVE SYSTEM

The valves are located in the cylinder block portion of the engine. Each valve stem rides in a valve

11

guide machined directly in the aluminum alloy cylinder block or in a replaceable bushing. If valve service is required, refer to the following sections.

Removal

Proceed as follows to remove the valves and springs for service.

> *NOTE*
> *All component parts of each valve assembly must be kept together.*

1. Remove the cylinder head.

2. Remove components as required for access to the crankcase breather (**Figure 28**). Remove the crankcase breather.

3. Rotate the flywheel so the piston is at the top of the cylinder and both valves are closed.

4. Using a valve spring compressor, compress the valve spring (**Figure 29**).

> *NOTE*
> *Several types of valve spring compressors are available. Be sure the compressor will work on a small engine.*

> *WARNING*
> *Safety eyewear should be worn when using a valve spring compressor. A compressed spring can travel several feet if it works free of the compressor.*

5. Remove the valve spring retainer, valve and valve spring.

6. Most engines are equipped with a slotted retainer that fits in a groove on the valve (**Figure 30**). The valve end will pass through the large end of the

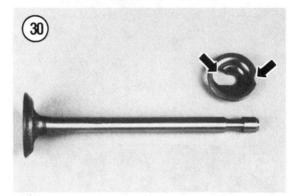

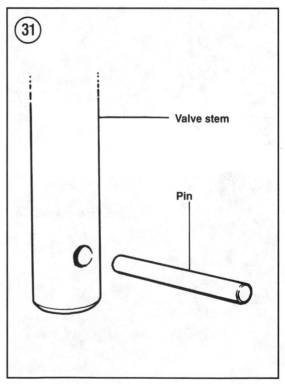

Valve stem

Pin

groove. Note that the large end of the slot is opposite the notch on the retainer edge.

NOTE
When removing a valve with a slotted retainer, position the big hole in the retainer slot over the valve stem, then pull out the valve.

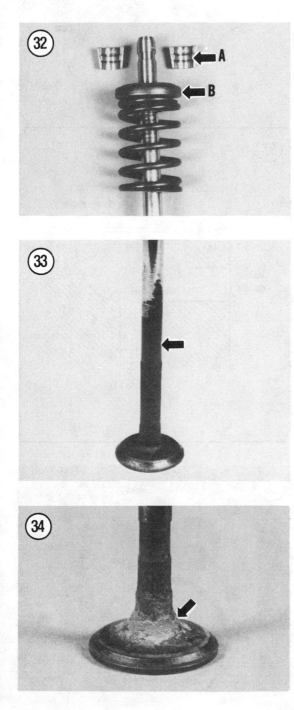

7. Some engines are equipped with a retaining pin that holds the valve spring retainer on the valve (**Figure 31**). Extract the pin to release the valve spring retainer and spring.

8. Some engines are equipped with automotive type valve spring retainer keys (A, **Figure 32**) that fit in a groove on the valve. After the valve spring is compressed, the keys can be pushed out of the groove to release the valve spring retainer and spring.

9. On some engines, a valve rotator (B, **Figure 32**) is located at the end of the exhaust valve in place of a valve spring retainer. A retaining pin or retainer keys are used to hold the rotator on the valve.

Inspection

1. Inspect the valve for damage and excessive wear. Inspect the valve before cleaning.

2. Gummy deposits on the intake valve (**Figure 33**) may indicate that the engine has run on gasoline that was stored for an extended period.

3. Hard deposits on the intake valve are due to burnt oil, while hard deposits on the exhaust valve (**Figure 34**) are due to combustion byproducts and burnt oil.

4. Moisture in the engine during storage can cause corroded or pitted valves which should be replaced.

5. Check the valve face for an irregular seating pattern. The seating ring around the face should be concentric with the valve head and equal in thickness all around the valve. If the seating pattern is irregular, the valve may be bent or the valve face or seat is damaged.

6. Remove deposits either with a wire brush or soak the valve in parts cleaner.

7. Run a fingernail down the valve stem and check for a ledge that would indicate that the valve stem is worn. Replace the valve if the valve stem is worn.

8. The valve stem must be perpendicular to the valve head. To check for a bent valve, carefully install the valve stem in a drill chuck and rotate the drill. Be sure the valve stem is centered in the drill chuck. Replace the valve if the valve head wobbles noticeably as the drill rotates.

9. Measure the valve head margin (**Figure 35**). The valve must be replaced if the margin is less than 1/64 in. (0.4 mm).

10. If the valve and valve seat (**Figure 36**) are worn, but serviceable, they can be restored by machining.

11

Take the valves and engine to a professional shop that is equipped to perform valve machine work. The valve face angle (**Figure 35**) and valve seat angle (**Figure 37**) should be 45°.

NOTE
The intake valve face angle and intake valve seat angle are 30° on some early engines.

11. Valve seat width (**Figure 37**) should be 3/64 to 1/16 in. (1.19-1.58 mm).
12. The valve seats are an insert type and may be replaced. If the valve seat is damaged to the extent that machining will not restore the seat, then a new valve seat insert must be installed. Installation should be performed by a shop equipped with the necessary tools.
13. Check the contact pattern on the valve face and valve seat. The pattern should be centered on the valve face and even all the way around. Unevenness indicates that the valve head is warped or the valve stem is bent.
14. Check for wear in the valve guides (**Figure 38**) by measuring the inside diameter at the top, middle and bottom of the guide. If the valve stem diameter is 1/4 in. (6.35 mm), the maximum allowable valve guide inside diameter is 0.266 in. (6.76 mm). If the valve stem diameter is 5/16 in. (7.94 mm), the maximum allowable valve guide inside diameter is 0.330 in. (8.38 mm). The valve rides directly in the aluminum of the engine block on some engines, while a renewable valve guide is used on other engines. In either case, if the valve guide is excessively worn or

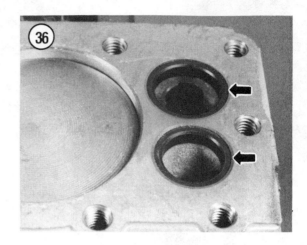

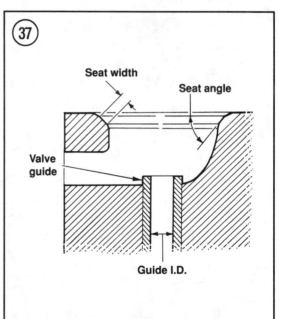

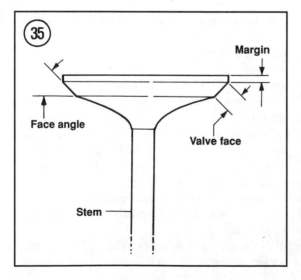

damaged, a new valve guide must be installed by a shop equipped with the necessary tools.

15. If valve machining is not necessary, the valve should be lapped against the valve seat to restore the seating surfaces.

16. Check the valve springs. The spring should be straight as shown in **Figure 39**. Some engines may be equipped with different valve springs for the intake and exhaust valves. The exhaust valve spring

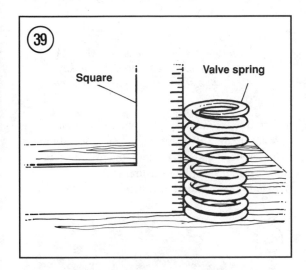

wire diameter is greater than the intake valve spring wire diameter.

17. Some engines may be equipped with a heavy duty exhaust valve or exhaust valve seat made of Cobalite. The Cobalite exhaust valve is marked on the valve head (**Figure 40**) with letters "TXS," "XS" or "PP-XS." The Cobalite exhaust valve and valve seat can be installed on all engines.

18. Some engines may be equipped with a rotator (B, **Figure 32**) on the exhaust valve. The rotator turns the valve a slight amount each time the valve opens, thereby wiping away deposits which can cause valve burning. A rotator can be installed on an engine not previously so equipped by changing the valve spring and retainer.

Valve Lapping

Valve lapping is a simple operation which can restore the valve seal without machining if the amount of wear or distortion is not too great. Lapping requires the use of lapping compound and a lapping tool (**Figure 41**). Lapping compound is available in either coarse or fine grade. Coarse compound is used first, followed by fine compound.

1. Apply small dabs of lapping compound to the valve face (**Figure 42**). Too much can fall into the valve guide and cause damage.

2. Insert the valve into the valve guide.

3. Moisten the end of the lapping tool suction cup and place it on the valve head.

4. Rotate the lapping tool back and forth between your hands several times (**Figure 43**). Lift and rotate the valve approximately 1/4 turn and repeat the lapping sequence.

11

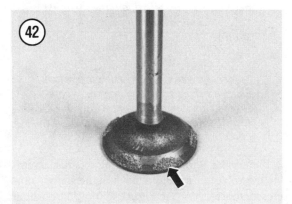

NOTE
When the grating sound lessens, reapply lapping compound.

WARNING
Do not use a drill to rotate the valve. The lapping compound may be forced out so quickly that metal-to-metal contact will occur, resulting in damage to the valve face and/or seat.

5. Clean compound from the valve and seat frequently to check progress of lapping. Lap only enough to achieve a precise seating ring around the valve head. The pattern on the valve face should be an even width as shown in **Figure 44**.

6. Closely examine the valve seat in the cylinder block. It should be smooth and even with a smooth polished seating ring.

7. After lapping has been completed, thoroughly clean the valves and seats using solvent to remove all grinding compound. Any lapping compound residue will cause rapid wear if left in the engine.

8. After the valve assemblies have been reinstalled into the engine, the valve seal should be tested. Check the seal for each valve by pouring solvent into the intake and exhaust ports. There should be no leakage past the seat. If fluid leaks past any of the seats, remove the valve and repeat the lapping procedure until there is no leakage.

Installation

1. Lubricate the valve stems before installation.

NOTE
The valve springs are identical for intake and exhaust on some engines, while others use a heavier spring (larger diameter spring wire) on the exhaust valve. Compare the springs before installing.

WARNING
Safety eyewear should be worn when using a valve spring compressor. A compressed spring can fly out with considerable force if it works free of the compressor.

2. If equipped with a slotted spring retainer, assemble the valve spring and retainer in the spring compressor tool as shown in **Figure 45** (note the position of the large hole of the retainer slot). Position the valve spring and retainer in the engine, then insert the valve so the valve stem passes through the large hole of the retainer slot. Then, push the retainer so the valve stem engages the narrow portion of the retainer slot.

3. If equipped with a spring retaining pin (**Figure 31**) or automotive type keys (A, **Figure 32**), position valve spring in engine and insert the valve so the valve stem passes through the spring. Install spring retainer pin or keys.

NOTE
If equipped with automotive keys (A, Figure 32), use grease to hold the keys in the valve stem groove during assembly.

4. Remove the valve spring compressor tool.

5. Measure the valve tappet gap before installing the cylinder head (all valve components must be installed for an accurate measurement).

6. Install the crankcase breather.

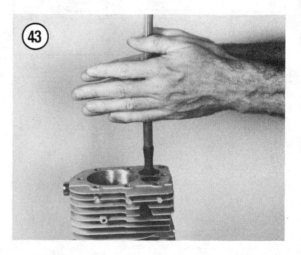

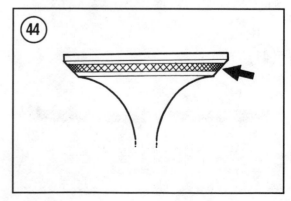

7. Install the cylinder head.

Valve Tappet Gap

The valve tappet gap should be checked whenever the valves are serviced. All valve components must be installed for an accurate measurement.

1. Turn the crankshaft until the piston is at the top of the cylinder on the compression stroke. Both valves should be closed.

NOTE
Turn crankshaft counterclockwise as viewed from pto end of crankshaft.

2. Continue turning the crankshaft counterclockwise until piston moves 1/4 in. (6 mm) down from top of cylinder. This position will place the tappets away from the compression release mechanism (if engine is so equipped) on the camshaft.

3. Measure the gap between the end of the valve stem and the tappet end for each valve using a feeler gauge (**Figure 46**).

4. The valve tappet gap for the intake valve should be 0.005-0.007 in. (0.13-0.18 mm). The valve tappet

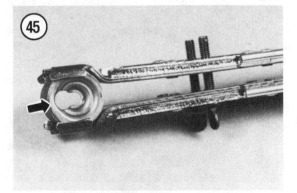

gap for the exhaust valve on engines with model series number less than 130000 should be 0.007-0.009 in. (0.18-0.23 mm). The valve tappet gap for the exhaust valve on engines with a model series number of 130000 or greater should be 0.009-0.011 in. (0.23-0.28 mm).

NOTE
On some 90000 model series engines, the exhaust valve gap should be 0.005-0.007 in. (0.13-0.18 mm). These engines are identified by the specified gap stamped on the inside of the crankcase breather.

NOTE
If a model 253400 or 255400 model series engine is equipped with only an electric starter and no rewind starter, the intake valve gap should be 0.009-0.011 in. (0.23-0.28 mm).

NOTE
On model series 286700 engines, the intake valve gap should be 0.004-0.006 in. (0.10-0.15 mm).

5. If the tappet gap is less than specified, the valve must be removed so the valve stem can be ground or filed to increase the gap. Be especially careful when grinding the stem as too much metal can be quickly removed. The end of the valve must be square with the stem after grinding. Dress the end of the valve stem to remove any burrs.

6. If the tappet gap is greater than specified, the valve seat must be ground to lower the valve or renew the valve and/or tappet to decrease the clearance.

11

OIL SEALS (SERVICE WITH CRANKSHAFT INSTALLED)

Oil seals at the flywheel end and at the output end of the crankshaft prevent the oil in the engine from leaking out. Wear or damage can reduce their effectiveness and oil leakage can become a problem, particularly if the oil contaminates the ignition breaker points or excessive amounts of oil are lost.

In some instances, it is possible to remove and install an oil seal without removing the crankshaft. Depending on the location of the engine and which oil seal is leaking, it may be necessary to remove the engine from the equipment.

If the oil seal at the flywheel end of the crankshaft is leaking, the flywheel must be removed (see previous *Flywheel* section). If the oil seal at the output end of the crankshaft is leaking, any parts attached to the crankshaft that prevent access to the oil seal must be removed.

> *NOTE*
> *Drain the engine oil if the working position will cause oil to run into the cylinder area.*

Removal/Installation

Before removing an oil seal, note the position of the seal in the crankcase, oil pan or crankcase cover. The oil seal in the crankcase cover on horizontal crankshaft engines may be recessed in the cover.

1. To remove an oil seal, insert a thin screwdriver or pick into the oil seal and pry out the seal. Special oil seal removal tools are available from automotive tool outlets.

> *CAUTION*
> *Care must be taken not to scratch the crankshaft or damage the metal behind the seal.*

2. Clean the seal seating area so the new seal will seat properly.
3. Check the oil seal bore in the engine and dress out any burrs created during removal. Remove only metal that is raised and will interfere with installation of the new seal. If a deep gouge is present, fill the depression with a suitable epoxy so it is level with the surrounding metal.
4. Apply nonhardening sealer to the periphery of the oil seal prior to installation.
5. Cover keyways and threads on the crankshaft with thin tape or a seal protector sleeve so the oil seal lip will not be cut when passing the oil seal down the crankshaft.
6. Lubricate the seal lip with clean engine oil or grease.
7. Position the seal so the seal lip is slanted toward the inside of the engine.
8. Use a suitable tool with the same diameter as the oil seal to force the oil seal into the engine. A deep-wall socket may work if the output end of the crankshaft is short. Suitable sizes of tubing or pipe may be purchased at a hardware store and used as

seal installing tools. Be sure the end of the tool is square and not sharp.

INTERNAL ENGINE COMPONENTS

The following discussion covers the following internal engine components: piston, piston rings, connecting rod, camshaft, tappets, crankshaft, bearings and governor. The overhaul procedure addresses a complete disassembly of internal engine

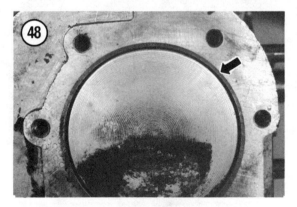

components. Although some components can be serviced without a complete disassembly, damage to one internal engine component often affects some or all of the other parts inside the engine. Failing to inspect all components may result in another repair that could have been avoided.

NOTE
The following procedures apply to a basic Briggs & Stratton engine. It may be necessary to modify a specific procedure to accommodate variations in engine components or special engine applications.

ENGINE DISASSEMBLY

Use the following procedure to disassemble the engine:

1. Drain the engine oil and remove the engine from the equipment.
2. Remove the electric starter motor, if so equipped.
3. Remove the muffler.
4. Remove the air cleaner, fuel tank and carburetor.
5. Remove the rewind starter and/or blower housing.
6. Remove the flywheel.
7. If equipped with a breaker point ignition system, detach the movable breaker arm and remove the breaker point plunger (**Figure 47**).
8. Remove the cylinder head and head gasket.
9. Remove the crankcase breather.
10. Remove the intake and exhaust valves.
11. If the cylinder has an iron sleeve (**Figure 48**), run a fingernail over the top portion of the cylinder and determine if a ridge exists. Use a ridge reamer (**Figure 49**) and remove the ridge at the top of the cylinder (ridge removal is not necessary on aluminum cylinders without an iron sleeve).
12. If not previously removed, remove any parts attached to the crankshaft and auxiliary pto shaft if so equipped.
13. Remove any rust or burrs from the crankshaft. This will prevent damage to the main bearing. A strip of emery cloth can be used as shown in **Figure 50** to remove rust. Burrs may be found adjacent to the keyways. It may be necessary to file down the end of the crankshaft to the original crankshaft diameter.
14. Unscrew the oil pan retaining screws on vertical crankshaft engines (**Figure 51** or **Figure 52**) or the crankcase cover retaining screws on horizontal crankshaft engines (**Figure 53**).

NOTE
On vertical crankshaft engines with an auxiliary drive shaft (except on Quantum model series 121000, 122000, 124000 and 126000), there is a hidden oil pan retaining screw behind the auxiliary shaft gear. Remove the cover

11

*shown in **Figure 54**, withdraw the shaft stop (**Figure 55**) and slide the gear and shaft towards the crankshaft to uncover the oil pan screw.*

15. Remove the oil pan on vertical crankshaft engines or the crankcase cover on horizontal crankshaft engines by tapping with a soft-faced hammer. Do not pry between the mating surfaces. Do not use excessive force against the oil pan or crankcase cover. Applying excessive force may damage the main bearing, oil pan or crankcase cover. If binding occurs, determine if an obstruction on the crankshaft, such as a burr, is causing the binding. If no obstruction is present, then the crankshaft may be bent. If the crankshaft is bent, then a replacement short block should be considered, depending on the condition of other internal engine components.

NOTE
Tools are available to straighten a bent crankshaft, however, Briggs & Stratton does not recommend straightening crankshafts, but states that a bent crankshaft must be discarded.

16. If so equipped, lift the oil slinger assembly (**Figure 56**) off the camshaft.

NOTE
*A spring washer (**Figure 57**) is located on the end of the camshaft on some model series 100900, 130700, 131700 and 130900 engines.*

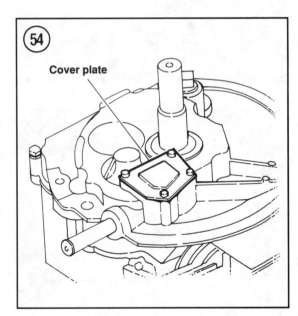

54

Cover plate

53

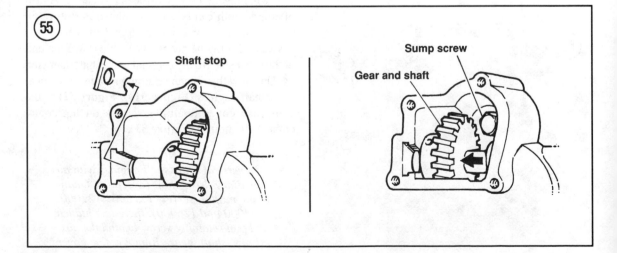

55

Shaft stop

Sump screw

Gear and shaft

17A. Proceed as follows if the engine does not have a ball bearing on the output end of the crankshaft:

    a. Position the engine so the tappets will not fall out.

    b. Rotate the crankshaft so the timing marks on the crankshaft gear and camshaft gear are aligned (**Figure 58**).

    c. Remove the camshaft.

    d. Mark the tappets, then remove the tappets from the cylinder block (**Figure 59**). The tappets must be marked so they can be reinstalled in their original positions.

    e. Bend back the lock plate tabs (**Figure 60**), then unscrew the connecting rod cap retaining screws and remove the rod cap and oil dipper, if so equipped.

NOTE
Care must be exercised not to damage the bearing surface of the connecting rod and rod cap.

    f. Push the connecting rod and piston out the top of the engine (**Figure 61**).

    g. Remove the crankshaft. Do not lose any shims mounted on the crankshaft; they are used to adjust crankshaft end play.

NOTE
*If the crankshaft is equipped with an oscillating counterbalance system (**Figure 62**), remove the crankshaft and balance components as a unit.*

17B. Proceed as follows if the engine has a ball bearing on the output end of the crankshaft (**Figure 63**):

11

a. Bend back the lock plate tabs (similar to **Figure 60**), then unscrew the connecting rod cap retaining screws and remove the rod cap and oil dipper, if so equipped.

b. Push the connecting rod and piston out the top of the engine (similar to **Figure 61**).

c. Position the engine so the tappets will not fall out.

d. Rotate the crankshaft so the timing marks on the crankshaft gear and camshaft gear are aligned (**Figure 64**).

e. Simultaneously withdraw the crankshaft and camshaft so they are removed together. Do not lose any shims mounted on the crankshaft; they are used to adjust crankshaft end play.

f. Mark then remove the tappets (**Figure 65**). The tappets must be marked so they can be reinstalled in their original positions.

18. The major components of the engine should now be removed from the engine crankcase. Refer to the following sections for further disassembly and inspection procedures.

PISTON, PISTON RINGS AND PISTON PIN

Two different types of piston are used depending on the metal used for the cylinder bore. The piston used in an aluminum cylinder bore is chrome plated while the piston used in an iron sleeve is tin plated. The tin plated piston is marked with an "L" on the piston crown (**Figure 66**). The pistons are not interchangeable.

Disassembly

If it is necessary to separate the connecting rod from the piston, use the following procedure.

1. Extract the piston pin retaining clip or clips (**Figure 67**). If there is only one clip, then the closed end of the piston pin abuts against an internal stop in the piston.

2. Push or tap out the piston pin. If the piston pin is closed at one end, force the pin out towards the open end.

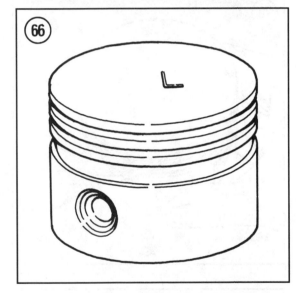

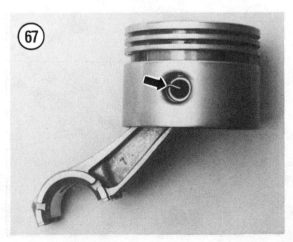

NOTE
*If the piston pin is stuck in the piston, and the pin is hollow, a puller tool like that shown in **Figure 68** can be fabricated to extract the pin. If the pin is a closed type, heat the piston with a small propane torch or hair dryer to about 140° F (60° C). The pin should then push easily out of the piston.*

3. A suitable piston ring expander tool (**Figure 69**) should be used to remove the piston rings. Although the rings can be removed by hand, there is less chance of piston ring breakage or gouging the piston ring grooves when the ring expander tool is used. When removing the rings, mark them so they can be returned to their original positions; note which side is towards the piston crown. Remove the top compression ring (closest to the piston crown) first, then the second compression ring and finally the oil con-

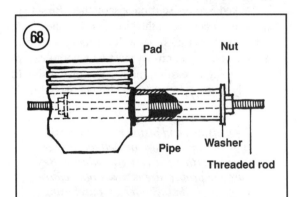

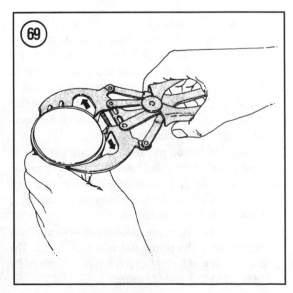

11

trol ring. Move the rings toward the piston crown for removal.

Inspection

1. Clean the top of the piston using a soft wire brush. Hard deposits can be loosened by soaking the piston in carburetor cleaner.

2. The piston ring grooves should be cleaned. One method for cleaning piston ring grooves is to pull the end of a broken piston ring through the groove as shown in **Figure 70**. Care must be used not to gouge or otherwise damage the groove. Piston ring groove cleaning tools are also available.

3. Piston diameter sizes are not specified by Briggs & Stratton. The cylinder bore should be measured as outlined in the *Cylinder* section. If an oversize piston is required, then piston inspection is unnecessary.

4. Inspect the piston for reuse. Replace the piston if it is cracked, scored, scuffed or scratched. Be sure to inspect the underside of the piston around the piston pin bosses for cracks, as well as the piston ring grooves. The piston crown must be smooth except for machining or casting marks. The piston should fit snugly in the cylinder bore with no "wobbling."

> *NOTE*
> *New pistons and piston rings are available in standard size as well as various oversizes to fit a resized cylinder. Be sure the proper size is available before machining the cylinder or purchasing components.*

5. Place a new piston ring in the clean top piston ring groove and measure the ring side clearance using a feeler gauge as shown in **Figure 71**. Replace the piston if a new top piston ring has a side clearance of 0.007 in. (0.18 mm) or more on engines with a displacement less than 14 cu. in. (229 cc) or 0.009 in. (0.23 mm) or more on engines with a displacement greater than 14 cu. in. (229 cc).

6. Inspect the piston pin and the piston pin hole in the piston for scoring and other damage. The piston pin is available in a standard size or an oversize, which permits reaming the piston and connecting rod holes if either is damaged.

7. Measure the piston pin diameter at several points to determine if the piston pin is out-of-round. The piston pin should be replaced if it is out-of-round by 0.0005 in. (0.013 mm) or more.

8. The standard size piston pin should be replaced with a standard piston pin or an oversize piston pin if it is worn to the reject diameter or less shown in **Table 1**.

9. The piston should be replaced or the piston pin hole in the piston should be reamed to accept an oversize piston pin if the hole diameter is equal to or greater than the dimension shown in **Table 1**.

10. The piston pin hole in the piston, as well as the connecting rod, can be enlarged with a reamer, presuming it is standard size, to accept a piston pin that is 0.005 in. (0.13 mm) larger in diameter than the standard piston pin. A reamer must be used that will provide a hole that allows a push fit for the piston pin in the piston or connecting rod. The cost for this

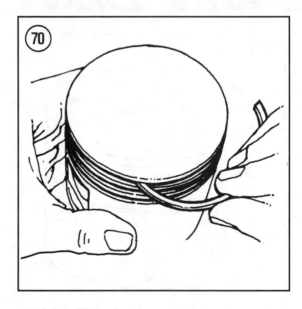

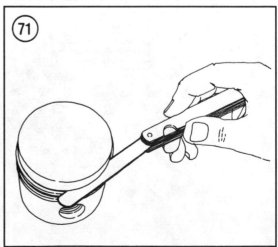

procedure should be compared with the cost of a new piston and/or connecting rod.

11. Measure the end gap of each piston ring. Place the piston ring in the cylinder bore, then push the piston ring down into the bore with a piston (**Figure 72**) so the ring is square in the bore. Position the piston ring 1 in. (25 mm) down in the bore from the top of the cylinder and measure the piston ring end gap as shown in **Figure 73**.

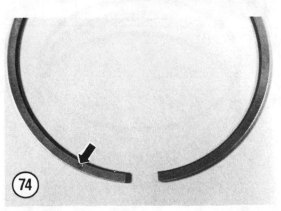

a. On engines with an iron sleeve in the cylinder bore, discard the piston ring if the end gap is 0.030 in. (0.76 mm) or more for a compression ring or 0.035 in. (0.89 mm) for the oil control ring.

b. On engines without an iron sleeve, discard the piston ring if the end gap is 0.035 in. (0.89 mm) or more for a compression ring or 0.045 in. (1.14 mm) for the oil control ring.

Assembly

1. When installing the piston rings, note that the top side (towards the piston crown) of some compression rings is marked with a dot (**Figure 74**) to identify the top side of the ring. Several piston ring configurations have been used. Refer to the information supplied with the new piston rings for proper ring placement. The chart in **Figure 75** shows the correct location of some piston ring combinations.

2. A suitable piston ring expander tool (**Figure 69**) should be used to install the piston rings. Although the rings can be installed by hand, there is less chance of piston ring breakage or gouging the piston ring grooves when the ring expander tool is used.

3. The oil control ring may be a one-piece ring or an assembled unit. The assembled oil control ring may consist of two pieces, the control ring plus an expander ring, or three pieces, two rails and an expander ring.

a. Two-piece oil control rings (**Figure 76**) may use a flat expander as shown in **Figure 76** or a coil wire expander as shown in **Figure 77**. The expander is placed in the piston ring groove first, then the oil control ring is placed in the groove over the expander ring so the end gaps of the oil control ring and expander ring are on opposite sides of the piston.

b. If a three-piece ring (**Figure 78**) is used, the expander ring (**Figure 79**) is first installed in the oil ring groove. The expander ring ends must abut, not overlap. Then, one of the rails is carefully twisted in a spiral and inserted in the top piston ring groove (**Figure 80**), then the center groove, and finally into the oil ring groove, placing the first rail against the bottom of the expander ring. The rail end gap must be 120° from the expander ring ends. Install the second rail using the same procedure so it fits along the top of the expander and the end gap is 120° from the bottom rail end gap. The

11

installed oil control ring should appear as shown in **Figure 81** and rotate without binding in the piston ring groove.

4. The piston and connecting rod can be assembled in either direction, except on pistons with a notch used in vertical crankshaft engines. If the piston on a vertical crankshaft engine has a notch in the piston

crown, then the piston and connecting rod must be assembled so the notch (A, **Figure 82**) and long side of the rod (B) are positioned as shown in **Figure 82**.

5. Before assembling the piston and connecting rod, determine if one or two piston pin retaining clips are

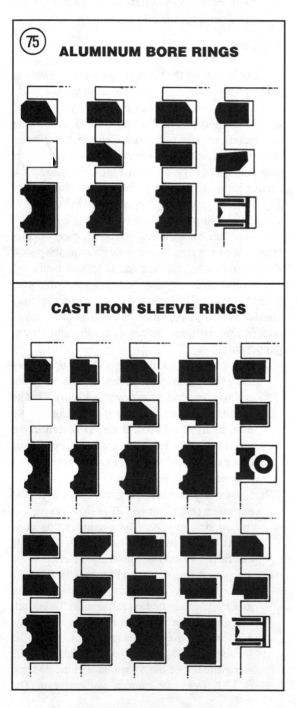

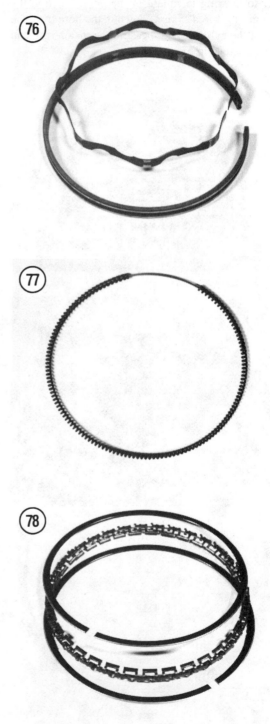

used (if only one clip is used, then an internal stop is located at one end of the piston pin bore).

NOTE
Do not reuse old piston pin retaining clips; install new clips. Used clips may not seat properly in the grooves and can pop out.

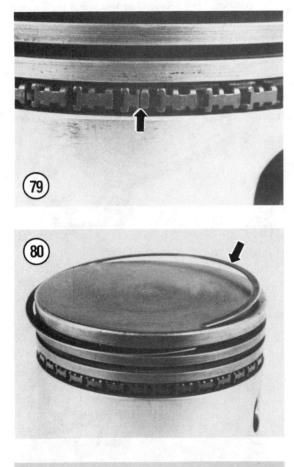

6. If two clips are used, proceed as follows:
   a. Install one of the clips in the piston pin bore.
   b. Position the connecting rod end in the piston.
   c. Insert the piston pin.
   d. Install the remaining piston pin retaining clip.
   e. Be sure the piston pin retaining clips are securely positioned in the piston grooves.
7. If only one retaining clip is used, proceed as follows:
   a. Position the connecting rod end in the piston.
   b. Insert the piston pin with the closed end entering first.
   c. Install the piston pin retaining clip; be sure the clip is securely positioned in the piston groove.

CONNECTING ROD

Disassembly/Inspection/Assembly

1. Refer to *Piston, Piston Rings and Piston Pin* section for procedure to separate the connecting rod from the piston.

2. On all engines, the connecting rod rides directly on the crankshaft crankpin. Inspect the bearing surfaces for signs of scuffing and scoring. If any damage is observed, also inspect the surface of the mating part, i.e., the crankpin or piston pin.

NOTE
If the rod bearing surface is worn due to abrasive particles (the surface texture is dull and rough), it should be replaced even if it is not worn beyond the specified wear limit. Grit may be embedded in the aluminum which will continue to cause wear on mating surfaces.

11

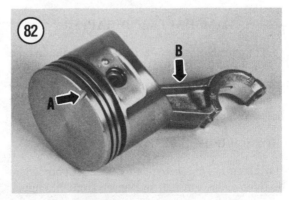

3. Inspect the connecting rod for cracks, twisting and other damage.

4. Measure the inner diameter of the connecting rod big end (**Figure 83**) after installing the rod cap (be sure the mating surface grooves on the rod and cap are aligned). Tighten the connecting rod screws to the torque listed in **Table 2**.

5. Replace the connecting rod if the big end diameter is equal to or greater than the dimension shown in **Table 1**.

> *NOTE*
> *On Quantum model series 100700, 121000, 122000, 124000 and 126000 engines, a connecting rod that is 0.020 in. (0.51 mm) undersize is available to fit a worn crankshaft crankpin. However, machining of the crankshaft is required. Instructions are included with the new rod.*

6. Measure the inside diameter of the small end of the connecting rod (**Figure 84**). The connecting rod should be replaced or the piston pin hole in the connecting rod should be reamed to accept an oversize piston pin if the hole diameter is equal to or greater than the dimension shown in **Table 1**.

7. The piston pin hole in the connecting rod, as well as the piston, can be enlarged with a reamer, presuming it is standard size, to accept a piston pin that is 0.005 in. (0.13 mm) larger in diameter than the standard piston pin. A reamer must be used that will provide a hole that allows a push fit for the piston pin in the piston or connecting rod. The cost for this procedure should be compared with the cost of a new piston and/or connecting rod.

8. Refer to *Piston, Piston Rings and Piston Pin* section for procedure to assemble the connecting rod to the piston.

CAMSHAFT AND TAPPETS

The camshaft rides directly in the aluminum bore of the crankcase, oil pan or crankcase cover. The camshaft gear is integral with the shaft, except on some later models that are equipped with a camshaft constructed of metal and plastic.

Removal/Inspection/Installation

1. Refer to engine *Disassembly* section for procedure to remove the camshaft and tappets from the engine.

2. The camshaft and gear should be inspected for wear on the journals, cam lobes and gear teeth. Measure the diameter of the bearing journals (**Figure 85**).

    a. On model series 60000, 61000, 80000, 81000 fitted with an auxiliary drive gear on the camshaft, replace the camshaft if the journal diameter for the end that fits into the crankcase is 0.498 in. (12.65 mm) or less, or if the journal diameter near the worm drive gear is 0.751 in. (19.08 mm) or less.

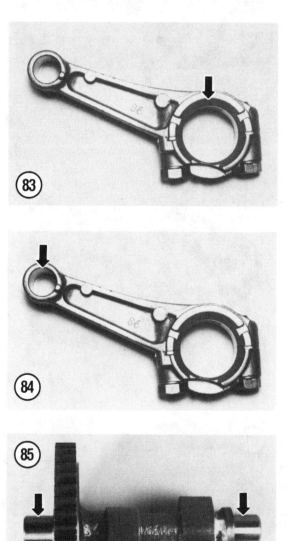

83

84

85

b. On model series 110000, 111000, 112000, 113000 and 114000, replace the camshaft if the journal diameter for the end that fits into the crankcase is 0.436 in. (11.07 mm) or less, or if the journal diameter nearer the cam gear is 0.498 in. (12.65 mm) or less.

c. Replace the camshaft on all other models if either camshaft journal is 0.498 in. (12.65 mm) or less.

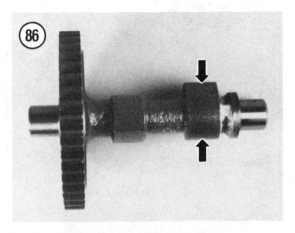

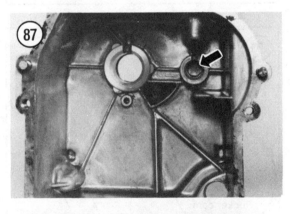

3. Measure the height of the cam lobes (**Figure 86**). Replace the camshaft if the cam lobe height of either cam lobe is equal to or less than dimension shown in **Table 1**.

4. Inspect the camshaft bearing surfaces in the crankcase and oil pan (on vertical crankshaft engines) or crankcase cover (on horizontal crankshaft engines). The surface must be smooth with no sign of abrasion.

5. Measure the inside bearing diameter in the crankcase (**Figure 87**) and oil pan or crankcase cover (**Figure 88**).

   a. On model series 60000, 61000, 80000, 81000 fitted with an auxiliary drive gear on the camshaft, replace the crankcase if the camshaft bearing diameter in the crankcase is greater than 0.504 in. (12.80 mm), or if the camshaft bearing diameter in the oil pan is 0.757 in. (19.23 mm) or more.

   b. On model series 110000, 111000, 112000, 113000 and 114000, replace the crankcase, oil pan or crankcase cover if the camshaft bearing diameter in the crankcase is 0.443 in. (11.25 mm) or more, or if the camshaft bearing diameter in the oil pan or crankcase cover is greater than 0.504 in. (12.80 mm).

   c. Replace the crankcase, oil pan or crankcase cover on all other models if the camshaft bearing diameter is greater than 0.504 in. (12.80 mm).

6. Some camshafts may be equipped with a compression release mechanism: the yoke type shown in **Figure 89** or the cam-weight type shown in **Figure 90**. The mechanism should move freely without binding. No individual components are available.

7. Some camshafts are also equipped with Easy-Spin starting. The intake cam lobe is designed to hold the intake valve slightly open on part of the compression stroke. To check compression, the crankshaft must be turned backwards.

NOTE
Easy-Spin camshafts (cam gears) can be identified by two holes drilled in the web of the gear. Where the part number of an older cam gear and an Easy-Spin cam gear are the same (except for an "E" following the Easy-Spin part number), the gears are interchangeable.

Some Easy-Spin camshafts are also equipped with a mechanically operated

11

*compression release on the exhaust lobe. With the engine stopped or at cranking speed, the spring holds the actuator cam weight inward against the rocker cam. See **Figure 90**. The rocker cam is held slightly above the exhaust cam surface which in turn holds the exhaust valve open slightly during the compression stroke. This compression release greatly reduces the power needed for cranking.*

*When the engine starts and rpm is increased, the actuator cam weight moves outward overcoming the spring pressure. See **Figure 91**. The rocker cam is rotated below the cam surface to provide normal exhaust valve operation.*

8. On some engines, a worm gear on the camshaft drives an auxiliary drive shaft that is used on self-propelled lawn mowers. The camshaft, worm gear and oil slinger are available only as a unit assembly. A thrust washer (**Figure 92**) is used to accommodate additional axial thrust of the camshaft. The thrust washer is located at the flywheel end of the camshaft if the auxiliary drive shaft rotation is clockwise. The thrust washer is located at the worm gear end of the camshaft if auxiliary shaft rotation is counterclockwise.

9. The tappets should be inspected for excessive wear on the contact surface with the camshaft. Check for excessive side play with the tappet installed in the crankcase bore.

10. Refer to the engine *Reassembly* section in this chapter for procedure to install the camshaft and tappets in the engine.

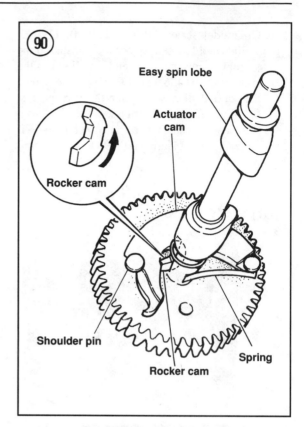

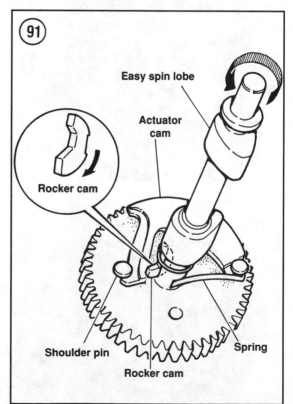

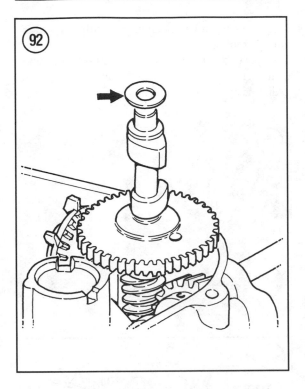

GOVERNOR

Removal/Inspection/Installation

Engines that use a mechanical governor are equipped with a flyweight assembly that is driven by the camshaft gear.

Model series 80000, 83400, 100200, 100900, 130000, 170000, 190000, 220000, 251400, 252400, 254400 and 280000

The governor flyweight assembly is mounted on a stub shaft on the crankcase cover (**Figure 93**).

1. Remove the crankcase cover.

2. The flyweight assembly can be removed by pulling it off the stub shaft. A thrust washer (**Figure 94**) is located between the flyweight assembly and the crankcase cover boss.

3. Inspect the flyweight assembly for broken components, worn gear teeth and excessive clearance on the stub shaft. Note that the flyweight assembly is available only as a unit assembly. The stub shaft is not removable.

4. To install the flyweight assembly, first install the flyweight assembly on the shaft, then install the wire clip (**Figure 95**).

5. Position the flyweight assembly near the end of the shaft so that the weights can be spread enough so the thrust sleeve can be installed in the flyweights. The flange on the thrust sleeve must engage the flyweight fingers as shown in **Figure 96**.

6. Installation of the crankcase cover and governor should be made with the crankshaft in the horizontal position. The governor lever internal arm should hang straight down so that the end of the thrust flange will contact the arm when the governor is installed.

11

7. Adjust governor lever as outlined in the engine *Reassembly* section in this chapter.

Model series 60000 and 80000

Some early horizontal crankshaft engines are equipped with a flyweight assembly that is contained within a governor housing (**Figure 97**) which is attached to the crankcase cover.

1. Remove governor housing mounting screws, remove the governor assembly and separate flyweight assembly from the housing. Refer to **Figure 98** for an exploded view of governor components.

2. To remove governor shaft, loosen governor lever clamp bolt and withdraw the lever (**Figure 98**).

3. Drive out the roll pin, then unscrew governor shaft from follower by turning shaft clockwise.

4. Inspect the flyweight assembly for broken components, worn gear teeth and excessive wear on the stub shaft.

5. To install governor assembly, thread governor shaft into the follower by turning shaft counterclockwise.

6. Position the governor shaft so the follower points downward as shown in **Figure 97**.

7. Place washer on outside of shaft and install roll pin. Note that the roll pin should be installed so leading end of pin is flush with surface of governor shaft.

8. Place thrust washer, governor flyweight and cup on the stub shaft in governor housing.

9. Assemble governor gear and housing to crankcase cover so that the point of the steel cup rests against the governor follower.

10. Install governor housing cap screws and tighten securely.

11. Assemble governor lever to governor shaft and adjust as outlined in the engine *Reassembly* section in this chapter.

Model series 91700, 94500, 94900, 111700, 113900, 114700 and 114900

The flyweight assembly on vertical crankshaft engines is mounted on the end of the camshaft along with the oil slinger (**Figure 99**).

1. The engine oil pan must be removed before the governor can be removed.

2. Loosen governor lever clamp screw and remove governor lever from the governor crank.

3. Remove the governor crank and withdraw governor assembly from engine.

4. Inspect governor unit for worn or broken components. The oil slinger and flyweight assembly are available as a unit assembly.

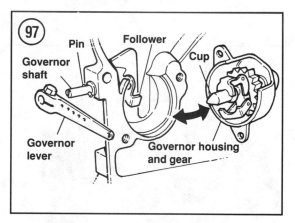

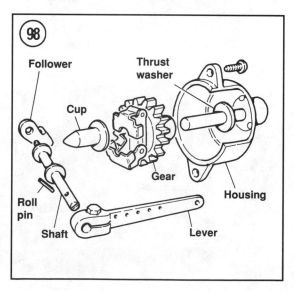

5. A new governor shaft bushing can be installed in the cylinder block if the old bushing is excessively worn. The new bushing must be reamed to correct size after installation using Finish Reamer, B&S Tool No. 19058. This operation should be performed by a properly equipped shop if you do not have the tools necessary to do the job correctly.

6. Install the governor flyweight and oil slinger assembly.

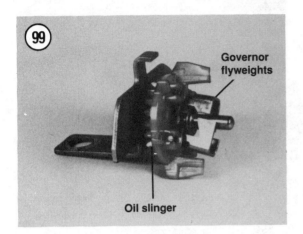

Governor flyweights

Oil slinger

7. Install the governor crank from inside the cylinder. Make certain that governor crank contacts the governor cup.

8. Install the oil pan.

9. Install governor lever on crank and adjust as outlined in the engine *Reassembly* section in this chapter.

CRANKSHAFT AND MAIN BEARINGS

Removal/Inspection/Installation

1. Refer to the engine *Disassembly* section in this chapter for procedure to remove the crankshaft from the engine.

2. Some crankshafts are equipped with a removable crankshaft gear that is driven by a pin or key in the crankshaft. It may be necessary to pry off the gear. Note that the gear must be installed on the crankshaft so the side with the timing mark (**Figure 100**) is visible (the chamfered side is towards the crankshaft counterweight). A crankshaft drive pin is not removable while a crankshaft drive key can be removed.

3. If the crankshaft is equipped with an oscillating counterbalance system (**Figure 101**), refer to the *Balancer Systems* section for removal of the balancer components.

4. If considerable effort was required to remove the oil pan or crankcase cover from the crankshaft, then the crankshaft is probably bent and must be discarded. If moderate effort was required during removal, then the crankshaft should be checked for straightness by a shop with the necessary equipment. If oil pan or crankcase removal was relatively easy, and the bearings are within specifications, then the crankshaft is probably straight.

5. Inspect all mating surfaces on the crankshaft for indications of scoring, scuffing and other damage.

6. Check any fastener threads, such as the flywheel nut and blade retaining screw, for damage and cross-threading and repair if possible.

7. Check keyways (**Figure 102**) and remove burrs. The keyway must be straight and unworn.

8. If the engine is equipped with ignition breaker points, check the plunger flat (**Figure 103**) which must be unworn for proper breaker point operation.

9. Check the crankshaft gear for broken or pitted teeth.

10. Measure the crankpin journal (**Figure 104**). The crankshaft should be replaced if the crankpin journal

diameter is equal to or less than the dimension shown in **Table 1**.

> *NOTE*
> *On Quantum model series 100700, 121000, 122000, 124000 and 126000 engines, a connecting rod that is 0.020 in. (0.51 mm) undersize is available to fit a worn crankshaft crankpin. However, machining of the crankshaft is required. Instructions are included with the new rod.*

11. On engines so equipped, inspect the ball bearing(s) for roughness, pitting, galling and play by rotating the bearing slowly by hand. If any roughness or play can be felt in the bearing, it must be replaced. The bearings are a press fit on the crankshaft. The crankshaft should be replaced if bearings are loose on journals. Ball bearing removal and installation can be performed by a shop equipped with a press. The new bearing must be installed so the bearing side with the metal shield is towards the counterweight as shown in **Figure 105**. An alternate method for bearing installation, is to warm the bearing in oil that is heated to no more than 250° F (121° C). The bearing must not contact the container. While hot, the bearing can be slipped down the crankshaft into place.

12. Measure the main bearing journals (**Figure 106**). The crankshaft should be replaced if the journal diameter is equal or less than the dimension shown in **Table 1**.

13. If not equipped with a ball bearing main bearing, the crankshaft rides directly in the aluminum of the crankcase and oil pan (on vertical crankshaft engines) or crankcase cover (on horizontal crankshaft engines), or the crankshaft rides in a renewable bushing. On some engines, a bushing can be installed if the aluminum is excessively worn or damaged. Most engines can be repaired using a bushing, but check parts availability on a specific engine. Main bearing bushing installation should be performed by a shop with the necessary experience and tools.

14. Inspect the main bearing (bushing) surfaces in the crankcase and oil pan (on vertical crankshaft engines) or crankcase cover (on horizontal crankshaft engines). The surface must be smooth with no sign of abrasion. Measure the inside bearing (bushing) diameter in the crankcase (**Figure 107**) and oil pan or crankcase cover (**Figure 108**). If the diameter

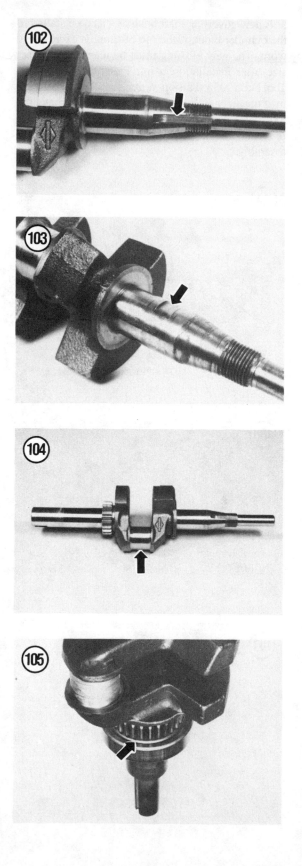

is equal to or greater than the specified dimension in **Table 1**, then a bushing must be installed or the crankcase, oil pan or crankcase cover must be replaced.

15. Refer to the engine *Reassembly* section in this chapter for procedure to install the crankshaft in the engine.

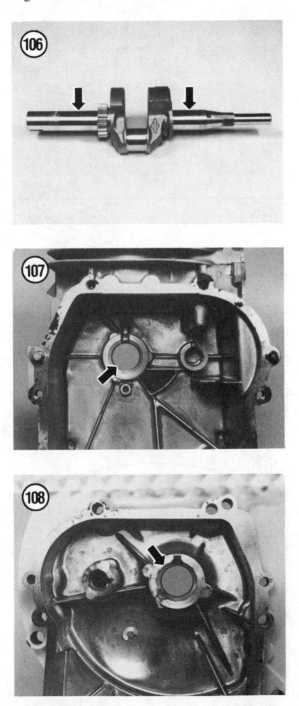

CYLINDER

Inspection/Reconditioning

The cylinder and crankcase are an integral casting. The cylinder bore is aluminum on some engines, while other engines are equipped with an iron sleeve that is cast in the aluminum cylinder block.

1. The cylinder bore should be inspected for scratches, scoring, scuffing and other damage. If the bore is excessively worn or damaged, the cylinder can be bored oversize and an oversize piston can be installed. Machining (boring) the cylinder to accept an oversize piston should be performed by a shop with the required equipment and experience. Compare the cost of another engine assembly (shortblock) with the cost of installing an oversize piston.

2. Measure the cylinder bore to determine if the bore is excessively worn, tapered or out-of-round. Measure the cylinder bore at the top, middle and bottom at several points around the cylinder. Compare the measurements to determine cylinder bore size, taper and out-of-round. The cylinder should be bored if the cylinder diameter is equal to or more than the dimension shown in **Table 1**.

> *NOTE*
> *A chrome piston ring set is available for slightly worn standard bore cylinders. No honing or cylinder deglazing is required for these rings. The cylinder bore can be a maximum of 0.005 in. (0.13 mm) oversize when using chrome rings.*

3. The cylinder must be bored if the cylinder bore is 0.0025 in. (0.06 mm) or more out-of-round.

> *NOTE*
> *New pistons and piston rings are available in standard size as well as various oversizes to fit a resized cylinder. Be sure the proper size piston and rings is available before machining the cylinder.*

4. If new piston rings are being installed in an engine with an iron sleeve (**Figure 109**), the cylinder bore surface should be reconditioned with a hone or deglazing tool (**Figure 110**) to restore the crosshatch pattern (**Figure 111**). The crosshatch pattern retains oil in the grooves while also promoting piston ring seating. The tool is driven by an electric drill. Push the tool in and out of the cylinder bore approxi-

11

mately 12 times at 300-700 rpm so an angle of 45°
between the intersecting lines of the crosshatch is
produced. The tool manufacturer may recommend a
specific stone grade and lubrication.

> *NOTE*
> *It is not necessary to deglaze the cylin-*
> *der wall when installing new piston*
> *rings in aluminum cylinder engines.*

5. After deglazing, thoroughly wash the cylinder
bore using a stiff brush with hot soapy water. If the
bore is an iron sleeve, lubricate the bore to prevent
rust formation.

> *NOTE*
> *Do not clean the bore with kerosene or*
> *solvent, as a residue of abrasive grit will*
> *remain.*

6. Note that the pistons used in an aluminum cylinder
bore and an iron-sleeved cylinder bore are different.
The piston used in an aluminum cylinder bore is
chrome plated while the piston used in an iron sleeve
is tin plated. The tin plated piston is marked with an
"L" on the piston crown (**Figure 112**). The pistons
are not interchangeable.

OIL SEALS

Removal/Installation

An oil seal is located adjacent to the main bearing
in both the crankcase and the oil pan or crankcase
cover. The oil seals should be replaced during any
overhaul.

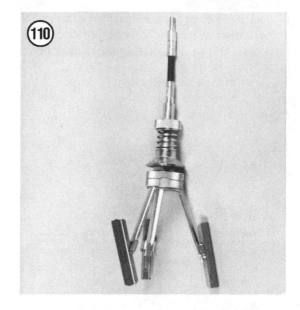

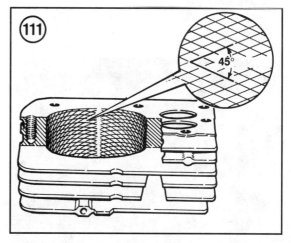

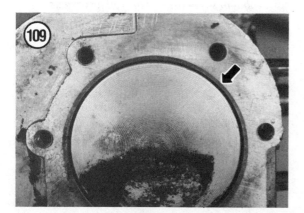

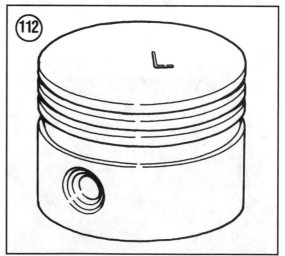

NOTE
Before removing an oil seal, note the position of the seal in the crankcase, oil pan or crankcase cover. The oil seal in the crankcase cover on horizontal crankshaft engines may be recessed in the cover.

1. To remove an oil seal, pry the oil seal out using a screwdriver as shown in **Figure 113**, but be careful so the metal of the crankcase, oil pan or crankcase cover surrounding the seal is not damaged.

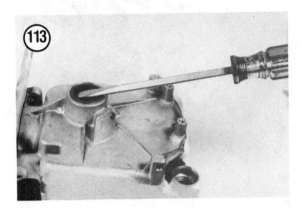

2. Clean the seal seating area so the new seal will seat properly.

3. Before installing the oil seal, apply a nonhardening sealer to the periphery of the seal.

4. To install the oil seal, position the seal so the seal lip is slanted toward the inside of the engine (**Figure 114**). Drive the seal into position using a seal driver or a wood block and a hammer.

5. The seal should be flush with the surrounding metal, except on some engines where a mounting flange attached to the crankcase cover requires that the seal be recessed 3/16 in. (4.8 mm). The seal must not block oil passages (**Figure 115**). If the seal is recessed, a socket with the same outside diameter as the seal makes a suitable seal driver.

NOTE
The oil seal lip must be lubricated with engine oil before inserting the crankshaft. Lack of lubrication when the engine is started may damage the seal lip.

OSCILLATING BALANCER

Disassembly

Some larger vertical crankshaft engines may be equipped with an oscillating balancer system. The balance weight assembly rides on eccentric journals on the crankshaft and moves in the opposite direction of the piston. The crankshaft and balance components are shown in **Figure 116**.

Refer to the engine *Disassembly* section in this chapter for procedure to remove the crankshaft and balancer unit from the engine.

11

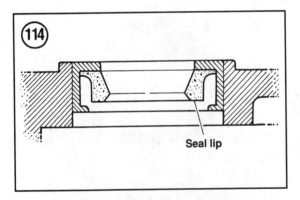

Seal lip

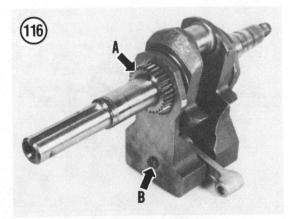

NOTE
Be aware when handling the balancer and crankshaft assembly that the eccentrics can fall out.

After the crankshaft and balancer unit are removed from the crankcase, disassemble the balancer as follows.

1. Remove the crankshaft gear (A, **Figure 116**) as outlined in the *Crankshaft* section.
2. Unscrew the retaining screw (B, **Figure 116**). On some engines, there are two screws holding the counterweights together.
3. Separate the weights and remove the link, dowel pins and spacers (**Figure 117**).
4. Slide the weights off the crankshaft.

Inspection

1. Inspect the eccentrics (**Figure 118**) on each side of the crankshaft. Replace the eccentrics if they are scored or discolored or otherwise damaged. On some engines the eccentrics can be replaced separately, while on other engines the crankshaft must be replaced along with the eccentrics.
2. Measure the eccentric diameter (**Figure 119**). Replace the eccentric if the diameter is equal to or less than the dimension shown in **Table 1**.
3. Inspect the bushing in the weight. The weight must be replaced if the bushing is damaged or worn to a diameter (**Figure 120**) that is equal to or greater than the dimension shown in **Table 1**.

Assembly

To reassemble the balancer on the crankshaft, proceed as follows:

1. Install the eccentrics on the crankshaft. The chamfered side (**Figure 121**) must be towards the crankshaft counterweight
2. Install the inner weight (the inner weight has a threaded hole or holes) on the flywheel end of the crankshaft.
3. Place the crankshaft in a vise (**Figure 122**) so the output end is up.

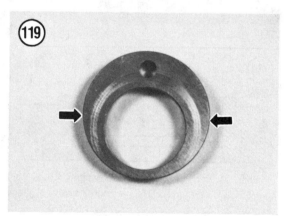

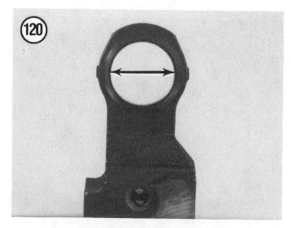

4. Install the dowel pin(s) and place the link on the pin (**Figure 123**). Note that the rounded edge on the free end of the link must be up.

5. Install the outer weight (**Figure 124**), spacers, lock and cap screws. Spacers and a lock plate are only used on units with two retaining screws.

6. Tighten the retaining screws, if two are used, to 80 in.-lb. (9 N•m) and secure with lock tabs. If only one retaining screw is used, tighten the screw to 115 in.-lb. (13.0 N•m).

7. Install the crankshaft key, if removed, and the crankshaft gear. Note that the gear must be installed on the crankshaft so the side with the timing mark is visible (the chamfered side is towards the crankshaft counterweight).

ROTATING COUNTERBALANCE SYSTEM

Some larger horizontal crankshaft engines may be equipped with two balancer gears that are in constant mesh with the crankshaft gear. The balancer gears are mounted in the crankcase cover and rotate in the opposite direction of the crankshaft (**Figure 125**).

The balancer gears ride on needle roller bearings. The gears and bearings are available only as a set.

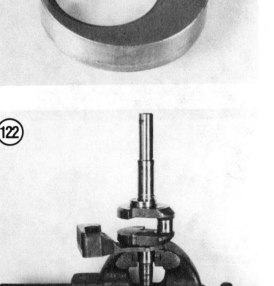

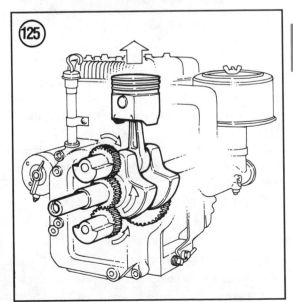

11

NOTE
If the balancer gears are removed from the crankcase cover, exercise care in handling or cleaning to prevent loss of the needle bearings.

The balancer gears must be positioned in time with the crankshaft gear during installation of the crankcase cover. See *Reassembly* procedure.

BREAKER-POINT PLUNGER HOLE

If the breaker-point plunger hole (**Figure 126**) on engines equipped with a breaker-point ignition system is excessively worn, the hole can be reamed to accept a bushing, or the existing bushing can be replaced.

NOTE
It may be worthwhile to install a new or used electronic ignition rather than install or replace the plunger hole bushing.

The maximum allowable plunger hole diameter is 0.189 in. (4.80 mm). If the bore is aluminum, then the hole should be reamed so a bushing can be installed. If a bushing is already in place, a new bushing should be installed. If bushing installation is required, the job should be performed by a shop equipped with the proper tools.

ENGINE REASSEMBLY

Before assembling the engine, be sure all components are clean. Any residue or debris left in the engine will cause rapid wear and/or major damage when the engine runs.

The following components should be assembled or installed before proceeding with assembly of the engine.

a. Piston, piston rings and connecting rod.

b. Oil seals.

c. Governor flyweight.

d. Bushings or bearings.

e. Camshaft and compression release.

f. Balancer.

Assembly (Engines with Ball-Type Main Bearings)

Proceed as follows if the engine has a ball bearing on the output end of the crankshaft.

1. Position the engine so the tappets will not fall out and install the tappets (**Figure 127**) in their original positions.

2. Lubricate the crankcase oil seal, crankshaft bearings, camshaft and camshaft bearings with engine oil.

NOTE
Thin tape or an oil seal protection sleeve should be used around the crankshaft

*keyway and threads (**Figure 128**) to protect the oil seal when the crankshaft is inserted.*

3. Mate the crankshaft gear with the camshaft gear so the timing marks are aligned (**Figure 129**), then simultaneously insert the crankshaft and camshaft along with any original shims.

4. Lubricate the piston, piston pin and piston rings with engine oil.

5. Position the piston ring end gaps so they are 120° apart and compress the piston rings with a piston ring compressor (**Figure 130**). Turn the ring compressor tightener so the piston will just rotate in the compressor.

6. Place the piston and connecting rod in the cylinder while noting the following:

    a. On horizontal crankshaft engines, position the connecting rod so the alignment mark on the big end of the rod is towards the camshaft gear on model series 60000 (**Figure 131**) or so the alignment mark on the big end of the rod is opposite the camshaft gear on model series 100200, 130000 and 170000 (**Figure 132**).

    b. On vertical crankshaft engines, position the piston and connecting rod so the long side of the rod is on the side of the engine opposite from the camshaft (**Figure 133**).

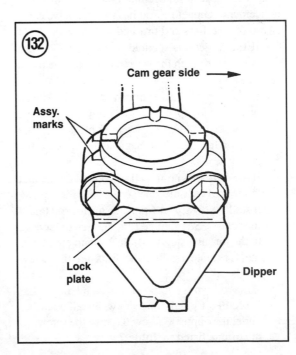

11

7. Rotate the crankshaft so the crankpin is towards the cylinder bore.

8. Lubricate the cylinder bore with engine oil.

9. Insert the connecting rod and piston through the top of the engine (**Figure 134**) so the piston ring compressor rests against the engine.

10. Push the piston into the cylinder bore while guiding the connecting rod onto the crankshaft crankpin.

> *CAUTION*
> *Do not use excessive force when install-*
> *ing the piston and rod. If binding oc-*
> *curs, remove the piston and rod and try*
> *again. Excessive force can damage or*
> *break the piston rings, piston ring lands,*
> *connecting rod or crankshaft.*

11. Liberally lubricate the connecting rod bearing and the crankshaft crankpin with engine oil.

12. Mate the connecting rod with the crankshaft crankpin, then rotate the crankshaft so the connecting rod cap can be installed.

13. Liberally lubricate the bearing surface of the connecting rod cap and install the cap on the connecting rod. Be sure the indexing notches on the rod and cap are properly meshed (**Figure 135**).

14. Refer to the following instructions to install the oil dipper, lockplate (a new lockplate should be installed), washers and retaining screws (if a new replacement connecting rod has two thick washers, discard the washers and proceed as follows):

   a. If the rod cap is secured by only screws with washers, tighten the screws to the torque listed in **Table 2**.

   b. If the rod cap is equipped with a lockplate, install the lockplate and the screws. Tighten the screws to the torque listed in **Table 2**. Bend the ears of the lockplate against the flats on the screw heads.

   c. If the rod cap is equipped with an oil dipper that is secured by only one screw and a lockplate, install the oil dipper first, then the lockplate and the screws. See **Figure 136**. Tighten the screws to the torque listed in **Table 2**. Bend the ears of the lockplate against the flats on the screw heads.

   d. If the rod cap is equipped with an oil dipper that is secured by only one screw, install a washer under the opposite screw. Tighten the screws to the torque listed in **Table 2**.

   e. If the rod cap is equipped with an oil dipper that is secured by two screws, tighten the screws to the torque listed in **Table 2**.

> *NOTE*
> *The oil dipper on horizontal crankshaft*
> *engines must be installed so the dipper*
> *portion is on the flywheel side of the*
> *connecting rod (**Figure 136**).*

Assembly (Engines With Plain Main Bearings)

Proceed as follows if the engine does not have a ball bearing on the output end of the crankshaft.

1. Lubricate the crankcase oil seal and crankshaft bearing with engine oil.

NOTE
Thin tape or an oil seal protection sleeve should be used around the crankshaft

*keyway and threads (**Figure 137**) to protect the oil seal when the crankshaft is inserted.*

2. Insert the crankshaft in the crankcase.

NOTE
*If the crankshaft is equipped with an oscillating counterbalance system (**Figure 138**), install the crankshaft and balance components as a unit. Be sure all moving parts of the balancer are lubricated.*

3. Lubricate the piston, piston pin and piston rings with engine oil.

4. Position the piston ring end gaps so they are 120° apart and compress the piston rings with a piston ring compressor (**Figure 130**). Turn the ring compressor tightener so the piston will just rotate in the compressor.

5. Place the piston and connecting rod in the cylinder while noting the following:

   a. On horizontal crankshaft engines, position the connecting rod so the alignment mark on the big end of the rod is towards the camshaft gear on model series 60000 (**Figure 131**) or so the alignment mark on the big end of the rod is opposite the camshaft gear on model series 100200, 130000 and 170000 (**Figure 132**).

   b. On vertical crankshaft engines, position the piston and connecting rod so the long side of the rod is on the side of the engine opposite from the camshaft (**Figure 139**). If there is a notch in the piston crown, then position the piston so the notch will be towards the fly-

11

wheel side of the engine after installation (**Figure 140**).

6. Rotate the crankshaft so the crankpin is towards the cylinder bore.

7. Lubricate the cylinder bore with engine oil.

8. Insert the connecting rod and piston through the top of the engine (**Figure 141**) so the piston ring compressor rests against the engine.

9. Push the piston into the cylinder bore while guiding the connecting rod onto the crankshaft crankpin.

> *CAUTION*
> *Do not use excessive force when installing the piston and rod. If binding occurs, remove the piston and rod and try again. Excessive force can damage or break the piston rings, piston ring lands, connecting rod or crankshaft.*

10. Liberally lubricate the connecting rod bearing and the crankshaft crankpin with engine oil.

11. Mate the connecting rod with the crankshaft crankpin, then rotate the crankshaft so the connecting rod cap can be installed.

12. Liberally lubricate the bearing surface of the connecting rod cap and install the cap on the connecting rod. Be sure the indexing notches on the rod and cap are properly meshed (**Figure 135**).

13. Refer to the following instructions to install the oil dipper, lockplate (a new lockplate should be installed), washers and retaining screws (if a new replacement connecting rod has two thick washers, discard the washers and proceed as follows):

  a. If the rod cap is secured by only screws with washers, tighten the screws to the torque listed in **Table 2**.

  b. If the rod cap is equipped with a lockplate, install the lockplate and the screws. Tighten the screws to the torque listed in **Table 2**. Bend the ears of the lockplate against the flats on the screw heads.

  c. If the rod cap is equipped with an oil dipper that is secured by only one screw and a lockplate, install the oil dipper (A, **Figure 142**) first, then the lockplate (B) and the screws. Tighten the screws to the torque listed in **Table 2**. Bend the ears of the lockplate against the flats on the screw heads.

  d. If the rod cap is equipped with an oil dipper that is secured by only one screw, install a washer

under the opposite screw. Tighten the screws to the torque listed in **Table 2**.

  e. If the rod cap is equipped with an oil dipper that is secured by two screws, tighten the screws to the torque listed in **Table 2**.

> *NOTE*
> *The oil dipper on horizontal crankshaft engines must be installed so the dipper*

*portion (A, **Figure 142**) is on the fly-wheel side of the connecting rod.*

14. Position the engine so the tappets will not fall out and install the tappets (**Figure 143**) in their original positions.

15. Lubricate the camshaft and camshaft bearings with engine oil.

16. Install the camshaft so the timing marks on the crankshaft and camshaft gears are aligned. Three sets of timing marks have been used as shown in the following illustrations:

   a. On some engines with a metal camshaft gear, the crankshaft gear may have a straight line and the camshaft gear may have a dimple (**Figure 144**).

   b. On some engines with a metal camshaft gear, both the crankshaft and camshaft gears may have a dimple (**Figure 145**).

   c. On engines with a plastic camshaft gear, the dimple on the crankshaft gear tooth should be positioned between the gear teeth on the camshaft gear marked by the two lines (**Figure 146**). Note that other marks (such as "O") on the camshaft gear face are molding impressions.

NOTE
*On engines with an auxiliary drive shaft, a thrust washer (**Figure 147**) is*

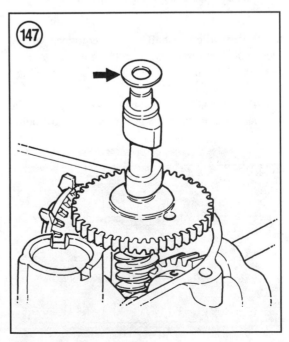

11

used on the camshaft. If the auxiliary drive shaft rotates clockwise, the thrust washer must be at the crankcase end of the camshaft. If the auxiliary drive shaft rotates counterclockwise, the thrust washer must be at the gear end of the camshaft.

17. If so equipped, place the oil slinger assembly (**Figure 148**) on the camshaft.

> *NOTE*
> *A spring washer (**Figure 149**) must be installed on the end of the camshaft on some models series 100900, 130700, 131700 and 130900 engines.*

Mechanical Governor Installation

1. Install the governor arm (A, **Figure 150**) and E-ring (B) in the crankcase.
2. Secure the governor arm with the spring clip (A, **Figure 151**) and washer (B). Note the relative position of the spring clip ends and the boss on the crankcase (C, **Figure 151**) on horizontal crankshaft engine or (C, **Figure 152**) on vertical crankshaft engine.

> *NOTE*
> *On Quantum engines, a shoulder on the governor arm shaft is used in place of an E-ring and a push nut is used in place of the spring clip.*

3. On vertical crankshaft engines equipped with a mechanical governor, be sure the governor arm is positioned against the governor thrust sleeve (**Figure 153**).
4. On horizontal crankshaft engines equipped with a mechanical governor, the governor arm must point

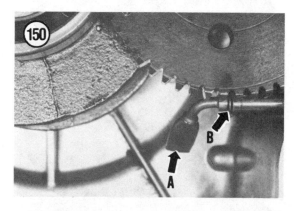

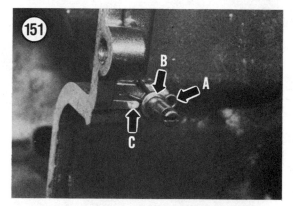

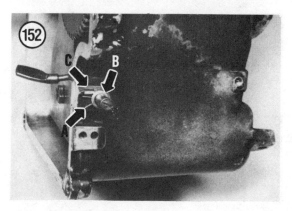

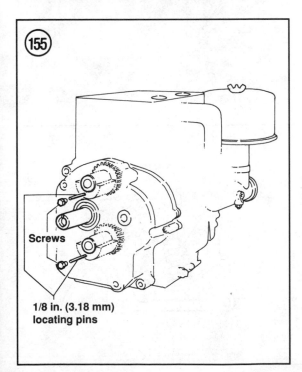

Screws

**1/8 in. (3.18 mm)
locating pins**

directly at the bottom of the crankcase as shown in **Figure 154**).

> *CAUTION*
> *If the governor arm is not in the position specified in the previous steps, internal damage may result when the engine runs.*

Crankcase Cover or Oil Pan Installation

1. Install the crankcase gasket with a nonhardening sealer. At least one 0.015 in. thick crankcase gasket must be installed.

2. Lubricate the crankshaft main bearing and camshaft bearing and crankshaft oil seal.

3. Install the oil pan (vertical crankshaft engines) or crankcase cover (horizontal crankshaft engines).

4. If a horizontal crankshaft engine is equipped with rotating balance weights in the crankcase cover, proceed as follows:

   a. Install balance weights on the shafts in crankcase cover.

   b. Remove two small screws from the cover and insert 1/8 in. (3.2 mm) diameter locating pins through the screw holes and into the timing holes in the counterweights as shown in **Figure 155**.

   c. Rotate the crankshaft so the piston is at top dead center.

   d. Install the crankcase cover with balance weights and new cover gasket.

   e. Remove the locating pins, coat the threads of the timing hole screws with nonhardening sealer and install the screws with the fiber sealing washers.

   f. Install the oil pan or crankcase cover on the crankcase.

> *NOTE*
> *Do not force the oil pan or crankcase cover onto the crankcase. If binding occurs, remove the oil pan or crankcase cover and determine the cause.*

5. Install the oil pan or crankcase cover retaining screws.

6. On vertical crankshaft engines with a mechanical governor, note the configuration of the oil pan and apply nonhardening sealer to the screw indicated in **Figure 156**, **Figure 157** or **Figure 158**.

11

NOTE
*On vertical crankshaft engines with an auxiliary drive shaft (except on Quantum model series 121000, 122000, 124000 and 126000), slide the gear and shaft toward the crankshaft to install the oil pan screw. After installing the screw, slide the gear and shaft into place, then install the shaft stop (**Figure 159**). Apply nonhardening sealer to the four auxiliary drive shaft cover screws (**Figure 160**).*

7. Tighten the oil pan or crankcase cover screws evenly in a crossing pattern to the torque listed in **Table 2**.

Crankshaft End Play Adjustment

Check and adjust crankshaft end play. End play is the distance the crankshaft can move along its axis.

1. Set up a dial indicator so in and out movement (end play) of the crankshaft can be measured. If the crankshaft is long, the dial indicator can be mounted on the crankshaft with the plunger against the oil pan or crankcase cover (**Figure 161**). If the crankshaft is

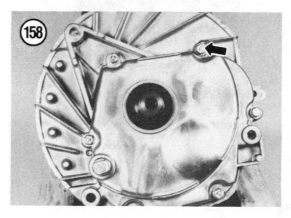

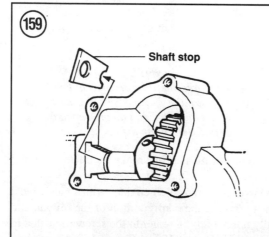

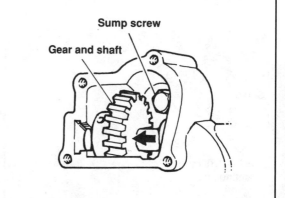

short, the dial indicator plunger should rest against the end of the crankshaft (**Figure 162**).

2. Move the crankshaft in and out and measure the movement (end play). Crankshaft end play should be 0.002-0.030 in. (0.05-0.76 mm) on models 92500 and 92900 with a next-to-last digit of "5" in the code number. Crankshaft end play should be 0.002-0.030 in. (0.05-0.76 mm) on Quantum model series 100700, 121000, 122000, 124000 and 126000. Crankshaft end play should be 0.002-0.008 in. (0.05-0.20 mm) for all other models.

3. Adjust end play by changing the thickness or number of crankcase gaskets. Gaskets in several thicknesses are available. Increasing the gasket thickness will increase end play.

4. If end play is excessive with the required 0.015 in. gasket installed on an engine not equipped with a ball bearing at the output end of the crankshaft, a thrust washer (shim) is available to reduce end play. Install a thrust washer next to the crankshaft gear (**Figure 163**), then check and adjust the end play as necessary using gaskets.

5. If end play is excessive with the required 0.015 in. gasket installed on an engine equipped with a ball bearing at the output end of the crankshaft, a thrust washer (shim) is available to reduce end play. The thrust washer must be installed at the flywheel end of the crankshaft between the crankshaft and crankcase, which will require removal of the crankshaft. Check and adjust the end play as necessary using gaskets.

NOTE
The thrust washers are sized according to their inside diameter to fit the crankshaft. Measure the crankshaft diameter before ordering the thrust washer. Diameter sizes are 0.875, 1.000, 1.181 and 1.378 in.

6. End play cannot be adjusted using thrust washers on engines with ball bearings at both ends of the

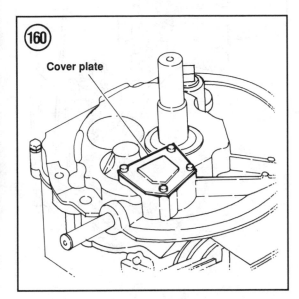

Cover plate

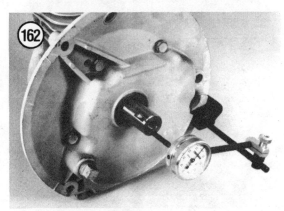

11

crankshaft. If end play is excessive, then there are worn parts which must be replaced.

Install External Components

1. Install the intake and exhaust valves, valve springs and retainers. Measure clearance between end of valve stems and tappets as outlined in *Valve System* section in this chapter.
2. Install crankcase breather.
3. Install the cylinder head with a new head gasket.
4. If engine is equipped with breaker point-type ignition system, install ignition coil, breaker points and condenser. Adjust ignition coil air gap and breaker point gap as outlined in Chapter Five.
5. If engine is equipped with solid-state (breakerless) ignition system, install ignition coil and module. Adjust ignition coil air gap as outlined in Chapter Five.
6. Install the flywheel. Tighten flywheel nut or starter clutch to torque specified in **Table 2**.
7. Install blower housing and rewind starter.
8. Install electric starter motor if so equipped.
9. Install carburetor, fuel tank and air cleaner.

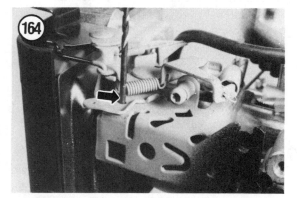

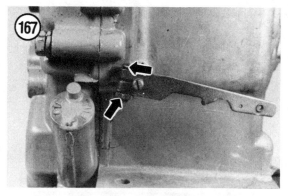

10. Install the muffler.

11. Fill crankcase to proper level with recommended engine oil as outlined in Chapter Five.

12. Check and adjust carburetor mixture settings and engine speed as outlined in Chapter Five.

Governor Lever Adjustment

On engines with a mechanical governor, adjust the position of the governor lever after assembly as follows:

1. On Quantum 121000, 122000, 124000 and 126000, move the speed control lever to "FAST" position and place an 1/8 in. (3 mm) rod through the holes in the governor control lever (**Figure 164**) and the bracket. Loosen the clamp bolt (**Figure 165**) then rotate the governor shaft counterclockwise until it stops. Hold the shaft and tighten the clamp bolt to 35-45 in.-lb. (4-5 N•m).

2. If the governor shaft is mounted on the crankcase cover as shown in **Figure 166**, loosen the governor lever clamp screw and move the governor lever so the carburetor throttle plate is in wide open position. Turn the governor shaft as far as possible counterclockwise, then tighten the clamp bolt.

3. On engines with less than 13 cu. in. displacement (except 80000, 83000, 100200, 100900 and engines previously specified), loosen the clamp bolt on the governor lever (**Figure 167**). Move the governor lever so the carburetor throttle plate is in wide open position. Using a screwdriver, rotate the governor shaft counterclockwise as far as possible and tighten the clamp bolt.

4. On engines with greater than 13 cu. in. displacement, as well as models 80000, 83000, 100200 and 100900, loosen the clamp bolt on the governor lever (**Figure 168**). Move the governor lever so the carburetor throttle plate is in wide open position. Using a screwdriver, rotate the governor shaft clockwise as far as possible and tighten the clamp bolt.

Table 1 ENGINE SERVICE SPECIFICATIONS

Alternator stator air gap	
90000, 100000	0.010 in. (0.25 mm)
120700	0.007 in. (0.18 mm)
Balancer (oscillating type)	
Eccentric diameter (min.)	
171700	1.870 in. (47.50 mm)
191700, 193700, 195700, 196700	1.870 in. (47.50 mm)
251700, 252700, 253700, 255700, 256700, 257700, 258700, 259700	2.120 in. (53.85 mm)
280700, 281700, 282700, 283700, 285700, 286700, 289700	2.202 in. (55.93 mm)
Weight bushing diameter (max.)	
171700	1.881 in. (47.78 mm)
191700, 193700, 195700, 196700	1.881 in. (47.78 mm)
251700, 252700, 253700, 255700, 256700, 257700, 258700, 259700	2.131 in. (54.13 mm)
280700, 281700, 282700, 283700, 285700, 286700, 289700	2.212 in. (56.18 mm)
Camshaft	
Bearing journal (min.)	
110000, 111000, 112000, 113000, 114000	
Crankcase end	0.436 in. (11.07 mm)
Gear end	0.498 in. (12.65 mm)
All other models	
Both ends[1]	0.498 in. (12.65 mm)

(continued)

11

Table 1 ENGINE SERVICE SPECIFICATIONS (continued)

Lobe height (min.)	
60000, 61000, 80000, 81000, 82000, 90000, 91000, 92000, 93000, 94000, 95000, 96000[2]	0.883 in. (22.43 mm)
100200, 100900	0.950 in. (24.13 mm)
100700, 121000, 122000, 124000, 126000[2], 110000, 111000, 112000, 113000, 114000	0.870 in. (22.10 mm)
130000, 131000, 132000	0.950 in. (24.13 mm)
140000	0.977 in. (24.82 mm)
170000, 171000	0.977 in. (24.82 mm)
190000, 191000, 192000, 193000, 194000, 195000, 196000	0.977 in. (24.82 mm)
Engines greater than 22 cu. in. (360 cc) displacement	1.184 in. (30.07 mm)
Camshaft bearing diameter (max.)	
110000, 111000, 112000, 113000, 114000	
Crankcase	0.443 in. (11.25 mm)
Crankcase cover or oil pan	0.504 in. (12.80 mm)
All other models[3]	0.504 in. (12.80 mm)
Connecting rod	
Big end diameter (max.)	
60000, 61000	0.876 in. (22.25 mm)
Engines less than 14 cu. in. (229 cc) displacement (except 60000, 61000)	1.001 in. (25.43 mm)
140000	1.095 in. (27.81 mm)
170000, 171000	1.095 in. (27.81 mm)
190000, 191000, 192000, 193000, 194000, 195000, 196000	1.127 in. (28.61 mm)
Engines greater than 22 cu. in. (360 cc) displacement	1.252 in. (31.80 mm)
Small end diameter (max.)	
Engines less than 14 cu. in. (229 cc) displacement (except 100200, 100900)	0.492 in. (12.50 mm)
100200, 100900	0.555 in. (14.10 mm)
140000	0.674 in. (17.12 mm)
170000, 171000	0.674 in. (17.12 mm)
190000, 191000, 192000, 193000, 194000, 195000, 196000	0.674 in. (17.12 mm)
Engines greater than 22 cu. in. (360 cc) displacement	0.802 in. (20.37 mm)
Crankshaft	
Crankpin diameter (min.)	
60000, 61000	0.870 in. (22.10 mm)
Engines less than 14 cu. in. (229 cc) displacement (except 60000, 61000)	0.996 in. (25.30 mm)
140000	1.090 in. (27.69 mm)
170000, 171000	1.090 in. (27.69 mm)
190000, 191000, 192000, 193000, 194000, 195000, 196000	1.122 in. (28.50 mm)
Engines greater than 22 cu. in. (360 cc) displacement	1.247 in. (31.67 mm)

	Flywheel end	Output end
Main bearing journal diameter (min.)		
60000, 61000	0.873 in. (22.17 mm)	0.873 in.[4] (22.17 mm)
80000, 81000, 82000	0.873 in. (22.17 mm)	0.873 in.[4] (22.17 mm)

(continued)

Table 1 ENGINE SERVICE SPECIFICATIONS (continued)

	Flywheel end	Output end
Main bearing journal diameter (min.) (continued)		
90000, 91000, 92000, 93000, 94000, 95000, 96000	0.873 in. (22.17 mm)	0.873 in.[4] (22.17 mm)
100200, 100900	0.873 in. (22.17 mm)	0.998 in. (25.35 mm)
100700	0.873 in. (22.17 mm)	1.060 in. (26.92 mm)
110000, 111000, 112000, 113000, 114000	0.873 in. (22.17 mm)	0.873 in.[4] (22.17 mm)
121000, 122000, 124000, 126000	0.873 in. (22.17 mm)	1.060 in. (26.92 mm)
130000, 131000, 132000	0.873 in. (22.17 mm)	0.998 in. (25.35 mm)
140000	0.997 in. (25.32 mm)	1.179 in. (29.95 mm)
170000, 171000	0.997 in.[5] (25.32 mm)	1.179 in. (29.95 mm)
190000, 191000, 192000, 193000, 194000, 195000, 196000	0.997 in.[5] (25.32 mm)	1.179 in. (29.95 mm)
Engines greater than 22 cu. in. (360 cc) displacement	1.376 in. (34.95 mm)	1.376 in. (34.95 mm)

Crankshaft end play	
100700	0.002-0.030 in. (0.05-0.76 mm)
121000, 122000, 124000, 126000	0.002-0.030 in. (0.05-0.76 mm)
All other models[6]	0.002-0.008 in. (0.05-0.20 mm)
Cylinder bore	
Standard diameter (max.)	
60000 (early), 61000 (early)	2.3155 in. (58.81 mm)
60000 (late), 61000 (late)	2.3780 in. (60.40 mm)
80000, 81000, 82000, 83000	2.3780 in. (60.40 mm)
90000, 91000, 92000, 93000, 94000, 95000, 96000	2.5655 in. (65.16 mm)
100200, 100900	2.5030 in. (63.58 mm)
100700	2.5655 in. (65.16 mm)
110000, 111000, 112000, 113000, 114000	2.7842 in. (70.72 mm)
121000, 122000, 124000, 126000	2.6915 in. (68.36 mm)
130000, 131000, 132000	2.5655 in. (65.16 mm)
140000	2.7530 in. (69.93 mm)
170000, 171000	3.0030 in. (76.28 mm)
190000, 191000, 192000, 193000, 194000, 195000, 196000	3.0030 in. (76.28 mm)
220000, 221000, 222000	3.4405 in. (87.39 mm)
251000, 252000, 253000, 254000, 255000, 256000, 257000, 258000, 259000	3.4405 in. (87.39 mm)
280000, 281000, 282000, 283000, 285000, 286000, 289000	3.4405 in. (87.39 mm)
Out-of-round (max.)	0.0025 in. (0.06 mm)
Electric starter motor	
Direct drive motor	
Brush length (min.)	
Briggs & Stratton motors	1/8 in. (3.2 mm)
Commutator diameter (min.)	
Briggs & Stratton motors	1.23 in. (31.24 mm)

(continued)

11

Table 1 ENGINE SERVICE SPECIFICATIONS (continued)

Electric starter motor (continued)	
Gear reduction motor (except model series 130000)	
Brush length (min.)	5/64 in. (2.0 mm)
Armature end play	0.005-0.025 in. (0.13-0.63 mm)
Gear reduction motor (model series 130000)	
Brush length (min.)	1/4 in. (6.4 mm)
Ignition breaker point plunger hole diameter (max.)	0.189 in. (4.80 mm)
Ignition breaker point plunger length (min.)	0.870 in. (22.10 mm)
Ignition coil armature air gap	
Three-leg armature	0.012-0.016 in. (0.30-0.41 mm)
Two-leg armature	
60000, 61000	0.006-0.010 in. (0.15-0.25 mm)
80000, 81000, 82000, 83000	0.006-0.010 in. (0.15-0.25 mm)
90000, 91000, 92000, 93000,	
94000, 95000, 96000	0.006-0.010 in. (0.15-0.25 mm)
100200, 100900	0.010-0.014 in. (0.25-0.36 mm)
100700	0.006-0.010 in. (0.15-0.25 mm)
110000, 111000, 112000, 113000, 114000	0.006-0.010 in. (0.15-0.25 mm)
121000, 122000, 124000, 126000	0.006-0.010 in. (0.15-0.25 mm)
Engines greater than 12 cu. in. (197 cc) displacement	0.010-0.014 in. (0.25-0.36 mm)

	Crankcase bearing	Oil pan or crankcase cover bearing
Main bearing diameter (max.)		
60000, 61000	0.878 in. (22.30 mm)	0.878 in.[7] (22.30 mm)
80000, 81000, 82000	0.878 in. (22.30 mm)	0.878 in.[7] (22.30 mm)
90000, 91000, 92000, 93000, 94000, 95000, 96000	0.878 in. (22.30 mm)	0.878 in.[7] (22.30 mm)
100700	0.878 in. (22.30 mm)	1.065 in. (27.05 mm)
100200, 100900	0.878 in. (22.30 mm)	1.003 in. (25.48 mm)
110000, 111000, 112000, 113000, 114000	0.878 in. (22.30 mm)	0.878 in.[7] (22.30 mm)
130000, 131000, 132000	0.878 in. (22.30 mm)	1.003 in. (25.48 mm)
140000	1.004 in. (25.50 mm)	1.185 in. (30.10 mm)
170000, 171000	1.004 in.[7] (25.50 mm)	1.185 in. (30.10 mm)
190000, 191000, 192000, 193000, 194000, 195000, 196000	1.004 in.[8] (25.50 mm)	1.185 in. (30.10 mm)
Engines greater than 22 cu. in. (360 cc) displacement	1.383 in. (35.13 mm)	1.383 in. (35.13 mm)

Piston pin	
Diameter (min.)	
Engines less than 14 cu. in. (229 cc) displacement	
(except 100200, 100900)	0.489 in. (12.42 mm)
100200, 100900	0.552 in. (14.02 mm)
140000, 170000, 171000, 190000,	
191000, 192000, 193000, 194000,	
195000, 196000	0.671 in. (17.04 mm)

(continued)

Table 1 ENGINE SERVICE SPECIFICATIONS (continued)

Piston pin (continued)	
Diameter (min.) (continued)	
Engines greater than 22 cu. in. (360 cc) displacement	0.799 in. (20.30 mm)
Out-of-round (max.)	0.0005 in. (0.013 mm)
Piston pin hole (max.)	
Engines less than 14 cu. in. (229 cc) displacement (except 100200, 100900)	0.492 in. (12.50 mm)
100200, 100900	0.554 in. (14.07 mm)
140000, 170000, 171000, 190000, 191000, 192000, 193000, 194000, 195000, 196000	0.673 in. (17.09 mm)
Engines greater than 22 cu. in. (360 cc) displacement	0.801 in. (20.34 mm)
Piston ring end gap (max.)	
Iron sleeve bore	
Compression rings	0.030 in. (0.76 mm)
Oil control ring	0.035 in. (0.89 mm)
Aluminum bore	
Compression rings	0.035 in. (0.89 mm)
Oil control ring	0.045 in. (1.14 mm)
Piston ring side clearance (max.)	
Engines less than 14 cu. in. (229 cc) displacement	0.007 in. (0.18 mm)
Engines greater than 14 cu. in. (229 cc) displacement	0.009 in. (0.23 mm)
Spark plug electrode gap	0.030 in. (0.76 mm)
Valve tappet gap (cold)	
Intake valve	0.005-0.007 in. (0.13-0.18 mm)
Exhaust valve	
Engines less than 12 cu. in. (197 cc) displacement[9]	0.007-0.009 in. (0.18-0.23 mm).
Engines greater than 12 cu. in. (197 cc) displacement[10]	0.009-0.011 in. (0.23-0.28 mm)
Valve	
Face & seat angles	45°[11]
Margin (min.)	1/64 in. (0.4 mm)
Valve seat width	3/64-1/16 in. (1.19-1.58 mm).
Valve guide inside diameter (max.)	
1/4 in. (6.35 mm) valve stem	0.266 in. (6.76 mm)
5/16 in. (7.94 mm) valve stem	0.330 in. (8.38 mm)

1. On model series 60000, 61000, 80000, 81000 fitted with an auxiliary drive gear on the camshaft, minimum camshaft bearing journal diameter is 0.498 in. (12.65 mm) at the crankcase end and 0.751 in. (19.08 mm) at the worm drive gear end.
2. Lobe height is not specified on models with plastic cam lobes. Replace camshaft if either lobe is pitted or galled.
3. On model series 60000, 61000, 80000, 81000 fitted with an auxiliary drive gear on the camshaft, maximum camshaft bearing diameter in the crankcase is 0.504 in. (12.80 mm) and maximum camshaft bearing diameter in the oil pan is 0.757 in. (19.23 mm).
4. All models equipped with an auxiliary drive have a rejection size for the main bearing journal at the output end of 0.998 in. (25.35 mm).
5. Models equipped with a balancer have a main bearing rejection size for the main bearing journal at the flywheel end of 1.179 in. (29.95 mm).
6. Crankshaft end play should be 0.002-0.030 in. (0.05-0.76 mm) on models 92500 and 92900 with a next-to-last digit of "5" in the code number.
7. All models equipped with an auxiliary drive have a rejection size for the main bearing in the oil pan of 1.003 in. (25.48 mm).
8. Models equipped with a balancer have a main bearing rejection size for the main bearing in the crankcase of 1.185 in. (30.10 mm).
9. On some 90000 model series engines, the exhaust valve gap should be 0.005-0.007 in. (0.13-0.18 mm). These engines are identified by the specification stamped on the inside of the crankcase breather.
10. If a model 253400 or 255400 engine is equipped with only an electric starter and no rewind starter, the intake valve gap should be 0.009-0.011 in. (0.23-0.28 mm). On model 286700 engines, the intake valve gap should be 0.004-0.006 in. (0.10-0.15 mm).
11. The intake valve face angle and intake valve seat angle are 30° on some early engines.

11

Table 2 SPECIAL TIGHTENING TORQUES

Connecting rod	
Engines less than 14 cu. in. (229 cc) displacement	100 in.-lb. (11.3 N•m)
Model series 140000, 170000, 171000	165 in.-lb. (18.6 N•m)
Engines greater than 17 cu. in. (279 cc) displacement	190 in.-lb. (21.5 N•m)
Crankcase cover or oil pan	
Engines less than 12 cu. in. (197 cc) displacement (except 100200, 100900)	85 in.-lb. (9.6 N•m)
100200, 100900	120 in.-lb. (13.6 N•m)
130000	120 in.-lb. (13.6 N•m)
Engines greater than 14 cu. in. (229 cc) displacement	140 in.-lb. (15.8 N•m)
Cylinder head	
Engines less than 15 cu. in. (246 cc) displacement	140 in.-lb. (15.8 N•m)
Engines greater than 15 cu. in. (246 cc) displacement	165 in.-lb. (18.6 N•m)
Flywheel nut or starter clutch	
Model series 100200, 100900	65 ft.-lb. (90 N•m)
Engines less than 12 cu. in. (197 cc) displacement (except 100200, 100900)	55 ft.-lb. (76 N•m)
Engines greater than 12 cu. in. (197 cc) displacement	65 ft.-lb. (90 N•m)
Spark plug	140-200 in.-lb. (15.8-22.6 N•m)

Table 3 INCH SERIES TORQUE CHART*

	SAE grade	Head markings	SAE grade	Nut markings
	SAE grade 1		2	
	SAE grade 2	No mark		No mark
	SAE grade 5			
	SAE grade 5.1		5	
	SAE grade 5.2			
	SAE grade 8		8	
	SAE grade 8.2			

		SAE grade 1		SAE grade 2	
Diameter	Wrench size	Oil in.-lb. (N•m)	Dry in.-lb. (N•m)	Oil in.-lb. (N•m)	Dry in.-lb. (N•m)
#6	—	4.5 (0.5)	6 (0.7)	7 (0.8)	10 (1)
#8	—	8 (0.9)	11 (1.2)	13 (1.5)	18 (2)

(continued)

Table 3 INCH SERIES TORQUE CHART* (continued)

Diameter	Wrench size	SAE grade 1		SAE grade 2	
		Oil ft.-lb. (N·m)	Dry ft.-lb. (N·m)	Oil ft.-lb. (N·m)	Dry ft.-lb. (N·m)
#10	—	12 (1.4)	16 (1.8)	19 (2)	25 (2.8)
#12	—	19 (2)	25 (2.8)	30 (3.4)	40 (4.5)
1/4	7/16	2.5 (3.5)	3.0 (4)	4.0 (5)	5.0 (7)
5/16	1/2	5.0 (7)	6.5 (9)	7.5 (10)	10.0 (14)
3/8	9/16	8.5 (12)	12.0 (16)	14.0 (19)	18.0 (24)
7/16	5/8	14.0 (19)	19.0 (26)	22.0 (30)	30 (41)
1/2	3/4	21.0 (24)	30 (41)	35 (47)	45 (61)
9/16	13/16	30 (41)	40 (54)	50 (68)	65 (88)
5/8	15/16	40 (54)	55 (75)	65 (88)	90 (122)
3/4	1-1/8	75 (102)	100 (136)	120 (163)	160 (217)
7/8	1-5/16	120 (163)	165 (224)	120 (163)	165 (224)
1	1-1/2	180 (244)	245 (332)	180 (244)	245 (332)
1-1/8	1-11/16	255 (346)	345 (468)	255 (346)	345 (468)
1-1/4	1-7/8	360 (488)	490 (664)	360 (488)	490 (665)
1-3/8	2-1/16	470 (637)	640 (868)	470 (637)	640 (868)
1-1/2	2-1/4	625 (848)	850 (1153)	625 (848)	850 (1153)

Diameter	Wrench size	SAE grade 5		SAE grade 8	
		Oil in.-lb. (N·m)	Dry in.-lb. (N·m)	Oil in.-lb. (N·m)	Dry in.-lb. (N·m)
#6	—	12 (1.4)	15 (1.7)	—	—
#8	—	21 (2.4)	28 (3.2)	—	—
#10	—	30 (3.4)	41 (4.6)	—	—
#12	—	48 (5.4)	65 (7.3)	—	—
		ft.-lb. (N·m)	ft.-lb. (N·m)	ft.-lb. (N·m)	ft.-lb. (N·m)
1/4	7/16	6.0 (8)	8.0 (11)	8.5 (12)	12 (16)
5/16	1/2	12.0 (16)	17.0 (23)	18.0 (24)	24 (33)
3/8	9/16	22.0 (30)	30 (41)	30 (41)	40 (54)
7/16	5/8	35 (47)	50 (68)	50 (68)	70 (95)
1/2	3/4	55 (75)	75 (102)	75 (102)	105 (142)
9/16	13/16	80 (108)	105 (142)	110 (149)	150 (203)
5/8	15/16	110 (149)	145 (197)	150 (203)	205 (278)
3/4	1-1/8	190 (258)	260 (353)	270 (366)	365 (495)
7/8	1-5/16	305 (414)	415 (563)	435 (590)	590 (800)
1	1-1/2	460 (624)	625 (848)	650 (881)	880 (1193)
1-1/8	1-11/16	575 (780)	780 (1058)	920 (1248)	1250 (1695)
1-1/4	1-7/8	810 (1098)	1100 (1492)	1300 (1763)	1765 (2393)
1-3/8	2-1/16	1061 (1438)	1440 (1953)	1705 (2312)	2315 (3140)
1-1/2	2-1/4	1410 (1912)	1910 (2590)	2260 (3065)	3070 (4163)

* Tighten cap screws having lock nuts to approximately 50 percent of amount shown in chart.

11

Table 4 is on the following pages.

Table 4 METRIC SERIES TORQUE CHART

Property class	Head markings	Property class	Nut markings
4.6		5	
4.8			
8.8		8	
9.8		10	
10.9			
12.9		12	

Diameter	Wrench size	4.6 Oil ft.-lb. (N·m)	Dry ft.-lb. (N·m)	4.8 Oil ft.-lb. (N·m)	Dry ft.-lb. (N·m)
M5	8 mm	1 (1.5)	1.5 (2.5)	1.5 (2.5)	2 (3.0)
M6	10 mm	2 (3.0)	3 (4.0)	3 (4.0)	4 (5.5)
M8	13 mm	5 (7.0)	7 (9.5)	7.5 (10.0)	10 (13.0)
M10	16 mm	10 (14.0)	14 (19.0)	15 (20.0)	18 (25)
M12	18 mm	18 (25)	26 (35)	26 (35)	33 (45)
M14	21 mm	30 (40)	37 (50)	41 (55)	55 (75)
M16	24 mm	44 (60)	59 (80)	52 (85)	85 (115)
M18	27 mm	59 (80)	81 (110)	74 (115)	118 (160)
M20	30 mm	85 (115)	118 (160)	122 (165)	166 (225)
M22	33 mm	118 (160)	159 (215)	167 (225)	225 (305)
M24	36 mm	148 (200)	203 (275)	210 (285)	288 (390)
M27	41 mm	218 (295)	295 (400)	306 (415)	417 (565)
M30	46 mm	295 (400)	402 (545)	417 (565)	568 (770)
M33	51 mm	402 (545)	546 (740)	568 (770)	774 (1050)
M36	55 mm	516 (700)	700 (950)	730 (990)	992 (1345)

Diameter	Wrench size	8.8 Oil ft.-lb. (N·m)	Dry ft.-lb. (N·m)	9.8 Oil ft.-lb. (N·m)	Dry ft.-lb. (N·m)
M5	8 mm	3.5 (4.5)	4.5 (6.0)	3.5 (5.0)	5 (7.0)
M6	10 mm	5.5 (7.5)	7.5 (10.0)	6 (8.5)	9 (12.0)
M8	13 mm	13 (18.0)	18 (25)	15 (21.0)	22 (30)

(continued)

Table 4 METRIC SERIES TORQUE CHART (continued)

		8.8		9.8	
Diameter	Wrench size	Oil ft.-lb. (N·m)	Dry ft.-lb. (N·m)	Oil ft.-lb. (N·m)	Dry ft.-lb. (N·m)
M10	16 mm	26 (35)	37 (50)	30 (40)	41 (55)
M12	18 mm	48 (65)	63 (85)	52 (70)	74 (100)
M14	21 mm	74 (100)	103 (140)	85 (115)	114 (155)
M16	24 mm	118 (160)	159 (215)	133 (180)	180 (245)
M18	27 mm	166 (225)	225 (305)	—	—
M20	30 mm	236 (320)	321 (435)	—	—
M22	33 mm	321 (435)	435 (590)	—	—
M24	36 mm	409 (555)	553 (750)	—	—
M27	41 mm	597 (810)	811 (1100)	—	—
M30	46 mm	811 (1100)	1103 (1495)	—	—
M33	51 mm	1106 (1500)	1500 (2035)	—	—
M36	55 mm	1420 (1925)	1925 (2610)	—	—

		10.9		12.9	
Diameter	Wrench size	Oil ft.-lb. (N·m)	Dry ft.-lb. (N·m)	Oil ft.-lb. (N·m)	Dry ft.-lb. (N·m)
M5	8 mm	4.5 (6.5)	6.5 (9.0)	5.5 (7.5)	7.5 (10.0)
M6	10 mm	8 (11.0)	11 (15.0)	9.5 (13.0)	13 (18.0)
M8	13 mm	18 (25)	26 (35)	22 (30)	33 (45)
M10	16 mm	41 (55)	55 (75)	48 (65)	63 (85)
M12	18 mm	70 (95)	97 (130)	81 (110)	111 (150)
M14	21 mm	111 (150)	151 (205)	129 (175)	177 (240)
M16	24 mm	173 (235)	232 (315)	203 (275)	273 (370)
M18	27 mm	236 (320)	321 (435)	277 (375)	376 (510)
M20	30 mm	356 (455)	457 (620)	395 (535)	535 (725)
M22	33 mm	457 (620)	620 (840)	535 (725)	726 (985)
M24	36 mm	583 (790)	789 (1070)	682 (925)	926 (1255)
M27	41 mm	852 (1155)	1154 (1565)	996 (1350)	1353 (1835)
M30	46 mm	1158 (1570)	1571 (2130)	1353 (1835)	1837 (2490)
M33	51 mm	1575 (2135)	2139 (2900)	1844 (2500)	2500 (3390)
M36	55 mm	2021 (2740)	2744 (3720)	2364 (3205)	3212 (4355)

11

CHAPTER TWELVE

BRIGGS & STRATTON TOOLS

Briggs & Stratton offers a wide range of tools and products to service and maintain their engines. Refer to Briggs & Stratton Service Tools Catalog MS-8746 for a complete list. Briggs & Stratton tools can be obtained through a dealer or distributor. See Chapter Three for a list of Briggs & Stratton distributors who can provide the name of a local dealer.

With the exception of flywheel holder tool Nos. 19310 and 19321, the Briggs & Stratton tools specified in this manual are available in the Briggs & Stratton Tool Kit 19300. The retail price for the tool kit at the time of this manual's printing was approximately $120. The tools included in the kit are listed in **Table 1**.

Table 1 TOOL KIT 19300

Description	Tool No.	Applicable model series
Carburetor nozzle screwdriver	19280	Flo-Jet carburetors
Flywheel brake band adjustment gauge	19256	90000, 110000, 130000 so equipped
Flywheel holder	19167	60000, 80000, 90000, 100200, 100900
Flywheel puller	19069	60000, 80000, 90000, 100700, 110000, 120000
Flywheel puller	19165	140000, 170000, 190000, 250000
Flywheel puller	19203	190000, 220000, 250000, 280000
Fuel mixture adjusting screwdriver	19263	Pulsa-Jet & Vacu-Jet carburetors
Ignition spark tester	19368	All engines
Piston ring compressor	19070	60000, 80000, 90000, 100000, 110000, 120000, 130000
Piston ring compressor	19230	140000, 170000, 190000, 220000, 250000, 280000
Starter clutch wrench	19244	All engines so equipped
Tachometer	19200	All engines
Tang bender	19229	130000, 140000, 170000, 190000, 220000, 250000, 280000
Valve guide lubricant	93963	All engines
Valve lapping compound	94150	All engines
Valve lapping tool	19258	All engines
Valve spring compressor	19063	All engines
ADDITIONAL TOOLS		
Description	Tool No.	Applicable model series
Flywheel holder	19310	100700
Flywheel holder	19321	280000